ADVANCE PRAISE FOR

Social Education
in the Twentieth Century

"This is an outstanding, wide-ranging collection that addresses virtually every significant issue within the social education field. It makes two particularly unique contributions: it approaches social education from a decidedly (and necessarily) broadened perspective, detailing the complexity of a 'range of activities, agents, and issues,' both inside and outside the public school classroom; and, with a scope that begins in 1893 and ends in the early twenty-first century, it does so by situating each topic within the evolving historical and social contexts that shaped it. Enjoyable and provocative to read, this comprehensive volume has the potential to significantly revitalize scholarship in the social education field."

Kenneth Teitelbaum, Professor and Chair of Education,
Kent State University, Ohio

"This enlightening and useful collection of essays provides an historical panorama of the key developments shaping social studies education in the twentieth century."

Kathleen Weiler, Professor of Education, Tufts University

"This new book is a much-needed addition to the history of the social studies in American schools. This book offers practitioners and scholars impressively researched and deftly written accounts and interpretations that extend understanding of some important elements of rhetoric and of a few practices of the field mainly during the twentieth century. These explorations, furthermore, display the high quality of scholarship that the field must continue to expect."

O. L. Davis, Jr., Catherine Mae Parker Centennial Professor
of Curriculum and Instruction, University of Texas, Austin

Social Education in the
Twentieth Century

HISTORY OF
SCHOOLS &
SCHOOLING

Alan R. Sadovnik and Susan F. Semel
General Editors

Vol. 32

PETER LANG
New York • Washington, D.C./Baltimore • Bern
Frankfurt am Main • Berlin • Brussels • Vienna • Oxford

Social Education
in the Twentieth Century

Curriculum and Context for Citizenship

Christine Woyshner, Joseph Watras,
and Margaret Smith Crocco,
EDITORS

PETER LANG
New York • Washington, D.C./Baltimore • Bern
Frankfurt am Main • Berlin • Brussels • Vienna • Oxford

Library of Congress Cataloging-in-Publication Data

Social education in the twentieth century: curriculum
and context for citizenship / edited by Christine Woyshner,
Joseph Watras, Margaret Smith Crocco.
p. cm. — (History of schools and schooling; vol. 32)
Includes bibliographical references and index.
1. Education—United States—Curricula—History—20th century.
2. Social sciences—Study and teaching—United States—History—20th
century. 3. Education—United States—Philosophy—History—20th
century. I. Title: Social education in the 20th century.
II. Woyshner, Christine A. III. Watras, Joseph. IV. Crocco, Margaret.
V. History of schools and schooling; v. 32.
LB1570.S645   370.11'5—dc21   2003003738
ISBN 978-0-8204-6247-9
ISSN 1089-0678

Bibliographic information published by **Die Deutsche Nationalbibliothek**.
Die Deutsche Nationalbibliothek lists this publication in the "Deutsche
Nationalbibliografie"; detailed bibliographic data is available
on the Internet at http://dnb.d-nb.de/.

Cover design by Joni Holst

The paper in this book meets the guidelines for permanence and durability
of the Committee on Production Guidelines for Book Longevity
of the Council of Library Resources.

© 2004, 2010 Peter Lang Publishing, Inc., New York
29 Broadway, 18th Floor, New York, NY 10006
www.peterlang.com

Printed in the United States of America

CONTENTS

ACKNOWLEDGMENTS

The process of bringing this book to publication has involved many people. Our project originated with the encouragement of O.L. Davis, Jr., who in 1995, in the journal *Theory and Research in Social Education,* posed a challenge to write the history of social studies and social education that extended its reach beyond the biographies of great men. In subsequent years we were a part of a group of scholars who presented their research at various national conferences in pursuit of this goal. This collection reflects, in part, the efforts of those of us who took up O.L.'s challenge.

We thank those who joined us on the journey, even though their work is not represented in this collection. O.L. Davis, Jr., Sherry Field, Jerry Ligon, Elizabeth Ann Yeager, and Skip Chilcoat shared our passion for examining the development of social studies within broader economic, social, and political trends. Some scholars, such as Jonathan Zimmerman, Daniel Perlstein, Joseph Newman, and Murry Nelson, were among a group of supporters to offer intelligent and useful suggestions for improvement. We like to think of this collection as a beginning that represents the aspirations of these and other scholars.

There are many others to thank. We were aided by the expert direction of Susan Semel and Alan Sadovnik, who brought our ideas to Lang Publishers and aided us along the way. Lisa Dillon and Chris Myers at Lang Publishers helped us see the project through to completion. Likewise, the authors who contributed to this volume offered their diligent cooperation throughout the process. We also thank Joseph Ducette at Temple University's College of Education, who awarded us a small grant to aid in production.

Likewise, each of us has benefited from funding that supported our research and this collection. Christine Woyshner's chapter on the PTA was supported in part by a Temple University Summer Fellowship that allowed her to visit PTA archives in Upstate New York. Christine also wishes to thank Aneta Pavlenko, Mary Vesey, Joseph Watras, and Margaret Smith Crocco for their feedback and encouragement. Temple also supported the travel to conferences so that she could present her developing ideas. Joseph Watras would like to acknowledge the support of the University of Dayton for travel support to conferences. Margaret Smith Crocco wishes to thank Stephen J. Thornton and Andrew Mullen for introducing her to the history of social studies and Teachers College, Columbia University for its support for her research and travel.

INTRODUCTION

I believe that education is a regulation of the process of coming to share in the social consciousness; and that the adjustment of individual activity on the basis of this social consciousness is the only sure method of social reconstruction.
JOHN DEWEY, 1897[1]

Individuals since Thomas Jefferson have long pondered how to use public education to promote and sustain democracy. More than two hundred years into the American experiment with republican governance, citizens today may be less fearful than Jefferson, Madison, and other founders about the fragility of democracy and its staying power. Despite contemporary concerns about the engagement of the civic polity, most citizens would concede that public education has played a critical role in nourishing American democracy throughout its history.[2]

During the early nineteenth century, educational theorists such as Hannah Adams, Samuel Morse, and Noah Webster devoted their energies to refashioning the school subjects of history, geography, language, and spelling for what they perceived to be the new demands of education in this democracy.[3] During the twentieth century, the subject dedicated to meeting the demands of citizenship preparation has become the social studies. Born of the progressive education movement, the social studies derives its curricular legitimacy from the commitment of American citizens to using formal education to prepare future generations for their role in this nation's political life, broadly conceived.[4] Still, this commitment means that, in theory, widespread public input, experimentation, and deliberation all play a role in shaping such education.

Over the course of the last century, the precise definition of the social studies, the fundamental aims of public education, and the best means of accomplishing these ends have all been highly contested and routinely re-imagined. We would expect no less of a school subject closely tied to citizenship within a large, vibrant, and complex democratic society. In addition, evolving twentieth century commitments to respect the many forms of diversity found in this nation have placed social studies in ever more complex relationships to its social and educational contexts. Even in periods when the social studies have ignored significant social movements such as civil rights and feminism, this disengagement holds historical significance in ways that one would not impute to other school subjects.

With the advent of compulsory public education in many states in the nineteenth century and the introduction of high schools in the twentieth, schools have become the chief settings where citizenship education occurs. Nevertheless, citizenship education by its very nature has also occurred in many other settings, from social settlements to Americanization schools to the freedom schools of the civil rights movement. To underscore the notion that education for citizenship takes place in multiple venues, both inside and outside the school, we use the term "social education" in this volume to signify "teaching and learning about how individuals construct and live out their understandings of social, political, and economic relations—past and present—and the implications of these understandings for how citizens are educated in a democracy."[5] Social education includes social studies but is not limited to the course of study aimed at citizenship conventionally found in public schools.

Over time, articulation may occur between social education and social studies, as an idea originating outside the schools works its way, typically rather slowly, into the formal K-12 curriculum. The most obvious example of this phenomenon is the influence colleges and universities have had on secondary curriculum.[6] As the number of students attending college has expanded over the last century, pressure has been placed on high schools to insure adequate preparation. The growth of the Advanced Placement program of The College Board over the last thirty years is a good example of this phenomenon. Academic disciplinary trends also play a role here, for example, the "new social history" movement of the sixties and seventies. National and global conditions also alter the context of schooling. In recent years, globalization has resulted in world history replacing European history and Western civilization courses in many schools. In some regions, business groups have promoted Junior Achievement programs in elementary and middle schools and parent associations have encouraged character education. During the nineteen fifties and sixties, advocates of vocational education, often in tandem with business interests, promulgated the life adjustment movement in curriculum, leading to what has been dubbed the "shopping mall high school."[7] In the eighties, conservative backlash against this trend led to the "back to basics" movement, also created within the context of a broad consensus of diverse concerned groups, many located outside formal educational institutions. In this case, publication of the book, *A Nation at Risk,* in 1983 galvanized these groups into action, which over the last twenty years has produced many other changes as part of a broad-based, often contradictory, school reform movement.[8]

Within the social studies, a tradition of responsiveness to broader social currents does exist—a phenomenon undoubtedly rooted in the very nature of social studies itself. A brief example of this process will demonstrate how concerns for the social and civic welfare of the nation have informed social studies from the outset. Thomas Jesse Jones, one of the field's founders, is reported to have first heard the term "social studies" around 1902, when he served as "head worker" at the Columbia University Settlement, a social welfare institution which published a journal by that name.[9] Jones introduced a course called "social studies" at Hampton Institute, a trade school for Native Americans and African Americans in Hampton, Virginia, because he believed this course of study would help assimilate these groups into their communities, although hardly on equitable terms, it should be noted. Another early example of such responsiveness was "community civics," an approach that sought to ameliorate social and political conditions in rural parts of the country. From its inception, social education took inspiration from a variety of sources, inside and outside the schools. Not surprisingly, therefore, the curriculum was sometimes quite responsive to perceived citizenship needs in local and regional settings.

Beyond social education, another concept central to this book is curriculum, a term generally taken to mean the "purposes, content, activities, and organization inherent in the educational program of the school."[10] We use curriculum here somewhat more broadly than this definition to mean any systematically conceived and implemented course of study within an organization that takes as part of its mission teaching and learning. We find curriculum created by government organizations, voluntary associations, and textbook publishers as well as formalized by educational administrators and curriculum theorists. As Herbert Kliebard once put it, "In any time and place, what we call *the* American curriculum is actually an assemblage of competing doctrines and practices."[11] Educational change in this country has been an endeavor with many entry points, due in part to the highly decentralized nature of formal educational policymaking in the United States as compared to many European and Asian nations. Curriculum thus is conceived at a variety of levels. In the case of social studies, however, avoidance of national centralization has been undercut to some degree by heavy reliance on textbooks and the impact of national standards and high-stakes testing movements.

This collection explores a range of the many manifestations of social education in the twentieth century. We consider both formal curriculum products, such as the textbook series of Harold Rugg, as well as broad, societal influences on curriculum re-formulation such as the civil rights, feminist, and gay rights movements. We include chapters on familiar topics in the historiography of the field, such as The Committee of Ten, as well as chapters on topics rarely found in social studies histories, the PTA and the Civilian Conservation Corps. One of our goals in shaping this volume has been to include treatment of diverse curriculum efforts related to social education, for example Jewish American educators' approaches to citizenship education in the early twentieth century. We also acknowledge the central role of teachers as "curricular-instructional gatekeepers"[12] in this volume by featuring a chapter about the work of one woman who championed intercultural education during the Second World War in the face of Japanese internment. Several chapters examine the effects of the cultural and sexual revolutions of the sixties and postmodernism in the eighties and nineties on social studies scholars. Towards the end of the book, one author provides an analysis of the century-long battle between historians and social studies scholars. The volume wraps up with an essay reflecting on the altered demands of citizenship education in a society fractured and still coping with the aftermath of the terrorist attacks on the United States of September 11, 2001.

Schooling and the Social Studies

Its various originators conceived of social studies as a school subject intended to increase students' affection for and understanding of democracy. Social studies was designed to serve alternately as a kind of moral, civic, character, vocational, and social education. In an early iteration it was aimed at helping students understand contemporary society and keeping them in school during an era of compulsory attendance laws and child labor concerns. Given various constituencies' interest in determining education for democracy, as well as changing conceptions of society, the definitions, approaches, and philosophies of the social studies have changed over time and looked very different even in different places during the same time period. One constant in the history of this subject area, and a central theme of this book, is how to teach about and for democracy in a nation of diverse peoples and political ideals.

Although teachers had long taught the material found in the fields now called history, economics, and political science, the subject that combined them and was called social studies began in 1916, when the Committee on the Social Studies produced its major report "The Social Studies in Secondary Education." This committee was one of fourteen committees the National Educational Association (NEA) established in 1913 to determine the appropriate content of various school studies, and the NEA formed the Commission on the Reorganization of Secondary Education (CRSE) to oversee their work.

According to the Committee on the Social Studies, the aim of the social studies was to develop citizenship without explicit attention to the teaching of what might be called ethnic diversity or pluralism. Still, the committee was careful to avoid overly narrow conceptions of citizenship. Instead of shallow patriotism, the committee called for students to develop feelings of membership in the human race and to desire that the different peoples in the world enjoy social justice. The 1916 social studies report took what might be called a liberal, progressive attitude that endeavored to show children how to shape a society to allow each person to have the opportunity to share in the benefits of social life without raising the troubling issues of economic, racial, and ethnic inequities.[13] This implied that members of different groups should recognize when their customs served their needs and when those traditional ways should give way to other, more beneficial methods. As a result, the report referred approvingly to Thomas Jesse Jones' efforts at Hampton Institute to encourage African American youth to accept their subordination in the social, economic, and political hierarchy.

The social studies committee published its report immediately before the United States entered World War I and its members finished their work before Frances A. Kellor and her National American Committee started a national movement to Americanize the immigrants. Yet, the social studies report still promoted Americanization ideals in communities and classrooms. When more than thirty states enacted Americanization measures by the late 1910s, these focused on efforts to reach adults. Thus, Americanization reached children through the new social studies curriculum and adults through the National American Committee. Classes appeared in factories; schools offered evening classes for adults; and elementary schools taught exclusively in English.[14]

Americanization as a focus of the social studies was not without its detractors. Once the United States entered the war, U.S. President Woodrow Wilson asked school officials to increase the training in community and national life for elementary and secondary school students. Charles Judd and Leon Marshall of the University of Chicago produced a series of lessons about such topics as the war, business organizations, and workers and wage systems. Educators praised these materials, but the director of the National Industrial Conference Board complained that the lessons were propaganda in favor of national insurance, labor unions, and governmental control of business.[15]

After the war, social studies appeared in schoolrooms in superficial ways, which prompted a revitalization of the subject by a well-known educator. As described in Chapter Two, Harold Rugg surveyed the content of social studies courses in almost 1,200 schools in 1922. Although he was pleased to find that most schools had courses in civics, he was appalled to find that the teachers did not encourage students to understand social problems. Complaining that students rarely learned how to investigate local conditions, Rugg wrote a series of textbooks organized around important social problems which were presented in an evolving order of complexity for students in grades three through twelve.

Although Rugg's approach satisfied the popular desire at that time to use education to improve social conditions, some scholars disagreed about organizing the curriculum around social problems. For example, historian Charles Beard complained that predicting future social problems was difficult and that many social problems resisted even well conceived solutions. Beard and other social scientists such as Leon Marshall and his daughter, Rachael Marshall Goetz, suggested that textbooks cover the essential social process found in every society, such as adjusting to the external world, developing agencies of social organization, and molding personality. Their hope was that if the students came to understand the many different ways societies sought to adjust to the external world or guide human motivation, they would be able to participate intelligently in efforts to improve their own society. In this way, students would not retain undue devotion to the traditions or customs of any group but would follow those practices that seemed to be most beneficial for all people. Still others who disagreed with Rugg, Beard, Marshall, and Goetz during the Great Depression wanted to help students understand the different types of relationships they formed in their lives.

To assist schools in reorganizing their social studies curriculum around this third idea, the Progressive Education Association (PEA) established the Commission on the Secondary School Curriculum, and this commission created a variety of subcommittees that provided information to faculty members in the schools. One of these subcommittees, the Committee on the Function of the Social Studies, defined the aim of the social studies as meeting student needs in ways that enabled them to develop the characteristics essential to democracy. The Committee also decided that teachers could best meet students' needs by helping them understand the different types of relationships they formed during their lives. Thus, although the report complimented Marshall and Goetz for constructing the social processes approach, the authors pointed out that this approach illuminated only one set of relations, which they called social-civic relationships. The social studies teacher had to be aware of other sets of relationships such as immediate personal-social relationships and personal living.[16]

Within the Committee on the Function of the Social Studies, explicit attention to understanding diversity first appeared in the social studies. According to the Committee, an essential characteristic students should develop was tolerance. The need for this attitude became clear to the committee as they considered the effects of the totalitarian movements sweeping over Europe. Thus, the committee urged that students learn the virtues of diversity and the contributions that minority groups made to the culture. For example, in studying economic relations, the committee recommended that students learn that intolerance grew from economic maladjustment as people tended to blame their economic failures on racial or religious minorities.[17]

In the second half of the twentieth century, social studies took various forms in schools, though the challenge of diversity and difference remained. Historian of education B. Edward McClellan suggests the concentration on moral, civic, and social education in the social studies curriculum faded after World War Two, as American citizens demanded that schools emphasize high-level academic and cognitive skills.[18] Nevertheless, life adjustment aims within education remained popular in many schools and vocational education grew throughout subsequent decades.[19]

Signaling a major shift in the field, in 1964, Jerome Bruner became director of the federally funded initiative to create a social studies program entitled "Man: A Course of Study" (MACOS). Bruner's aim was to teach children to think in the manner used by scholars in the disciplines. To him, this meant that the students should begin with specific concrete information and then form hypotheses or wider governing principles from the available evidence. Using silent films about the Netsilik Eskimo or about baboons in Nairobi game parks, Bruner asked the children to use the power of contrasts to determine what it means to be human.[20]

In 1970, conservative politicians complained that the cultural relativism found in MACOS threatened traditional American values. To make this charge, conservatives cited the different films Bruner developed to show that MACOS taught children that primitive cultures were as good as civilized ones. Although this charge distorted Bruner's intentions, it does show that Bruner expressed a value orientation that served moral education. Like the authors of the 1916 report of the Committee on the Social Studies, Bruner wanted the children to locate the common humanity that all peoples shared. Bruner thought the children could attain this perspective by refraining from making judgments about cultures while thinking deeply about the practices they observed in the films. On the other hand, the conservatives who attacked Bruner wanted the schools to reinforce the values they supposed the parents held.[21]

By the 1970s, some scholars within social studies began to promulgate a new approach to the matter of cultural difference, one informed by the work of earlier twentieth-century Black scholars and educational theorists W.E.B. DuBois and Carter G. Woodson. The later generation of scholars introduced what was called "ethnic studies" in the sixties and seventies and "multicultural education" in the eighties and their work took a more pluralistic stance than what was found in earlier social studies approaches to diversity. For example, instead of asking students to evaluate the reasonableness of cultural practices, the texts asked the students to affirm the ongoing validity of these cultural differences within the American national context.

The movement to explore culture and ethnic differences in the social studies curriculum took on a particular salience in the decades after the U.S. Supreme Court's groundbreaking decision in *Brown v. Board of Education* (1954). Having overturned the "separate but equal" doctrine that had sanctioned segregation in public schooling, by 1971 the U.S. Supreme Court approved busing students to achieve racial balance in public elementary and secondary schools. Due to extensive public protests against busing, various politicians, including U.S. President Richard Nixon, sought ways to halt school desegregation. At the same time, various minority groups called for opportunities to control their own schools in their own communities. In this context of racial divisiveness, multicultural education provided one avenue for learning about racial and ethnic group differences, even where opportunities for contact were limited. Clearly, those scholars promoting multicultural education hoped that such learning would undercut the racism often fueling public outrage at school desegregation efforts.

A representative example of the multicultural approach might be the text, *Teaching Strategies for Ethnic Studies,* written by James Banks in 1975. Arguing that the melting pot had been a myth, Banks urged teachers to help students form valid generalizations about America's ethnic groups. The aim was to teach students that human beings have the same basic needs but different groups use different methods to satisfy them. Banks contended such understanding could lead students to develop tolerant attitudes because they learned that certain behaviors or cultures were functional in one setting and dysfunctional in other settings.[22]

In claiming that human beings in diverse cultures have similar needs, Banks expressed ideas similar to the social process approach advanced by Marshall and Goetz, though he sought different aims. While Marshall and Goetz wanted students to understand basic social processes in order to participate in changing society, Banks wanted students to develop accepting attitudes of cultural difference. In this way, Banks showed some affinity to the PEA model as well as the intercultural education movement described in Chapter Four.

As some state departments of education began to require local school districts to purchase textbooks reflective of multiculturalism, political conservatives complained that multicultural education trivialized religion, made patriotism appear foolish, and portrayed dialects of English as acceptable.[23] To try to prevent schools from using such books, some parents and citizens organized public demonstrations and other conservatives sued in federal courts arguing that the texts imposed a religion they called secular humanism. Usually, these suits failed either because the plaintiffs failed to prove the imposition of a religion or the judges declared that controversies about school texts should be decided by elected school boards not courts.[24]

Scholars, too, disagreed in their judgments about the wisdom of educational changes tied to the widespread social change during the closing decades of the twentieth century. Some complained that the discipline of social studies had "endured 40 years of confusion."[25] Others wrote about a "century of failed school reforms" and generations of children "left back" due to progressive education's misguided efforts to promote social change through the schools.[26] In addition, a number of historians complained that efforts to increase cultural sensitivity had replaced more traditional historical studies in schools and universities, which had damaged school children's grasp of the basic tenets of American democracy and key episodes of American history.

As Chapter Twelve explains, these historians urged the reduction of social studies classes in schools arguing that traditional history provided the information children needed to become intelligent citizens in a democratic society. As had been the case earlier in the twentieth century, conservative citizens and historians endorsed social studies programs that emphasized transmission-oriented instruction in history, but not programs of study aimed at social amelioration. Nevertheless, as the century ended, widespread public support existed within both groups for using schools to promote tolerance and understanding. This orientation reflects the same democratic spirit that prompted social educators in 1916 to construct materials emphasizing the avoidance of narrow loyalties and promoting appreciation for human dignity. As a school subject that emerged from the impulse to promote a vision of the good society, social studies ended the century as it began, with public debate about how best to enact this vision.

Curriculum and Contexts

Scholars who have written about the history of social studies often have underplayed the role of broader historical, social, economic, and political contexts in shaping the curriculum.[27] Writing in 1981 in the yearbook of the National Society for the Study of Education, editor O. L. Davis, Jr. called for a history of the field that moved beyond a collection of anecdotes told by senior scholars to an interpretive analysis of the ways in which various forces, external to the field, influenced educators' efforts to construct and reconstruct the social studies.[28] Obviously, the development of any school subject does not occur in a vacuum.[29] But to understand the social studies it is essential to place its development within multiple social, political, and intellectual contexts; not to do so is an "absurdity," according to Catherine Cornbleth.[30]

Context plays a pivotal role in this story in several respects: First, change in social studies has occurred over time, albeit sometimes slowly, and with much constancy alongside change.[31] Second, context is important because many agents contribute to producing change in the social studies, some of them situated outside educational institutions. Finally, context is important because we often take for granted the special status of social studies as school subject; its intimate engagement with democracy means that historians must attend closely to changes in the purposes of schooling and notions of citizenship.

Theories about what constitutes good citizenship and who is included as full citizens have changed over the twentieth century. So have visions of the good society.[32] Advocates for change in these matters as well as conservatives supporting the status quo have both viewed schools as pivotal to their positions. Like the canary in the proverbial coal mine, social studies can be taken as a bellwether of the health and direction of American democracy, which undoubtedly explains why disagreements over its content so often provoke uproar in the popular press.

Not surprisingly, therefore, politicians, interest groups, religious institutions, concerned parents, and professional educators have all played a role in shaping social education.[33] The controversy over the U.S. history standards provides a good illustration of the involvement of a broad array of groups who felt they should have a voice in shaping the content of the history curriculum.[34] Some organizations with targeted curricular interests, such as enhancing U.S.-Japanese relations or promoting appreciation of the Bill of Rights, work in cooperation with the National Council for the Social Studies or the National Education Association. Others, for example, fundamentalist religious groups, may be interested in alternative versions of social education and steer clear of involvement with mainstream, professional organizations.

In assessing the growth of social studies, readers should remember that this intellectual domain remained a relatively young field throughout the first half of the twentieth century. Education and curriculum studies were also in their early stages of development as forms of academic inquiry throughout these years.[35] Practitioners and scholars in all these domains worked throughout the first half of the century to define themselves and secure legitimacy and acceptance for their academic enterprises within the largely centuries-old curriculum found in American colleges and universities.[36]

As the processes of definition and refinement proceeded, advocacy for citizenship education accelerated in times of rapid social, political, or economic change. Times of turmoil create pressures for change on all curricula, but most particularly, on social education. In 1977, educational scholar R. Freeman Butts identified two sets of agents affecting education for citizenship in singular ways. One includes liberal reformers who wish to "mobilize disparate groups" to promote change. The other encompasses conservative individuals who "see the need for social cohesion to rally round their version of the American way of life and to stave off threats to it from alien sources."[37] These comments reflect the broader patterns within curriculum history, what has been described as a pendulum swing between the "hard" and "soft," between "back-to-the-basics education" and "progressive education," and between "meritocratic" and "democratic" notions of educational "excellence" and "equity."[38]

These swings result from the fact that curriculum making is not only a normative undertaking but one that inevitably involves the exercise of power in order to enact a particular vision of good schooling for the good society. Thus, curriculum making can rightfully be said to be a political enterprise.[39] Well-known critical theorist Michael W. Apple defines curriculum as "official knowledge,"[40] a formulation that highlights the social legitimacy conferred by the ability to get one's curriculum platform accepted by educational policymakers. In this process, "curriculum functions to privilege certain sets and orders of knowledge over others."[41] Obviously, those with power in society will be in the best position to promote their vision of what knowledge is of greatest value. By gaining public recognition and acceptance, a particular curricular vision becomes "official knowledge," thus leading to a form of incumbency in the educational decision making process that may be hard to overcome. Still, change is possible, but the process is likely to be slow, deliberative, incremental, and when the subject is social studies, highly contentious.[42]

Over the last thirty years, feminist and multicultural demands for curricular transformation have illustrated this dynamic quite vividly. And, given the highly politicized and publicized nature of these processes today, public perception of the degree of such change may be overblown. In point of fact, the amount of multicultural and feminist content in contemporary social studies textbooks remains generally at the level of tokenism, despite what pundits have alleged about such material having dramatically altered the curriculum. Likewise, even when multicultural content works its way into textbooks and state mandates, teachers exercise the ultimate control over what gets taught, or not, in their classrooms.[43]

A similar point needs to be made about schools in the U.S. For some students, schools have served as a "vast engine of democracy;" for others, especially in urban areas, schools have functioned instead as a "form of social control,"[44] or worse yet, as "subtractive" experiences robbing children of diverse backgrounds of their cultural patrimony.[45] Perhaps the bifurcated nature of students' experiences in American education can be explained not only by means of personal identity characteristics such as race, gender, class, and their interactions with dominant school structures, but also in terms of access to alternative approaches, for example, the socialist schools of the early twentieth century[46] or African American schools of the segregated South.[47] As we shall see, social education has admitted of more variation than was previously reported, especially when we look beyond what was prescribed by the official documents promulgated within social studies.

Given the thin and uneven nature of the historiographic evidence found in social studies, it would be easy to draw overly simplistic conclusions about the field's past. Similarly, to consider social education without acknowledging the complexity of American education in general—its diverse agents and multiple pressure points—is to do injustice to the historical record. In this regard, we are well cautioned to remember Herbert Kliebard's caveat that the "labels we give school subjects do not tell the whole story since those labels do not nearly reflect the diversity that actually exists in terms of curricular practice."[48] Nor do we claim, by any means, to tell the whole story here. For example, we do not consider the effects on students of the curricular approaches highlighted in this book or consider systematically their implications for teacher education. Our aim lies, instead, in illuminating certain facets of the history of social studies in the twentieth century by examining the creation of curriculum in historical context. In so doing, a picture emerges of the range of activities, agents, and interests involved in the messy, democratic process of curriculum making in social education.[49]

Portraits of Social Education

Presented in loose chronological order from 1890 to 2000, these chapters provide a new historical understanding of changes in thinking about social education by diverse individuals and groups as articulated within the changing set of contexts pertinent to each stage of this historical development.

The first two chapters set the stage by highlighting a period of intense effort to develop a school program in social education. Chara Bohan begins by analyzing the origins of social studies with its emphasis on civic education and citizenship by means of the National Education Association committees assigned the tasks of providing curriculum frameworks for the nation's schools. Her premise holds that, contrary to more recent interpretations of the Committees of Ten and Seven, these bodies were more progressive in their leanings than previously imagined, as they sought to incorporate Dewey's philosophy of education for life. Bohan argues further that these and other committees employed social science methods to understand the contemporary state of citizenship and history education in order to prescribe course outlines.

Andra Makler investigates the years between the world wars in order to chart the course of social education. According to Makler, citizenship education in the

1920s and 1930s oscillated between the social cohesion efforts during the Red Scare to the social reconstructionism of social studies theorists Harold Rugg and George Counts during the Depression. She concludes that the fate of citizenship education entering World War II was caught up in patriotic fervor, leaving social reconstructionism foundering in the wake of accusations of communism, and thereby leaving culture, social issues, and social critique on the fringe.

Several chapters examine social education in settings outside the public schools. As a group, they suggest that further research must be undertaken in disparate educational settings, such as government programs, religious and cultural schools, and national membership associations. In Chapter Five, Benjamin Jacobs examines the tension between education for Jewish heritage and education for citizenship in Jewish schools between 1910 and 1940. His research reveals how educators in these schools were influenced by progressive developments in social education. Jacobs concludes that Jewish educators successfully struck a balance between identification with a Jewish heritage and acculturation into American ways that allowed students to understand and accept their responsibilities within both societies.

Christine Woyshner considers changes in social education from 1900 to 1950 in what may be the largest voluntary education association in this country, the National Parent-Teacher Association (PTA). Arguing that the PTA had a widespread impact on public education by promoting various curricular innovations, she marks changes in the PTA's social education curriculum, from assimilation prescriptions in the first half of the twentieth century to initiatives in support of cultural pluralism beginning in the late 1940s. Efforts by PTA leaders to be more inclusive in the association, in schools, and in the curriculum were undercut by the organization's segregationist policies. Woyshner concludes that the PTA was an important link between changing approaches to social education in schools and the American public.

The Civilian Conservation Corps (CCC) and its parallel endeavors is examined by Steven Jay Gross, who traces the tensions between social reconstructionism and indoctrination in the CCC and its African American, American Indian, and women's auxiliaries. Gross notes how social education theory was applied and reinterpreted in the CCC setting, especially in terms of social efficiency, vocationalism, and life adjustment, which won out over the social reconstructionist platform of early CCC programs. This chapter and several others show the widespread influence of social education theory in community, governmental, cultural, and religious settings. Much more work remains to be done in these and other areas.

The remaining chapters consider changing political, intellectual, and social forces in the second half of the twentieth century and their impact on education for democracy. Collectively, they reveal the professionalization and formalization of the field of social studies as it became the chief subject through which citizenship was deliberated in the schools.

In Chapter Four Yoon Pak explores one teacher's application of intercultural understanding in the Pacific Northwest in the 1940s. Pak first reviews intercultural education as developed by social studies leader Rachel Davis DuBois, and then demonstrates how teacher Ella Evanson applied such ideas in her classroom. Pak concludes that such efforts, although limited by twenty-first century standards, suggest much about the earnest efforts of individuals who, in the crisis precipitated by the Second World War, applied social education theory to schooling in order to bridge dangerous cultural chasms.

Andrew Mullen continues with a chapter considering another contentious set of years in American twentieth century history, 1957 to 1972. Linking the transformation occurring within social studies to wider political and economic changes, Mullen notes what occurred in the social studies followed similar upheaval in mathematics and the natural sciences. Content and instructional strategies were the major areas of revision during these decades, as attention to anthropology, sociology, and psychology was increased, and new instructional methods borrowed from the natural sciences. Mullen considers two innovative approaches to the social studies: the so-called "new social studies" and the social problem/self-realization approach. He concludes on an unsettled note, as his chapter sets the tone for further discussions of what other authors take to be the ongoing, troubled nature of social studies curriculum.

Tyrone Howard next explores the meaning of social education within the context of the Civil Rights Era. Beginning with John Hope Franklin's observation that the principles upon which social studies were based stand in direct opposition to the under-representation of African Americans in the curriculum, Howard examines how the discipline of social studies gradually came to address issues of racial difference within the context of African American struggles for equality between 1955 and 1975. He begins with the challenge that heated up in the 1950s with the *Brown* decision, as theorists grappled with how to create more inclusive social studies. He argues that by the late 1960s key individuals played important roles in persuading social studies scholars to incorporate new paradigms that would debunk traditional, racist views of African Americans. Howard concludes that shifting research and scholarship to a multicultural stance was not a smooth process and remains a challenge today.

Avner Segall considers the impact of postmodernist theory on social studies scholars and publications. He argues that while many academic disciplines have embraced postmodernist thinking, including other subfields within education, social studies has remained relatively untouched by this phenomenon. Segall concludes by suggesting that in the twenty-first century incorporating critical postmodern sensibilities into the social studies has the power to transform methodology and content within the field. Whether that will happen remains open to question.

Margaret Smith Crocco analyzes the impact of feminism on social studies by examining the leaders and agenda of the National Council for the Social Studies (NCSS) during the decades following from the women's movement of the 1970s. She begins by considering the challenges women faced in gaining advanced education, joining college faculties, and serving as leaders of professional organizations, and moves to an assessment of the effects of these changes on women's visibility within the field. Crocco indicates that feminist activity within social studies had only a brief period of visibility, finding decline by the mid-nineties. She attributes this casualty to the culture wars and a return to traditionalism in education.

Sexuality and the social education curriculum is the focus of Jackie Blount's contribution, which covers the twentieth century. She begins with the premise that schools have played powerful roles in assuring the normative sexuality and gender of their charges, and they typically have tackled these responsibilities through curricular approaches that include sex education courses and life adjustment courses that promote traditional gender roles. Blount argues that public education has supported the control of students' sexual and gender development by singling out homosexuals for specific treatment, by defining and regulating acceptable gender identities, and by hiring school workers who model acceptable sexuality and gender norms for their students. Blount concludes that through these means, schools have provided compelling social education for normative sexuality and gender within the deeply sexualized and gendered contexts of American culture.

Examining the interactions between social studies scholars and historians over the course of the twentieth century, Joseph Watras presents an overview of their debates about the best ways to shape the agenda of social education. He argues that the common interpretation of two groups at odds is facile, because historians and social studies scholars disagreed among themselves, and often the two worked cooperatively. Watras concludes that changes in the social education curriculum came not from disagreements among scholars, but from the tendencies of social studies educators to imitate the ways certain historians chose to do their work.

This collection concludes with Stephen J. Thornton's consideration of the meaning of these chapters for twenty-first century social education. Thornton structures his analysis around ten hypotheses regarding curriculum change in the social studies. He follows this with a discussion of the meaning and goals of citizenship education in the social studies curriculum, and suggests future directions for curriculum change in the wake of the terrorist attacks of September 11, 2001.

Taken together, these essays address three broad and related questions: First, how did external influences shape and alter the social education curriculum in and out of schools? Second, what has been the role of changing intellectual, social, political, and economic trends in defining education for citizenship and democracy and framing debates about the content and pedagogy of social education? Third, how were changes in social education over time shaped by the politics of difference such as gender, race, class, religion, and region? Despite its many gaps, we hope the book will serve as catalyst for other scholars interested in contributing to a more comprehensive understanding of the history of our field.

Notes

1. John Dewey, "My Pedagogic Creed," *The School Journal* 54, no. 3 (1897): 77–80.
2. Robert D. Putnam, *Bowling Alone: The Collapse and Revival of American Community*

(New York: Simon and Schuster, 2000) and Thomas E. Patterson, *The Vanishing Voter: Public Involvement in an Age of Uncertainty* (New York: Alfred Knopf, 2002).

3. Sherry Schwartz, "Hannah Adams: The Pioneer Intellect," (Ed.D. diss., Teachers College, Columbia University, 1999).

4. Christine Woyshner argues in "Political History as Women's History: Toward a More Inclusive Curriculum," *Theory and Research in Social Education* 30, no. 3 (2002): 354–380, that political activity needs to be conceptualized broadly and calls on feminist theorists, especially Paula Baker, to reconsider what it means to be political in American society. An important subfield within social studies education has been, since its formalization as a school subject, civic education, with its explicit orientation towards promulgating democratic values by means of one or more courses dealing with citizens' responsibilities in a democracy. These courses are often called "Problems of Democracy," "Participation in Government," or simply "Civics." A prominent contemporary social studies educator working in this vein is Walter Parker. See, in particular, his book *Teaching Democracy* (New York: Teachers College Press, 2002).

5. Margaret Smith Crocco and O. L. Davis Jr., eds., *"Bending the Future to Their Will": Civic Women, Social Education, and Democracy* (Lanham, MD: Rowman & Littlefield Publishers, Inc., 1999), 1.

6. For a description of the enormous influence of colleges on private schools, see Arthur G. Powell, *Lessons from Privilege: the American Prep School Tradition* (Cambridge, MA: Harvard University Press, 1996). Innovations such as the Advanced Placement program first gained widespread acceptance in prep schools, but have gradually made their way into many public schools as well. See, also, Nicholas Lemann, *The Big Test: The Secret History of the American Meritocracy* (New York: Farrar, Straus, and Giroux, 1998).

7. Arthur G. Powell, Eleanor Farrar, and David K. Cohen, *The Shopping Mall High School: Winners and Losers in the Educational Marketplace* (Boston: Houghton Mifflin, 1985). See also, David L. Angus and Jeffrey E. Mirel, *The Failed Promise of the American High School, 1890–1995* (New York: Teachers College Press, 1999).

8. National Commission on Excellence in Education, *A Nation at Risk* (Washington, DC: Author, 1983); for a review of the long term impact of this publication, see David T. Gordon, ed., *A Nation Reformed?: American Education 20 Years after A Nation at Risk* (Cambridge, MA: Harvard Education Publishing Group, 2003).

9. Michael B. Lybarger, "Need as Ideology: A Look at the Early Social Studies," in *The Formation of School Subjects: The Struggle for Creating an American Institution,* ed. Thomas S. Popkewitz (New York: Falmer Press, 1987), 176–190.

10. Decker F. Walker and Jonas F. Soltis, *Curriculum and Aims,* 3rd edition (New York: Teachers College Press, 1997), 1.

11. Herbert M. Kliebard, "The Effort to Reconstruct the Modern American Curriculum," in *The Curriculum: Problems, Politics, and Possibilities, 2nd edition,* eds. Landon E. Beyer and Michael W. Apple (New York: State University of New York Press, 1998), 21–33; emphasis in original, p. 21.

12. Stephen J. Thornton, "Social Studies Teachers as Curricular Instructional Gatekeepers," in *Handbook of Research on Social Studies Teaching and Learning,* ed. James Shaver (New York: McGraw Hill, 1991), 237–248.

13. Arthur W. Dunn, *The Social Studies in Secondary Education* (Washington, DC: The National Education Association, 1916), 54–56.

14. John F. McClymer, "The Federal Government and the Americanization Movement, 1915-1924," *Prologue* 10 (Spring 1978): 28–42.

15. Edward A. Krug, *The Shaping of the American High School, 1880–1920* Vol. I (Madison: University of Wisconsin Press, 1969), 410, 411, 420.

16. American Education Fellowship. Commission on the Secondary School Curriculum, *The Social Studies in General Education* (New York: D. Appleton-Century Co., 1940), 129–130, 171–173.

17. American Education Fellowship, *The Social Studies*, 46–47, 233.

18. B. Edward McClellan, *Moral Education in America: Schools and the Shaping of Character from Colonial Times to the Present* (New York: Teachers College Press, 1999), 59, 73.

19. Herbert M. Kliebard, *The Struggle for the American Curriculum, 1893–1958* (New York: Routledge, 1995), Chapter 9.

20. Peter B. Dow, *Schoolhouse Politics: Lessons from the Sputnik Era* (Cambridge: Harvard University Press, 1991), 79–81.

21. Dow, *Schoolhouse Politics*, 178–187.

22. James A. Banks, *Teaching Strategies for Ethnic Studies* (Boston: Allyn and Bacon, 1975), 3–21.

23. Jonathan Zimmerman provides an overview of educational problems related to the social change of the seventies, eighties, and nineties in *Whose America? Culture Wars in the Public Schools* (Cambridge, MA: Harvard University Press, 2002).

24. Edward B. Jenkinson, *The School Protest Movement* (Bloomington, IN: Phi Delta Kappa Educational Foundation, 1986).

25. Joe L. Kincheloe, *Getting Beyond the Facts: Teaching Social Studies/Social Science in the Twenty-First Century,* 2nd edition (New York: Peter Lang, 2001).

26. Diane Ravitch, *Left Back: A Century of Failed School Reforms* (New York: Simon and Schuster, 2000).

27. For example, see Murry R. Nelson, "Emma Willard: Pioneer in Social Studies Education," *Theory and Research in Social Education* 15, no. 4 (1987): 245–256; Stuart A. McAninch, "The Educational Theory of Mary Sheldon Barnes: Inquiry Learning as Indoctrination in History Education," *Educational Theory* 40, no. 1 (1990): 45–52; Michael Whelan, "Albert Bushnell Hart and the Origins of Social Studies Education," *Theory and Research in Social Education* 22, no. 4 (1994): 423; and Michael Whelan, "Social Studies for Social Reform: Charles Beard's Vision of History and Social Studies Education," *Theory and Research in Social Education* 25, no. 3 (1997): 288–315. Others have focused on committees or programs, such as David Warren Saxe, *Social Studies in Schools: A History of the Early Years* (Albany, NY: SUNY Press, 1991). Saxe relies almost exclusively on the documents of the various social studies committees of the National Education Association.

28. O. L. Davis, Jr., "Understanding the History of the Social Studies," in *The Social Studies: Eightieth Yearbook of the National Society for the Study of Education* (Chicago: University of Chicago Press, 1981), 19–20.

29. Daniel Tanner and Laurel Tanner, *History of the School Curriculum* (New York: Macmillan, 1990), 20. Look, for example, at the impact of the Cold War on science education found in John L. Rudolph, *Scientists in the Classroom: The Cold War Reconstruction of American Science Education* (New York: Palgrave Macmillan, 2002).

30. Pinar, 243–44; Catherine Cornbleth, "Curriculum in and out of Context," *Journal of Curriculum and Supervision* 3, no. 2 (1988), 85.

31. We acknowledge James Shaver's comment that change in social studies resembles ripples across a large lake: much surface movement yet little that gets disturbed under-

neath the surface. In *Handbook of Research on Social Studies Teaching and Learning* (New York: McGraw-Hill, 1991).

32. Excellent examinations of these changes may be found in Rogers M. Smith, *Civic Ideals: Conflicting Visions of Citizenship in U.S. History* (New Haven, CT: Yale University Press, 1997); Linda Kerber, *No Constitutional Right to Be Ladies* (New York: Hill and Wang, 1998); Eric Foner, *The Story of American Freedom* (New York: Oxford University Press, 2002); and Alice Kessler-Harris, *In Pursuit of Equity: Women, Men, and The Quest for Economic Citizenship in 20th Century America* (New York: Oxford, 2001).

33. Pinar, 14.

34. Lynda Symcox, *Whose History? The Struggle for National Standards in History* (New York: Teachers College Press, 2002).

35. Mary Louise Seguel, *The Curriculum Field: Its Formative Years* (New York: Teachers College Press, 1966).

36. Ellen C. Lagemann, *An Elusive Science: The Troubling History of Education Research* (Chicago: University of Chicago Press, 2000).

37. R. Freeman Butts, "Historical Perspectives on Civic Education in the United States," in *Education for Responsible Citizenship,* ed. National Task Force on Citizenship Education (New York: McGraw-Hill, 1977), 47.

38. Kenneth Sirotnik, "What Goes on In Classrooms? Is This the Way We Want It?," in Beyer and Apple, *The Curriculum,* 1988, 59.

39. Michael W. Apple, "Social Crisis and Curriculum Accords," *Educational Theory* 38, no. 2 (1988): 201. See also Michael W. Apple, *Ideology and Curriculum,* 2nd edition (New York: Routledge, 1990).

40. Michael W. Apple, *Official Knowledge,* 2nd edition (New York: Routledge, 2000).

41. Pinar, 251. See also Apple, *Ideology and Curriculum.*

42. See, for example, the comments of David Warren Saxe on multiculturalism in "Patriotism versus Multiculturalism in Times of War," *Social Education* 67, no. 2 (2003): 107–109. Saxe's point of view seems to be a clear indicator that he believes multiculturalism to have become "official knowledge" within the social studies.

43. Thornton, "Social Studies Teachers as Curricular Instructional Gatekeepers."

44. Apple, *Official Knowledge,* 43.

45. Angela Valenzuela, *Subtractive Schooling: U.S.-Mexican Youth and the Politics of Caring* (New York: State University of New York Press, 1999); Paula S. Fass, *Outside In: Minorities and the Transformation of American Education* (New York: Oxford University Press, 1989); and Joel Spring, *Deculturalization and the Struggle for Equality* (New York: McGraw-Hill, 1997).

46. Kenneth Teitelbaum, "Outside the Selective Tradition: Socialist Curriculum for Children in the United States, 1900–1920," in *The Formation of School Subjects: The Struggle for Creating an American Tradition,* ed. Thomas S. Popkewitz (New York: The Falmer Press, 1987), 238–268.

47. Susan E. Noffke, "Multicultural Curricula: 'Whose Knowledge?' and Beyond," in *The Curriculum: Problems, Politics, and Possibilities,* 2nd edition, eds. Landon E. Beyer and Michael W. Apple (New York: SUNY Press, 1998), 101–116, and Adam Fairclough, *Teaching Equality: Black Schools in the Age of Jim Crow* (Athens, GA: University of Georgia Press, 2001).

48. Kliebard, *The Struggle for the American Curriculum,* xiv–xv.

49. Sirotnik, "What Goes on in Classrooms? Is This the Way We Want it?" In Beyer and Apple, *The Curriculum,* 1988, 58–79.

1

Chara Haeussler Bohan

EARLY VANGUARDS OF PROGRESSIVE EDUCATION: THE COMMITTEE OF TEN, THE COMMITTEE OF SEVEN, AND SOCIAL EDUCATION

In 1896, X-rays were used in the United States for the first time in the treatment of breast cancer, the Spanish American War approached as the U.S. Congress granted belligerent status to revolutionaries in Cuba, *Plessy v. Ferguson* was affirmed by the U.S. Supreme Court, thereby upholding the "separate but equal doctrine," and Utah entered the Union as the 45th state with a constitution that included women's suffrage.[1] On the verge of the twentieth century, the United States was not a superpower, but increasingly a nation of recent immigrants filled with complexities and contradictions, striving to achieve prominence. How could women be granted rights in one state, while at the same time blacks could be denied rights by the federal government? How could scientists make progress in the treatment of disease, while at the same time scientific knowledge further the massive killing of humans in war? How were such paradoxes possible in the United States? How did public education, and in particular the late nineteenth-century history and social science curricula, address these social issues and contribute to changing notions of citizenship? Clearly, the 1890s brought change and transformation, sprinkled with attempts to cling to the past and preserve the status quo.

Public education, and social education especially, played an essential role in the dramatic transformation of American society. By the early twentieth century, a new citizenship education curriculum had emerged, which endorsed a significantly broadened definition of citizenship. The hallmark of progressive era educational change was the development of new social science methods of research and investigation, expanded social studies course sequences, innovative experiential teaching methods, social studies curricula designed for younger children, and new community civics courses which "completely ignored formal politics and government in favor of themes of cooperation and community."[2] By emphasizing the cultural concept of citizenship rather than a narrow legal conception, groups such as women, blacks, and children, who traditionally had not possessed political rights, such as voting, were included in the new social education curricula. Notions of improving society through cooperation, community works, and social activism were essential components of the progressive era legacy. Today, the high school social studies curricula throughout the United States differs only slightly from that recommended by progressive era educators who served on national committees to propose modifications to the school curricula. The antecedents of this educational change were evidenced in the 1880s.

In the 1890s, the progressive movement in the United States was in its infancy. Progressivism was largely conceived as a democratic reform movement response to the problems and paradoxes evident in the Gilded Age. The post–Civil War era witnessed rapid industrialization, massive immigration, the rise of "robber barons," the growth of corporate business, increased corruption among big city bosses, and rampant tenement conditions among the poor and working classes. Progressives, although not a uniform group, sought to correct these pernicious evils through increased democracy, regulation of big business, public service, social justice, conservation, and public service.[3] Progressivism soon embraced reform of the education system. Although Lawrence Cremin claims in *The Transformation of the School: Progressivism in American Education 1876–1957* that a capsule definition of progressive education did not exist, for "progressive education meant different things to different people, and these differences were only compounded by the remarkable diversity of American education," he contends that progressive education was a "vast humanitarian effort" and a "many-sided effort to use the schools to improve the lives of individuals."[4] More recently, William Reese also argues that the origins of progressive education "were part of a larger humanitarian movement [that] sought both social stability and social uplift."[5]

During the late nineteenth century, in the education arena, important events developed as part of the progressive movement. Progressive educators and citizens sought not only to improve the quality of education but also to increase access to education. This laboratory of democracy began with the school. In 1892, the National Education Association (NEA) created the Committee of Ten to report on the status of secondary education and to recommend standards in the various school subjects. Its special subcommittee on History, Civil Government, and Political Economy met at Madison, Wisconsin, and developed recommendations to the larger Committee for the teaching of social science subjects in high schools. Four years later, in 1896, the American Historical Association's Committee of Seven evaluated and further developed recommendations for the teaching of historical studies in secondary schools. The work of these committees and several subsequent committees, such as the Committee of Five (1911), the Committee of Eight (1912), and the Commission on the Reorganization of Secondary Education

(CRSE, 1918), helped to lay the foundation for educational curriculum in general, and the teaching of social studies in particular, that exists in most American schools today.[6]

Clearly, the fundamental transformation of American education during the progressive era facilitated the United States' growth as a global power. Providing educational opportunities to all students essentially differentiated the United States from most other countries. Even if the paths of opportunity were not equal for all students, as established in 1954 by *Brown v. Board of Education,* the increased access to education as evidenced by the growth in the number of schools and the number of students attending schools, and the development of a broadened curriculum designed to meet the needs and interests of all students, helped create a more informed citizenry, a more educated workforce, and a broadened understanding of citizenship, in general.

Reese traces the origins of progressivism to a "rising ethos of caring within emergent capitalism, which increased human misery, but also [promoted] empathy, compassion, and social action."[7] He claims that progressivism had antecedents in Romanticism and the eighteenth- and nineteenth-century reform movements of the Western world. For example, a growing fascination with the child can be found in the Enlightenment and the Romantic-era writings of John Locke, Jean Jacques Rousseau, Ralph Waldo Emerson, Henry David Thoreau, and more specifically in the arena of education, to the work of Johann Pestalozzi and Friedrich Froebel.[8] The origins of universal American education, and romantic ideals of kinder, more active pedagogy date back to Horace Mann's vision of public schooling. Nonetheless, common schools were not preordained. Real educators, politicians, and leaders had to make decisions that affected untold millions. As Lawrence Cremin writes in the beginning of his work *American Education: The Metropolitan Experience,* Americans in the late nineteenth century faced "the challenge of modernism" but "inherited a commitment to popular education that was extraordinary for its time."[9] The notion of popular education was an instrumental part of the progressive education movement.

Throughout the later half of the twentieth century through the present, progressive education has been subject to criticism from educators such as Arthur Bestor (1953), Richard Hofstadter (1962), and to more recent attacks from Diane Ravitch (2000).[10] Yet, progressive education has also had its supporters, most notably Lawrence Cremin (1964), Arthur Zilversmit (1993), Susan Semel and Alan Sadovnik (1999), and most recently William Wraga (2001).[11] Perhaps if the debate over progressive education were framed as an argument about whether or not one favored universal public education the dispute would not have become so polemical. Despite champions and critics, William Reese suggests that scholars should be "humbled by the magnitude of the subject."[12] The social studies curriculum certainly has been a large part of the debate. As discussed herein, progressivism meant more than universal education, and social education soon developed a broader focus than the traditional study of political and military history from which the subject originated.

Many factors contributed to the growth of public schooling in the United States in the late nineteenth and early twentieth century. The larger national progressive movement, with origins in the 1880–1890s, certainly influenced the nature and development of U.S. schools. Indeed, schools with Deweyan progressive notions of pedagogy, child-centeredness, social reconstruction, reform, broadened conceptions of citizenship, and studies that emphasize preparation for life, predate the work of the CRSE report of 1918.[13] Evidence of the progressive movement's influence on education can be traced back to the work of the Committee of Ten and the subsequent work of the Committee of Seven. One outgrowth of the progressive education movement, the comprehensive high school model, still in place today, can trace its origins to the 1890s and a subsequent "four decades in a series of reports."[14] Furthermore, the subject of social studies did not originate suddenly with the ideas of "social studies insurgents" and the 1913–1916 Committee on Social Studies, as David Warren Saxe claims,[15] but rather derived from the early progressive movement and the early progressive educators of the 1880s and 1890s who gradually helped to initiate changes in school curriculum and pedagogy.

Progressive Precursor: The Committee of Ten

In 1892, the National Education Association (NEA) authorized the Committee of Ten to recommend standards for the various subjects in the secondary school curriculum.[16] The Committee of Ten was comprised of nine separate conferences based upon the academic disciplines of (1) Latin, (2) Greek, (3) English, (4) Modern Languages, (5) Mathematics, (6) Physics, Astronomy, and Chemistry, (7) Natural History, (8) History and Civil Government, and Political Economy, and (9) Geography.[17] The special subcommittee on History, Civil Government, and Political Economy, meeting in Madison, Wisconsin, developed recommendations to the larger Committee for the teaching of history in the schools. The Committee of Ten included several prominent historians, many who became vanguards of the so-called "New Social History." College professors at the Madison Conference included Albert Bushnell Hart, Charles Kendall Adams, James Harvey Robinson, Edward Bourne, Jesse Macy, William Scott, and future U.S. President Woodrow Wilson, while Frederick Jackson Turner assisted the members.[18] These historians advocated a broadened conception of history that was not confined solely to descriptions of military and political events. Later, in 1904 at the International Congress of Arts and Sciences, many of these same historians, including Woodrow Wilson, James Harvey Robinson, and Frederick Jackson Turner argued for interpretive history that incorporated all aspects of human life rather than traditional narrative political histories.[19] Robinson coined this approach to history, "the new history" and in 1912 published a book on the topic of the same name.[20] Other members of the Madison Conference headed secondary schools and included Abram Brown, Ray Green Huling, and Henry Warren.[21] A distinct conference on geography was held at Cook County Normal school in Illinois, and included college and secondary school teachers, a member of the Weather Bureau, and progressive educators, such as Francis W. Parker.[22] With an array of membership on the Committee of Ten that included college and secondary school educators and government leaders, much deliberation ensued at the meetings over the nature and plan for historical and social education in the schools. Yet, membership on the Committee of Ten has often been portrayed as elitist, furthering the depiction that the "Committee of Ten report failed to consider the full implications of what a system of mass secondary education would entail."[23]

Ultimately, the college professors, secondary school leaders, and government officials who authored the report of the Committee of Ten called for a more complete program in history, similar to what had been common in Europe for more than fifty years.[24] At the time, such recommendations were quite progressive.[25] History was a relatively new subject in the secondary school curriculum, compared with classical subjects such as Greek, Latin, and mathematics. Members of the Committee of Ten at Madison argued that the amount of history taught in nationwide secondary schools needed to be broadened. History was not a universally established secondary school subject in 1892, and such suggestions indicated a transformation of the traditional classical curriculum. For example, some schools did not teach history as a separate subject but incorporated historical topics in classics courses, other schools offered a single year of general history, while other schools provided a more extensive social education curriculum. Evidently, little uniformity existed among the secondary school offerings. In large part, the Madison conferees attempted to establish a degree of cohesion and uniformity among the secondary school history course offerings.

Although the Report of the Committee of Ten recommended a more comprehensive program of history education, it endorsed two specific programs of history curricula. The first began with fifth grade and included eight years of historical study, and a second began when applicable and recommended six years of historical study.[26] At a minimum, students could study two years of required history and one year of elective history in American high schools. However, the Committee members suggested that having students study history each year of high school would be preferable. In addition, the report stated that teachers should use new teaching methods that engaged students and encouraged students to "broaden and cultivate the mind" rather than employ the traditional method of having students engage in rote memorization.[27] Finally, the report noted that the purpose of historical study was to prepare students for life, not for college. Such statements clearly reveal progressive educational thought and the influence of leading progressive thinkers such as John Dewey and Jane Addams. The school curricula needed to be broadened, not only to stimulate students' interest, but also to serve a functional need. In addition, by recommending that the social education curricula be extended into the elementary grades to teach younger students, the curricula necessarily was more egalitarian than elitist.[28] More students would receive social education instruction, even if they did not attend high school.

The Committee of Ten report was a germinal, early progressive document. Diane Ravitch portrays the Committee of Ten's report as supportive of the traditional academic curriculum[29] while William Wraga states that such claims misrepresent the historical record and work of the Committee of Ten. Although Wraga claims that the Committee of Ten viewed high school as an elite institution, rather than "envisioning secondary education for all youth, as progressives later would do," the seeds for educational change were planted with the Committee's report, and with the inescapable growth and changes transpiring in American society.[30] Although only 3.5 percent of American youth graduated from high school in 1889–1890,[31] a few years before the Committee began its work, the massive immigration during this time period must have made the Committee of Ten authors keenly aware that the numbers of high school students were dramatically increasing even as they wrote their report. In fact, Ellis Island's Immigrant Station had opened January 1, 1892, to handle the immense influx of immigrants into the United States.[32] Indeed, G. Stanley Hall's contemporaneous criticism of the report, that it failed "to take into account that 'great army of incapables' who were then invading the schools," stands as evidence that educators were aware of the rising number of students in American schools.[33]

However, if the members of the Committee of Ten and later the Committee of Seven had hoped to retain an elitist curriculum they would not have extended their recommendations to the elementary history and social education curriculum, where a much larger percentage of students were enrolled. The Committee of Ten declared, "Anyone who reads these nine reports consecutively will be struck with the fact that all these bodies of experts desire to have elements of their several subjects taught earlier than they now are; and that all the Conferences on all the subjects except the languages desire to have given in the elementary schools what may be called perspective views."[34] These recommendations to modify primary school curricula ultimately led to the American Historical Association's Report of the Committee of Eight (1912), which specifically addressed the study of history in the nation's elementary schools. In fact, the Committee of Eight Report explicitly credits the Committee of Ten and the Committee of Seven with beginning the earlier formulation of a program of history in elementary schools.[35] According to the Committee of Eight, the six-year course of historical study for elementary schools, prepared by Lucy M. Salmon, however, had not received the attention it deserved.

The authors of the Committee of Ten report should be viewed as the vanguards of early progressive thought, not traditionalists committed to upholding the status quo. They sought to create a prominent place for history in the school curriculum, and they produced a document that recommended *changes* to history education in schools, which included broadening the focus and extending the history and social education curricula. These adjustments included revisions in the purpose, methods, and curricula sequence of history and social science education. These modifications continued later with the work of the Committee of Seven, a group that was charged with furthering the work of the Committee of Ten. In fact, Albert Bushnell Hart served on both the Committee of Ten and the Committee of Seven. James Harvey Robinson served on the Committee of Ten and the later 1916 Committee on Social Studies, a subcommittee of the Commission on the Reorganization of Secondary Education (CRSE). Obviously, there was continuity of progressive educational thought and membership on these committees.

The progressive educational reform that resulted from the work of these committees was fortuitous because the number of students who entered American schools dramatically rose throughout the progressive era. As American students increased in number and diversity the need for change became more profound. By 1900, shortly after the Committee of Seven published its report, the number of high school graduates as a percentage of the U.S. population had nearly doubled to 6.4 percent. Remarkable increases in high school graduation continued throughout the progressive era, during the early part of the twentieth century. In 1920 graduates comprised 16.8 percent of the population; in 1930 they comprised 29.0 percent of the population; in 1940 they were 50.8 percent of the population.[36] The progressive era witnessed unprecedented growth in the numbers of students attending school, unlike any expansion before or since. American schools were compelled to respond to increased enrollment and changing demographics.

Progressive era changes to school curricula, however, did not result solely from rising enrollment in American public schools. A subtle egalitarian sentiment that the recommendations should be the same for all, that education was preparation for life and therefore suitable preparation for college, and that all students were entitled to the best methods of teaching the various subjects, pervaded the Committee of Ten report.[37] Indeed, the committee noted,

> . . . our interest is in the school children who have no expectation of going to college, the larger number of whom will not even enter a high school. This feeling is strengthened by the consideration that proportionally a much smaller number of girls go to college than of the boys, and it is important that both sexes shall be well grounded on these subjects. An additional responsibility is thrown upon the American system of education by the great number of children of foreigners, children who must depend on the schools for their notions of American institutions . . .[38]

Finally, the Committee of Ten report mentioned that the methods teachers employed should cultivate the mind and teach the individual to think, rather than to promote rote memorization. The Committee added that historical studies were particularly well suited to develop good citizens and promote moral character.[39] These ideals were hallmarks of progressive era reform movements. More specific elaboration of progressive changes in the study of history in the schools was expanded upon by the Committee of Seven.

The Deliberations of the Committee of Seven

Members of the Committee of Seven hailed from the American Historical Association (AHA). Founded in 1884 at Johns Hopkins University, the AHA was the first national association dedicated to promoting an interest in the study of history.[40] Concerned about the status of historical studies in secondary education, August F. Nightingale, Chairman of the National Education Association's Committee on College Entrance Requirements, had asked historians at the 1896 meeting of the American Historical Association to provide a report detailing the practice of teaching history in American schools.[41] In order to make an accurate evaluation, committee members conducted a nationwide survey of the subject of history in schools, analyzed the resultant data, and made appropriate recommendations based upon the social science findings. The Committee of Seven's report had a significant and lasting impact on the practice of history and social education in American schools, and vestiges remain in public schools today. For example, a three- or four-year sequence of social science courses in high school remains the typical program of study in most of the nation's public high schools.

As its charter, the Committee planned to make recommendations about the teaching of history and to foster more uniformity in secondary school history. The Committee of Seven considered the scope and sequence of history offerings in secondary schools and suggested college entrance requirements.[42] The report recommended a four-year course of study that included Ancient History, Medieval and Modern European History, English History, American History, and Civil Government. The report also proposed that amount of time students engaged in historical studies increase. The members of the Committee of Seven were: Andrew McLaughlin (chairman), Herbert B. Adams, George L. Fox, Albert Bushnell Hart, Charles H. Haskins, H. Morse Stephens, and Lucy M. Salmon.[43] Six members were prominent historians. Herbert B. Adams had organized the American Historical Association at its founding in 1884. Harvard historian, Albert Bushnell Hart, a prolific author, had written a popular guide on the study of American History.[44] Hart later was elected President of the American Political Science Association (1912) and the AHA (1909).[45] George L. Fox, Headmaster of the Hopkins Grammar School in New Haven, Connecticut, was the only individual practicing in a secondary school.[46] The only woman on the committee, Lucy Maynard Salmon, was chair of the history department at Vassar College.[47] In 1915, Salmon became the first woman elected to the Executive Council of the AHA, at a time when women in most states remained disenfranchised. Salmon's election to the AHA Executive Council highlights the membership's support for a broadened conception of citizenship. Had election been reserved only to those with the legal right to vote, Salmon could not have served on the AHA Executive Council.

Initially the members of the conference conducted a nationwide survey of secondary history curricula in the United States. After expanding their examination of history instruction to an international level, these historians made general recommendations, primarily in the form of a report, to improve history education in the U.S. This author's chapter in the *International Review of History Education, Vol. 3* examines in detail the considerable international dimensions of the Committee of Seven's work.[48] The committee explored the teaching of history in Germany, England, France, and Canada as a means of comparing practices, methods, curricula, teacher preparation, and pedagogy, with those employed in the United States. Clearly, the Committee of Seven sought a broad base of comparison, rather than an inward-looking, myopic perspective that might have resulted from merely examining U.S. schools. Nonetheless, the Committee also had to ascertain the common practices of teaching history in American schools, for no nationwide study heretofore had been undertaken.

Conducting a survey, or "Circulars of Inquiry" as the members referred to their initial method of gathering data on the status of history education in U.S. schools, was the subject of the very first meeting of the Committee of Seven held in Cambridge, Massachusetts, on April 16–17, 1897.[49] The committee wanted to develop questionnaires addressed to teachers and decided to "secure lists of representative schools, through state education agencies." U.S. regional territory was divided among the seven members of the Committee so that the resultant workload could be evenly divided among the group. The Committee of Seven researched the condition of historical study by sending out several hundred circulars to schools asking for information. Rather than distributing questionnaires at random, the committee requested that state educational authorities suggest selected lists of schools, which fairly represented the teaching of history in the state.[50] Approximately two hundred and fifty responses were received and the data was then analyzed to determine the status of history curricula and instruction.[51] Survey questions addressed the conditions of the school, nature of history courses taught, the time allotted for history instruction, methods of instruction, the selection of textbooks, the use of collateral reading and source materials, library facilities, written work required of students, teacher preparation, and potential difficulties encountered.[52] A follow-up inquiry was sent to respondents that probed even further. These questions tackled some of the more controversial issues with respect to history education at the time. For example, questions from the second circular of inquiry included,[53]

1. Courses. What is your practice and what is your opinion on having a separate course in history for those only who expect to go to college; and another course for others?
2. Order of Courses. What do you consider the best order in which to take up the five subjects most frequently offered; viz American, English, General, Greek, Roman?
3. General History. What is your practice and what is your opinion on a one year's course (of five exercises a week) in "general history?"
4. Sources. Do you use sources for any purpose—either as collateral reading or as material for written work? What do you consider the advantages and disadvantages of the method?
5. Teachers. Are your teachers of history especially prepared for that work, as your teachers of languages or science are expected to be prepared?

The Committee of Seven members boldly employed newly developed social science methods to investigate the status of history instruction. Methods such as collecting surveys and analyzing statistical data were rare forms of conducting historical inquiry, particularly in the late 1800s. However, these methods were typical of the work of the new progressive professional social scientists, such as Lester Frank Ward, Florence Kelley, Jane Addams, and Carroll Wright.[54] Clearly, the members of the Committee of Seven were "progressive" in their approach to researching the status of history in schools. Nor were they afraid to address controversial issues. Some of the criticisms later heaped upon the Committee of Seven were topics that heatedly were debated among the members of the Committee at their meetings. The historical record indicates that many of the criticisms were topics argued and debated by the members of the Committee of Seven themselves. These deliberations were not issues that only later were addressed by social studies insurgents.[55] Committee members vocalized many differences of opinions about history education, especially with regard to tracking, course sequencing, the study of general history, the use of primary sources (sometimes referred to as the Nebraska method), and the preparation of teachers. In order to produce a report that all could support committee members reached compromises.

Through deliberation and inquiry, the members of the Committee of Seven were able to negotiate the tenuous line between what Schwab and Reid later described as, "inquiry suited to problems arising from states of mind and inquiry suited to problems arising from states of affairs."[56] In other words, the Committee members tried to negotiate the path between theoretical beliefs about an ideal history curriculum in schools and the practical realities of adopting a history program suited to the needs of a wide variety of schools throughout the country. The Committee of Seven's use of questionnaires represented a shift from the work of the Committee of Ten's largely theoretical inquiry to a more powerful engagement in practical inquiry. The Committee of Seven's recommendations had a profound and enduring impact on history and social education.

The dialogue at the first meeting of the Committee of Seven in Cambridge, Massachusetts about economics, civil government, and biographical studies reveals that the social sciences had gained enough distinction to be part of the Committee's deliberations. Members discussed various aspects of the history and social science curricula during two full day sessions. On several topics, such as writing a report, developing circulars of inquiry, conducting foreign investigations, and teaching American and English history, there was unanimous agreement and, therefore, limited discussion.[57] On other issues, however, members held vast differences of opinion. Pointed debate ensued. For example, the committee fervently discussed the issue of whether or not economics should be taught as a separate course. The committee resolved that, "Economics ought not to be considered a part of history; but that economic conditions were a necessary part of historical study."[58] Therefore, economic conditions were not to be neglected in historical studies, but economics was not to be recommended as a separate course. Apparently, many Committee members believed the study of economics was too advanced for high school study, and thought it should be reserved for college coursework.

Members also discussed the proposition that civil government be taught as a separate subject. The proposition was withdrawn, however, in favor of a resolution that civil government be taught in connection with American History. At a later meeting in Cleveland, Ohio, in December 1897, the Committee continued its discussion on the teaching of American History "with collateral study of Civil Government," and noted that at the elementary grades "it is desirable to teach American History and Civil Government with some preliminary or collateral study of biography."[59] The discussion about social science subjects and the use of social science methods in conducting an inquiry regarding historical studies in schools highlights the notion that the social studies did not suddenly appear, as depicted by David Warren Saxe, with the "social studies insurgents"[60] and the Committee on the Reorganization of Secondary Education report of 1918, but instead social sciences had been gaining prominence and consideration throughout the 1890s. Indeed, by 1909, one of the modifications of the Committee of Seven's report that had gained considerable support from the New England Teachers Association and that was printed in *The History Teacher's Magazine* was the recommendation that Civil Government be offered as a distinct course, separate from the teaching of American History.[61]

The Committee also debated at great length whether or not to recommend the teaching of a course called "General History." Members held sharp differences of opinion about the validity of such a course. Problems arose because various definitions of general history existed. In some schools general history was taught as a universal history course from the fall of the Roman Empire, in others the course was taught in connection with a particular country (as had been recommended by the Madison conference), and in others it was taught as a European history course.[62] Initially, the Committee could not reach agreement about general history, other than state that European history was a suitable subject for schools and that it would continue discussions on the topic at later meetings. Clearly, not all members of the Committee agreed on this matter. At a subcommittee meeting, held at Vassar College in Poughkeepsie, on November 26, 1897, Lucy Salmon voiced her support for general history because she had seen it taught with success in Germany.[63] At the Cleveland meeting, however, the Committee voted 3–0 (presumably the 4 others abstained as all were present) against recommending a course in general history.[64] This was probably one of the Committee's most controversial decisions, because its own data revealed that general history was taught in approximately half the nation's schools. Nonetheless, in the final report, the Committee noted that they could not recommend a course in general history because,

> ... such a course necessitates one of two modes of treatment, neither of which is sound and reasonable. By one method, energy is devoted to the dreary, and perhaps profitless, task of memorizing facts, dates, names of kings and queens, and the rise and fall of dynasties. ... By the second method, pupils are led to deal with large and general ideas which are often quite beyond their comprehension. ... we do believe that, if the time devoted to a period of history be sufficiently long to enable him to deal with the acts of individual men and to see their work, he can be taught to group

his facts; and that a power of analysis and construction, a capacity for seeing relation-ships and causes, and ability to grasp a general situation and to understand how it came to be, can be developed in him.[65]

The primary objection of the Committee, therefore, was the manner in which general history was typically taught. Several members of the Committee objected to the common, traditional practice of employing rote memorization in the teach-ing of history. Furthermore, they believed that the general history course, taught in one year's span of time, frequently was offered as the only history course in a school. In seeking to gain prominence and augment the study of history, the Com-mittee believed that one year was simply not enough time to devote to historical studies in schools.

The Committee of Seven sought to increase the amount of time students stud-ied history and also found it necessary to extol the legitimacy of history in the school curriculum. Members decided that "one year" of study would represent five exercises a week throughout the school year, but that "in framing its program, make possible to arrange the work in combinations of three or five periods a week, as may be convenient to particular schools."[66] If a class met three times a week, the course should extend over two years. The Committee recommended a four-year history curriculum which included (1) Ancient History, (2) Medieval and Modern European History, (3) English History, and (4) American History and Civil Gov-ernment. History coursework also was designed to accommodate the four differ-ent plans for earning high school degrees that were known as "Classical," "Latin or Modern Language," "Scientific," and "English."[67] The Committee of Ten and the Committee of Seven's acknowledgment of different high school plans suggests that the comprehensive high school, designed to meet the needs of distinct stu-dent interests and abilities, did not originate in 1918 with the CRSE, but had clear antecedents in the late 1800s.

The Committee believed that the purpose of historical study was for students "to become, not scholastics, but men and women who know their surroundings and have come to a sympathetic knowledge of their environment" and that "the most essential result of secondary education is acquaintance with political and so-cial environment, some appreciation of the nature and state of society, some sense of the duties and responsibilities of citizenship" and "something of the broad and tolerant spirit which is bred by the study of past times and conditions."[68] Yet, the discussion regarding pedagogical methods of achieving this stated purpose re-vealed the Committee's strong divergence of opinion. Some members preferred to use only the textbook in first-year history courses, while others urged a large amount of collateral work.[69] Nonetheless, a consensus held that historical study was not intended to encourage rote memorization of meaningless facts. Instead, historical thinking was to be fostered through textbook and collateral readings, written work, oral reports, map making and reading, notebook preparation, and the appropriate use of original source material. With regard to the use of source material, Committee members held significant differences of opinion. Some favored considerable readings from original source documents, also known as the Nebraska method, as advocated by prominent historians Fred Morrow Fling and Mary Sheldon Barnes. Other members, however, believed that high school students' minds were too inexperienced and immature to "form correct notions without some systematic survey of the field."[70] After considerable deliberation, the Committee reached a compromise. Students should read sources in connection with a good textbook, so students could learn, not the art of historical investigation, so much as "the art of thinking historically."[71]

At the third meeting of the Committee of Seven, held in Ann Arbor, Michigan, on April 8–9, 1898, the Committee held long discussions about college entrance requirements in history. After all, the main impetus for the NEA's appointment of the Committee was to recommend a uniform history course curriculum. Importantly, the Committee noted that the majority of secondary students did not attend college and, therefore, the primary purpose of historical study was not to prepare students for college, but rather to prepare students "for the duties of daily life and intelligent citizenship."[72] For those students who did plan to enter college, the Committee of Seven established college entrance guidelines for secondary historical study.

The Committee of Ten and the Committee of Seven reports reveal the influence of many educational leaders' progressive thought, including Francis W. Parker, Frederick Jackson Turner, Lucy Salmon, Albert Bushnell Hart, and perhaps, John Dewey. Educational historians have debated whether expressions about education's purpose in preparing for life, enumerated in the *Cardinal Principals* report and authored by the CRSE, reveal the influence of John Dewey. William Wraga argues that the *Cardinal Principals* is a Deweyan-progressive achievement.[73] However, Herbert Kliebard finds Dewey's influence tenuous because no direct evidence, such as a citation to Dewey, exists in the report.[74] Wraga responds that the connection between the *Cardinal Principals* and Dewey was intended to demonstrate "a congruence of ideas."[75] While there may not be direct citations to Dewey's writings in either the Committee of Ten report or the Committee of Seven report, Dewey traveled in the same circles with these progressive educational leaders. Despite the growth in the number of colleges and universities in the 1890s, the total number of college professors remained small and they certainly exchanged ideas at the conferences, meetings, and dinners they attended.[76] Lucy Salmon was entertained in Dewey's home at the University of Michigan.[77] An unambiguous portrayal of early progressive ideas, however, is evidenced in the writings and deliberations of the members who wrote the reports.

Significance of the Committee of Ten and the Committee of Seven

The significance of the Committee of Ten and the Committee of Seven's work clearly has been neglected in the literature on progressive education. The work of the Committee of Ten has received considerably more attention than the report of the Committee of Seven from educational historians, although Kliebard notes in his most recent work that the significance of the Committee of Ten "lies more in the mythology of interpretation that followed its publication than in the actual recommendations espoused by the Committee under its esteemed chairman, Charles W. Eliot, president of Harvard University."[78] Kliebard argues that the main objective of the Committee of Ten was to make curricula recommendations that helped prepare students for "life" but that more recent interpretations reflect "latter-day ideas about what constitutes an appropriate curriculum for life" rather than accurately portraying the reality of the Committee of Ten's recommendations.[79] At least the work of the Committee of Ten has received limited attention, albeit potentially misinterpreted. The work of the Committee of Seven has been all but forgotten.

It is surprising that modern education literature has paid so little attention to the work of the Committee of Seven, because the Committee's work was heralded in the several decades following the publication of the report. Many articles in *The History Teacher's Magazine* lauded the Committee of Seven's work and made teaching recommendations based upon the Committee of Seven's report. Henry Johnson, a prominent historian in the early twentieth century noted that the Committee of Seven's report, "was the ablest document relating to history for schools ever produced in America."[80] A possible reason for the neglect is that the Committee of Seven's work has been summarily categorized and grouped with the Committee of Ten. Hence, the Committee of Seven, like the Committee of Ten, is heralded as the product of those who favored academic, humanist curricula, or derided as an elitist document lacking progressive recommendations for educational change. Depicting the members of the Committee of Ten and the Committee of Seven as "traditional historians" in contrast with the "insurgent" members of the later 1916 Committee on Social Studies of the Commission on the Reorganization of Secondary Education bifurcates the portrayal.[81] Neither accurately describes the Committee of Ten and the Committee of Seven's deliberations and recommendations.

Both reports shed light on an early progressive spirit. Both the Committee of Ten and the Committee of Seven recommended that subject matter be extended to elementary schools, in order to reach a greater number of students at younger ages. The Committee of Ten explicitly stated that females and children of foreigners, those without political power, should receive the same benefit of social education as the males destined to exercise legal rights. Such recommendations reveal egalitarian, if not also paternalistic, ideas of citizenship that had broadened to redefine citizenship in nonpolitical terms.[82] The Committee of Ten's egalitarian character is evident in its commitment to providing the best curriculum and teaching methods to all students, rather than differentiating the coursework. Nonetheless, students could select from diverse degree graduation plans based upon their interests. The influence of the Committee of Ten in the nation's secondary schools was far reaching, and the Committee of Seven's work significantly affected the history curriculum in the nation's schools.

The Committee of Seven recommended a four-year sequence of study, despite awareness that such comprehensive curricula courted criticism. Nonetheless, the Committee believed that history and social education warranted increased attention in high school course offerings and sought to implement such change in the secondary curriculum. Today, the high school social studies curriculum differs only slightly from that recommended in the report of the Committee of Seven. Course titles may reflect more modern interests, but the study of history continues to dominate the present social studies curriculum in most states. Furthermore, a three- or four-year sequence of study remains the norm.

The work of the Committee of Ten and Committee of Seven ought to be viewed as an early part of a larger progressive movement that helped to gradually transform the schools. The Committee of Ten and the Committee of Seven did not recommend maintenance of the status quo, but suggested moderate progressive reform. These changes included increased support for universal public education, expanded notions of citizenship, extension of subject matter studies to elementary students, curriculum reform, acknowledgement that the purpose of secondary education was not to prepare for college but to prepare for life, development of curricula guidelines that broadened secondary courses of study (antecedent of the comprehensive high school), recommendations of progressive pedagogies rather than reliance on traditional methods such as rote memorization, augmented history course requirements, strengthened social science studies, and a reliance on social science methodologies to gather data and support for the Committee report recommendations. Clearly, late nineteenth and early twentieth century reform and change was part of a continuum, in U.S. history in general, and educational history in particular. Transformation of the school began early in the progressive era with the Committee of Ten, continued with the Committee of Seven, and culminated with the Commission on the Reorganization of Secondary Education. Perhaps a reconsideration of the progressive legacy is warranted.[83]

Notes

1. Arthur Schlesinger, ed., *The Almanac of American History* (New York: G.P. Putnam's Sons, 1983), 381–382.
2. Julie A. Reuben, "Beyond Politics: Community Civics and the Redefinition of Citizenship in the Progressive Era," *History of Education Quarterly* 37, no. 4 (1997): 399.
3. George Tindall, *America: A Narrative History* (New York: W. W. Norton & Co., 1988), 940; Lawrence Cremin, *The Transformation of the School: Progressivism in American Education, 1876–1957* (New York: Knopf, 1962), viii–x.
4. Cremin, *The Transformation of the School*, viii–x.
5. William Reese, "Origins of Progressive Education," *History of Education Quarterly* 41, no. 1 (2001): 3.
6. National Education Association, *Report of the Committee on Secondary School Studies* (Washington, DC: GPO, 1893). Hereafter cited as The Committee of Ten. American Historical Association, *The Study of History in Schools: Report to the American Historical*

Association by The Committee of Seven (New York: The Macmillan Co., 1899). Hereafter cited as The Committee of Seven. American Historical Association, *The Study of History in Schools: Report of the Committee of Five* (New York: The Macmillan Co., 1899). Hereafter cited at the The Committee of Five. American Historical Association, *The Study of History in the Elementary Schools: Report to the American Historical Association by The Committee of Eight* (New York: Charles Scribner's Sons, 1912). Hereafter cited as The Committee of Eight.

7. Reese, "Origins of Progressive Education," 4.

8. Ibid, 5–16.

9. Lawrence Cremin, *American Education: The Metropolitan Experience, 1876–1980* (New York: Norton, 1987), 19, 153.

10. See Arthur Bestor, *Educational Wasteland: The Retreat from Learning in our Schools* (Urbana: IL, 1953); Richard Hofstadter, *Anti-intellectualism in American Life* (New York: Vintage, 1963); and Diane Ravitch, *Left Back: A Century of Failed School Reform* (New York: Simon and Schuster, 2000).

11. Cremin, *The Transformation of the School;* Arthur Zilversmit, *Changing Schools: Progressive Education Theory and Practice, 1930–1960* (Chicago: University of Chicago Press, 1993); Susan Semel and Alan Sadovnik, *"Schools of Tomorrow," Schools of Today: What Happened to Progressive Education* (New York: Peter Lang, 1999); and William Wraga, "A Progressive Legacy Squandered: The *Cardinal Principles* Report Reconsidered," *History of Education Quarterly* (Winter 2001): 494–519.

12. William J. Reese, "Origins of Progressive Education," *History of Education Quarterly* 41, no. 1 (2001): 1

13. Semel & Sadovnik, *"Schools of Tomorrow," Schools of Today,* xiii; Wraga, "A Progressive Legacy Squandered," 517.

14. Wraga, "A Progressive Legacy Squandered," 511.

15. David Warren Saxe, *Social Studies in Schools: A History of the Early Years* (New York: SUNY Press, 1991), 1, 15.

16. See, Henry Johnson, *Teaching of History in Elementary and Secondary Schools* (New York: The Macmillan Co., 1917); Herbert M. Kliebard, *The Struggle for the American Curriculum* (New York: Routledge & Kegan Paul, 1987); Edward Krug, *The Shaping of the American High School* (New York: Harper & Row, 1964); Michael Whelan, "A Particularly Lucid Lens: The Committee of Ten and the Social Studies Committee in Historical Context," *The Journal of Curriculum and Supervision* 12 (Spring 1997): 256–268; Saxe, *Social Studies in Schools;* and Diane Ravitch, *The Schools We Deserve* (New York: Basic Books, 1985).

17. The Committee of Ten, 8–11.

18. The Committee of Ten, 10, 166; Saxe, *Social Studies in Schools,* 39; Whelan, "A Particularly Lucid Lens," 260.

19. Chara Haeussler Bohan, "Go to the Sources: Lucy Maynard Salmon and the Teaching of History," (Ph.D. diss., The University of Texas at Austin, 1999), 155.

20. James H. Robinson, *The New History: Essays Illustrating the Modern Historical Outlook* (New York: Macmillan, 1912).

21. The Committee of Ten, 10.

22. Ibid., 11.

23. Herbert M. Kliebard, *Changing Course: American Curriculum Reform in the 20th Century* (New York: Teachers College Press, 2002), 40.

24. Johnson, *The Teaching of History in Elementary and Secondary Schools,* 134.

25. Whelan, "A Particularly Lucid Lens," 264.

26. The Committee of Seven, 163–201.

27. Ibid., 166–167.

28. Reuben, "Beyond Politics," 407.

29. Ravitch, *Left Back*.

30. William Wraga, "Left Out: The Villainization of Progressive Education in the United States," *Educational Researcher* 30 (October 2001): 34.

31. U.S. Department of Education, National Center for Education Statistics, Education Digest 2000, Table 101, on-line at http:nces.ed.gov/pubs2001/digest/dt003.html.

32. Liberty State Park, "Ellis Island Great Hall: The Immigrant Journey." On-line at www.libertystatepark.com/immigran.htm.

33. Kliebard, *Changing Course*, 43.

34. The Committee of Ten, 14.

35. The Committee of Eight, vi- vii.

36. U.S. Department of Education, National Center for Education Statistics, Education Digest 2000, Table 101, on-line at http:nces.ed.gov/pubs2001/digest/dt003.html.

37. The Committee of Ten, 167; Kliebard, *The Struggle for the American Curriculum*, 12.

38. The Committee of Ten, 167–168.

39. Ibid., 169–170.

40. Charles H. Haskins to Lucy Salmon, 31 October 1902, Special Collections, Vassar College Libraries, Lucy Maynard Salmon Papers, box 47, folder 12 (hereafter cited as Salmon Papers). Haskins, Corresponding Secretary of the AHA, was trying to increase membership and included in his letter to Salmon a pamphlet detailing the founding history of the AHA.

41. Saxe, *Social Studies in Schools*, 53–54; Howard Boozer, "The American Historical Association and the Schools, 1884–1956," (Ph.D. diss., Washington University, 1960), 51, 55.

42. The Committee of Seven, v.

43. Ibid., iii.

44. Michael Whelan, "Albert Bushnell Hart and the Origins of Social Studies Education," *Theory and Research in Social Education* 22 (Fall 1994): 423–440.

45. Whelan, "A Particularly Lucid Lens," 260.

46. Boozer, "The American Historical Association and the Schools," 53; The Committee of Seven, v.

47. Bohan, "Go to the Sources"; Chara Bohan, "Lucy Maynard Salmon: Progressive Historian, Teacher, and Democrat," in *"Bending the Future to their Will": Civic Women, Social Education, and Democracy*, eds. Margaret Smith Crocco and O. L. Davis, Jr. (New York: Rowman & Littlefield, 1999), 47–92.

48. Chara Bohan, "Historical and International Dimensions of History Education: The Work of the Committee of Seven," *Raising Standards in History Education: International Review of History Education*, 3, eds. Alaric Dickinson, Peter Gordon & Peter Lee (London: Woburn Press, 2001), 56–72.

49. Records of the American Historical Association, Library of Congress, Box 459, from the minutes of the Cambridge meeting, April 16–17, 1897, recorded by Albert Bushnell Hart, Secretary of the Committee of Seven. Most examinations of the Committee of Seven have been based upon the published report of the Committee. This is the first undertaking, to the author's knowledge, to examine the deliberations of the Committee of Seven.

50. Records of the American Historical Association, Library of Congress, Box 459, Committee of Seven Official Questionnaire to Schools.

51. The Committee of Seven, 5.
52. Records of the American Historical Association, Library of Congress, Box 459, Committee of Seven Official Questionnaire to Schools; The Committee of Seven, 152–153.
53. Ibid.
54. Dorothy Ross, *The Origins of American Social Science* (Cambridge: Cambridge University Press, 1991), 158.
55. Saxe, *Social Studies in Schools*, 81–98.
56. William Reid, *Curriculum as Institution and Practice: Essays in the Deliberative Tradition* (Mahwah, NJ: Lawrence Erlbaum, 1999), 9.
57. Records of the American Historical Association, Library of Congress, Box 459, from the minutes of the Cambridge meeting, April 16–17, 1897.
58. Ibid.
59. Records of the American Historical Association, Library of Congress, Box 459, from the minutes of the Cleveland meeting, Dec. 27–30, 1897.
60. Saxe, *Social Studies in Schools.* "Social studies insurgents" is a term Saxe employs throughout his book to describe the authors of the CRSE report of 1918.
61. Saxe, *Social Studies in Schools*, 88.
62. Records of the American Historical Association, Library of Congress, Box 459, from the minutes of the Cambridge meeting, April 16–17, 1897.
63. Records of the American Historical Association, Library of Congress, Box 459, from the minutes of the Poughkeepsie meeting, November 26, 1897, recorded by Franklin S. Edwards, Secretary of the Educational Club of Philadelphia, December 1897.
64. Records of the American Historical Association, Library of Congress, Box 459, from the minutes of the Cleveland meeting, Dec. 27–30, 1897.
65. The Committee of Seven, 44–47.
66. Records of the American Historical Association, Library of Congress, Box 459, from the minutes of the Cambridge meeting, April 16–17, 1897, and the minutes of the Ann Arbor meeting, April 8–9, 1898.
67. The names of the high school tracks differed slightly in the meeting minutes and the published report. The meeting discussion referred to "Classical, Latin-Scientific, Modern Language and English," while the published report referred to "Classical, Latin/Modern Language, Scientific and English." Records of the American Historical Association, Library of Congress, Box 459, from the minutes of the Cambridge meeting, April 16–17, 1897.
68. The Committee of Seven, 16–17.
69. Records of the American Historical Association, Library of Congress, Box 459, from the minutes of the Cambridge meeting, April 16–17, 1897.
70. The Committee of Seven, 101.
71. Ibid., 102.
72. Ibid., 122.
73. Wraga, "A Progressive Legacy Squandered," 511.
74. Herbert M. Kliebard, "Letter to the Editor," *History of Education Quarterly* (Summer 2002): 309–310.
75. William Wraga, "Letter to the Editor," *History of Education Quarterly* (Summer 2002): 311.
76. Laurence R. Vesey, *The Emergence of the American University* (The University of Chicago Press, 1965), 264.
77. Linda Robinson Walker, "John Dewey at Michigan," *Michigan Today* (Fall 1997): 18.

78. Kliebard, *Changing Course,* 52.
79. Kliebard, *Changing Course,* 53.
80. Johnson, *Teaching of History in Elementary and Secondary Schools,* 59.
81. Saxe, *Social Studies in Schools.*
82. Reuben, "Beyond Politics," 420.
83. Wraga, "A Progressive Legacy Squandered," 494–519.

2   *Andra Makler*

"PROBLEMS OF DEMOCRACY" AND THE SOCIAL STUDIES CURRICULUM DURING THE LONG ARMISTICE

> *[T]here is only one possible position for the citizen and especially for the educator. He must inculcate day in and day out the attitude of critically studying the system, its historical development, the factors that produced it, the most objective exhibit . . . of its resources, its productiveness, its weaknesses and its excellences. One supreme loyalty will emerge from such a point of view—that of following the facts to their inescapable conclusion, whether that conclusion be to perpetuate the existing ordering or to reconstruct it drastically. On no other basis can a humane and democratic society be permanently founded. . . . This can be done only by building the school program about controversial issues and by keeping those crucial issues of changing social life ever in the forefront of discussion.*
> HAROLD RUGG, *American Life and the School Curriculum*, 1936[1]

It is no easy task to educate for the perpetuation of a dynamic democratic society. It requires commitment to popular participation in policy-making and implementation, and to change. In the United States, where control of education is vested in the individual states, the worthy ideal of local control has generated a struggle to control curriculum content among majority and minority interests, with the deck most often stacked in favor of established elites. The economic and social dislocations that shook the U.S. following World War I were reflected in struggles to "democratize" the curriculum to better serve large numbers of students from differing immigrant, ethnic, religious, economic, rural, and urban communities. Then, as now, housing patterns assured that some schools would serve students from very similar backgrounds (whether professional, immigrant, or rural) and some, mostly urban high schools, would serve a diverse student body. A key question was, and is, who should control the content of curriculum: Parent? Student? School administrator? Teacher? Public opinion? Legislature?

In this chapter, I present a brief overview of the status of the civic/social education curriculum in the interbellum years and assess some implications of the ideology of local control of schools upon the social education curriculum, as illustrated by the work of Harold Rugg, considered by colleagues and historians to be the pre-eminent social studies educator of the time. It is important to situate Rugg's work in the social context of his time and to consider the difficult implications of the tensions between democracy and expertise embedded in his work.

Democratic theory enshrines the idea that the people should govern themselves. The U.S. constitution tweaks this idea by establishing a democratic republic run by a government of elected representatives. The people tell their representatives how they want the country run by giving or withholding their consent, through voting, on choices framed by their representatives. In *American Life and the School Curriculum*, Harold Rugg wrote that exercise of this consent was "the essence of democratic government":

> The education we set up must be one that will perpetuate the democratic culture . . . he who dares to affirm a faith in democracy . . . must be aware of the assumptions upon which the practice of democratic government rests. The supreme one . . . is that the preponderance of individuals who make up society must have the capacity to give intelligent consent to the acts of their chosen governors. . . . they should have the capacity and the trained ability to understand their collective problems in sufficient measure to choose representatives to deal with these problems in their names, to review the acts and policies of their representatives in office, and to dismiss them from office or continue them in it. Such practice is the very essence of democratic government. . . . [2]

A linchpin of Rugg's stance as an educator, whether assisting teachers with curriculum revision or developing materials for students, was that ordinary people made decisions in a democracy and therefore needed sufficient information to debate knowledgeably all sides of an issue. However, his experience administering I.Q. tests to soldiers during the First World War caused him to believe that a significant number of adults were unable to reason abstractly at the level required to make important decisions. Rugg thus decided that the general populace should be guided by expert opinion, being unable to untangle the complexities of an issue on their own.[3] He lobbied unceasingly for the proposition that curriculum-making (his term for curriculum design and development) was a separate professional field requiring special doctoral level studies and therefore supported the use of expert consultants to lead teachers in district-level curriculum revision efforts. Rugg regarded the tension between the ideal of trusting the people to decide and the reality of needing expert informed opinion in order to make good decisions as a key issue in modern American life; he called this "the problem of democratic consent."

The "long armistice" was a time of intense contradiction and change in all aspects of life: in morals, dress, technology, women's roles, and forms of government. Increasing industrialization and urbanization; new psychological theories that located control over behavior in the individual rather than in religious authority; the emerging image of success of communism and social planning in the Soviet Union; and fear that the self-regulatory mechanism of the market had been shattered by the excesses of monopoly capitalism all contributed to a sense of social instability. Public intellectuals, academics, journalists, and school administrators pressed for curriculum reform. National committees of professors of education, history, economics, and sociology agreed that the curriculum, kindergarten through college, had to change; but there were wide differences about the nature and procedures of such reform.

Curriculum historian Herbert Kliebard has documented the conflicted co-existence of three primary strands of curriculum thought during this time, all of which developed in response to the stultifying effects of traditional education's focus on memorization and discipline.[4] One group of educators saw development of the child's inner potential as the primary aim of schooling; some practitioners in this group eschewed all pre-selection of study topics and relied solely on student-generated themes and activities as the curriculum. A second group took their cue from business efficiency experts who promoted "scientific" management of industry. These educators supported the use of scientific methods, such as IQ and other standardized tests, to sort students into curriculum tracks that best fit students' aptitudes, career goals, and academic abilities. A third group of "social meliorists" believed the primary goal of schooling should be the betterment of society. An off-shoot of this group, the "social reconstructionists," wanted the school curriculum to further social and economic justice.

Social reconstructionism was a philosophy of educating premised on the idea that social change directed to the end of equalizing a democratic society's benefits and burdens was better than waiting for possible social change to occur on its own. Rugg and all social reconstructionists shared the central assumption that the United States had the technological and productive capacity to provide the entire population with an adequate standard of living; they saw the Depression as a crisis brought about by lack of central control over economic cycles of recession and unemployment, combined with an unfair and unequal distribution of wealth and income.[5] The crisis of the Depression showed that the market was incapable of sufficient self-correction; therefore some social planning to achieve a more democratic and desirable society was necessary.

In the 1920s and 1930s, social reconstructionists believed some form of collectivist society to be inevitable in the United States. Social studies educators Hunt and Metcalf summarized their key ideas as follows: Social change is inevitable. Since the future decreed some sort of collectivism—with a choice between authoritarianism (communist or fascist) and democracy—some groups needed to push for democratic collectivism. As schoolteachers were the group in the U.S. most dedicated to democratic values, most knowledgeable about cultural trends, and in the most strategic position to direct social change, they should be "the architects of the new social order."[6]

University of Chicago professor George S. Counts represented the more radical wing of social reconstructionists. In 1932, he stunned the Progressive Education Association in a speech challenging teachers to lead the charge for a more democratic economic, social, and political system through outright indoctrination of students. Counts rejected the possibility of "complete neutrality" and the idea that education could be "completely divorced from politics." He wanted students to be taught to take a stand and commit themselves to act.[7] Unwilling to support indoctrination, but in agreement that teachers should help students to understand and accept their responsibility to restructure society for a more open, just, and democratic society, Harold Rugg and other social reconstructionists tried to redefine citizenship education to focus on critical analysis and discussion of America's contemporary social and economic problems. Conservative interest groups and America's entry into World War II deflected their efforts.

The NSSE and The First National Assessment of Curriculum

The public school curriculum is a primary vehicle for socialization to national and local values, codes of ethics and behavior, and implicit and explicit preparation of young people to fulfill gendered adult roles as family members, workers, and citizens. The European conflicts that erupted into the Great War prompted educators to downplay the value of competition and to encourage students to cooperate for the social good. Public support increased for patriotism, social conformity and a unified country, better working conditions for women and children, and the extension of political democracy (through reforms such as woman suffrage, the referendum, initiative and recall).

In the 1920s and 1930s, the National Society for the Study of Education (NSSE) published several yearbooks on curriculum issues; the most famous and influential of these was the 26th Yearbook on "curriculum-making," organized by Harold Rugg, a professor of education at Teachers College.[8] Contributors surveyed hundreds of schools across the U.S. to assess the state of the curriculum and make "objective" recommendations for revision and reform.[9] The Yearbook presented exemplary models of experimental progressive practice in private and public schools and an outline of principles and procedures for scientific curriculum design, thereby establishing curriculum-making as a new field of professional expertise. Despite deep philosophical differences, Rugg persuaded contributors to sign off on a consensus statement describing scientific curriculum-making (their term) as requiring the testing of new curriculum in school sites before adoption, grounded in research on child development and social analysis, and including three technical tasks of major importance: the determination of the ultimate and immediate objectives of education; the experimental discovery of appropriate child activities and other materials of instruction; and the like discovery of the most effective modes of selecting and organizing the activities of the respective grades in the school.[10]

The Committee also agreed on the need for "expert analysis" of adult activities and children's interests, the need for materials directed at the "conscious improvement of society," and "the teacher's need for an outline of desirable experiences planned in advance."[11]

In response to surveys sent by Yearbook committee members, hundreds of school districts, urban, rural, large, and small, reported on-going revision of curricula, usually initiated by the superintendent to better meet students' needs. Reasons for revision included rising juvenile delinquency, changes in the economy, and increasing retention in high schools of a diverse group of non-college bound students. Despite the push to save time by integrating content from several courses into one new course, the high school curriculum remained rigidly divided into subject matter courses based on textbook and lecture. Civics and social studies courses were the most-revised subjects, with textbook history and lectures as the staple offerings.

Most districts reported "democratic" procedures to revise curriculum; this meant superintendents formed committees of teachers, principals, subject supervisors with expertise in particular academic fields, and outside consultants to write curriculum.[12] Sometimes parents were asked to review new materials before formal publication as a course of study. Scores of new courses were added but few were dropped, creating a cafeteria of options for the non-college-bound. Progressive ideas, such as activity or project-based curriculum, student research in their own communities, and use of drama, story, and arts and craft projects to demonstrate student understanding of material, were used sporadically in public elementary schools and rarely in senior high schools. Materials written specifically for junior high students were lacking.[13]

The Special Case of Rural Schools

Educators across the country recognized the inadequacy of the curriculum in preparing rural students, often in one-room and/or under-funded schools, to make a realistic, informed career choice to stay on or leave the farm. New "community schools," established first in Great Britain, focused on cooperation and encouraged students actively to serve the school and the wider community in which they lived. In the rural southern United States, community schools worked for social change and community improvement especially in depressed areas, teaching modern methods of poultry breeding, animal husbandry, and public health along with academics. Elsie Clapp, a colleague of Dewey's at the University of Chicago Laboratory School, founded such a community school in Arthurdale, West Virginia. The school housed a community canning kitchen and doctor's office, established a labor exchange, set up a community fire brigade, and developed a community market. Arthurdale was a model for public community schools that "concerned themselves with community betterment . . . in health, government, occupation and recreation from nursery to adulthood." The curriculum of these schools was the "community's on-going experience."[14]

Although local control of schools was both a symbol of democracy and a legal right, George Counts noted "the various minorities in the community appear[ed] on the whole to have little influence."[15] This held true for urban ethnic and religious minorities, for Native Americans on and off the reservation, for linguistic minorities such as Spanish-speaking children in the Southwest, and for African Americans.[16] Despite publicly expressed resistance, curriculum was imposed upon minority groups, especially in segregated rural schools. For example, the General Education Board (funded by John D. Rockefeller, a supporter of Hampton Institute and Tuskegee) set up a system of industrial training for rural Blacks with specially trained "Jeanes teachers" and County Training Schools under White supervisors.[17] The Training Schools' mission was to ensure a continuing supply of Black agricultural and domestic workers for the White economy.[18]

By 1935, 44.2 per cent of all Southern Black high school students lived in counties where County Training Schools were "either the only secondary schools or the ones with the most number of grades."[19] Their goal was directly opposed by "Black schools controlled by missionary societies and black religious organizations [which] placed top priority on traditional academic education. . . ."[20] Black colleges, which educated most Black teachers, Black teachers in the County Training Schools who "subverted" the industrial curriculum by teaching academic courses, and Black parents who sought "established textbooks" agreed: they wanted book learning, not training for physical labor. However, the White administration of the Training Schools removed the academic courses from the curriculum.[21]

In his Yearbook chapter, George Works, professor of education at Cornell University, concluded that most rural schools were like those in Texas, adapting courses developed elsewhere to local conditions. Texas authorities believed the aim of education was to supply children with "the essential conditions of growth lacking in [their] normal environment." Concerned about the gap between "the subject matter of daily lessons and the child's interests and experiences," teachers and superintendents sought "special curricula" for rural children, especially for "Mexican and Negro" children.[22] Prefiguring evaluation expert Ralph Tyler's community studies, Texas teachers assessed home life and language, health standards, reading habits, young peoples' social life, adult attitudes and ideals, and the appearance of the farmstead to develop "more meaningful" differentiated curricula. Noting that children "imbibe" social attitudes as babies, the Texas teachers charged with curriculum reform wrote:

As long as there is local indifference or bitterness among neighbors, it is practically impossible to realize the larger spirit of human brotherhood in the child. As long as outside local contacts are limited to purchasing things over a counter or standing as strangers on street corners, the social sympathy and understanding basic to a democracy is next to impossible. Once these details of the local situation were known and appreciated by the teacher, the work in civics would never descend to the formal recitation of facts about political machinery.[23]

The teachers' remarks were so guarded it is hard to tell whether they supported identical reforms of the civics curriculum in White and "other" schools. In Texas in 1930, a group of first generation Mexican American parents began a series of challenges to separation of their children from schools "maintained for children of other white races" on the grounds that the segregated schools were inferior and illegal.[24]

Criticism of the Curriculum Status Quo and the Rise of "Social Meliorism"

Harold Rugg stated the Progressive critique of traditional education: From the beginning, the American public school curriculum had always been "tinkered" into a "patchwork . . . assembly of parts" that "ignored almost totally the emerging economic, political and cultural problems and institutions."[25] Journalist Agnes de Lima was blunter; traditional schools treated children as an enemy, requiring stultifying obedience and memorization of content disconnected from their lives. She saw the high school curriculum as hostage to college admission requirements.[26]

In our postmodern climate of cynicism, it is hard to credit the faith of 1920s educators that through scientific studies and methods, they could create differentiated better curricula for all. Sincere in promoting character education for a "good life" of the "highest grade" as the school's primary goal, they aimed to produce students who would leave school with the knowledge, skills, and desire to be good citizens and workers and pursue the educators' vision of a high quality life.[27] The "Eight Year Study," launched in 1933, showed that students who took new experimental courses were as successful in college as those who followed the classical academic curriculum. This eroded college control of high school curriculum and encouraged a new central aim for public education, preparation for different adult futures.[28] As the Depression deepened, more Americans accepted as plausible the critique of public intellectuals, academics, artists, and some politicians that the U.S. system of laissez faire capitalism needed fixing. More educators supported changing curriculum to promote greater student awareness of U.S. social and economic inequities, and to encourage students to see themselves as agents of social change. Improvement of society also became a central aim of education.

Democracy, Equity, and the Civics Curriculum

By 1923, 23 states had laws requiring teaching of the U.S. Constitution, often alongside the state constitution and state history. Despite the increasing popularity of "community civics" courses which stressed the government's role in promoting social welfare and students' responsibility to participate in local community life, civic education typically meant reading about the structure and function of government, rather than actual contact with government in action.[29] In the decade following World War I, recitation of the Pledge of Allegiance became routine. History textbooks portrayed the American republic as the form of government most favored by God, and the Westward march of the flag as a victory for God and the free market over heathen peoples.[30] Progressive educators fretted that students acquired more of their ideas about social relationships, the meaning of participation in a democratic community, and a sense of values and good character through sports, clubs, and school social life than from the formal curriculum.

To satisfy democratic tenets of equity for all students, vocational, technical, and commercial courses, industrial training for boys and home economics for girls, and a new civics curriculum of "core" classes were developed. Reformers' "steadfastly middle class perspective" led them to believe the remedy for problems such as "the unequal distribution of income . . . overcrowded and run-down housing, disease and malnourishment, or even the ignorance of proper means of ventilation" was to instruct daughters, especially those from immigrant and poor families, in the principles of domestic science.[31] Civics education expanded to include fire drills and accident prevention, physical education, hygiene, the effects of narcotics and stimulants, prevention and cure of communicable diseases, and a long list of good character traits (e.g., thrift, industry, honesty, manners, piety, obedience to parents, humane treatment of animals, chastity). The curriculum provided was often sexist, racist, middle-class in values, and biased against certain ethnic, religious, and cultural groups, but it was not State indoctrination.

Who Should Control Curriculum in a Democracy?

Surveys conducted for the 26th NSSE Yearbook confirmed that classroom teachers, no matter how poorly educated or overworked, were the primary agents of curriculum revision. Rugg criticized this so-called democratic practice on the grounds that most teachers had insufficient subject matter background and lacked training in scientific procedures of curriculum design. Education professors were alarmed as more states passed laws to specify "the amount of time to be devoted to specific instructional curriculum content," its grade placement, and penalties for non-compliance despite legislators' lack of qualifications as educators.[32] Thus, Part II of the Yearbook specified a procedure for curriculum-making that shifted control to a group of curriculum experts, and would, over time, severely restrict public school teachers' ability to experiment with curriculum. Small private elementary schools, often founded by women and grounded in a specific theory of learning, remained the locus of child-centered, activity-based, teacher-developed, and spontaneous, unplanned curriculum. Public schools with reform reputations (Detroit, Denver, Winnetka, St. Louis, Los Angeles) usually hired consultants from a college of education (e.g., UCLA, University of Missouri, University of Iowa, University of Illinois, Teachers College) to help teachers and principals revise and develop curricula.

The NSSE Committee wrote a "platform of *practical forward steps* in curriculum-making . . . [with] principles being phrased to fit the difficult administrative conditions of public education, namely, large classes, wide individual differences, heavy teaching programs, inadequate facilities, lack of well-trained teachers."[33] The professors agreed that teachers needed "an outline of desirable experiences planned in advance" and listed a series of steps for the scientific production of curriculum. Professor Bagley of Teachers College argued "for a reasonable degree of uniformity in the grade-placement of the *crucial* subjects and topics of the elementary curriculum" to form the nucleus of a common culture in the face of increasingly high rates of family mobility.[34]

Many of the school district curriculum reforms detailed in the 26th Yearbook used procedures similar to those advocated in Bobbitt's textbook, *How to Make a Curriculum*. As the man responsible for organizing the Yearbook and writing the template of steps for scientific curriculum construction presented therein, Harold Rugg is credited with establishing curriculum-making as a separate domain of professional expertise. He argued for "objective" selection of content and use of a specific method of approach in planning curriculum, and urged the use of scientific experiments to establish the content students most needed to study, ways to save time by creating new integrated courses from currently distinct subjects, and the optimum grade-level placement for specific content. He and Counts argued that small curriculum–writing committees of expert teachers and principals released from other duties should serve under the authority of central office curriculum specialists.[35] Centralization of control at the district level helped to standardize curriculum content, providing more uniformity across schools. This resulted in better education for some students; but it also made it harder for low income and minority parents to shape their children's education.

The Emergence of "Social Reconstruction" as a Curriculum Platform

The brash confidence of the 1920s masked growing social problems in the U.S, including a stunning increase in lynchings, a legislated quota system to restrict immigration, and the Palmer raids on suspected "Reds." The Stock Market crash, the Depression, and the specter of another large-scale conflict in Europe fostered the growth of an already-present critique of market capitalism, along with a call to give study of contemporary life and issues more time than history. Historian Larry Cuban believes that the propensity to see the school as a tool for social reform is directly related to the ideology of capitalist democracy:

> Since individual choice is central to the economic and political belief systems of capitalism and democracy, school becomes crucial to the shaping of public and private values in understanding the rights and duties held by each individual. Thus, when there are national political, economic, or social problems that have been defined publicly as crises, schooling is viewed as a natural way of improving individual behavior which would then lead to a lessening or solution of national ills.[36]

In the early 1920s, a group of progressive educators, including Rugg, began to promote a new social studies agenda—the "problems of democracy" (POD) course, centered on analyzing social, economic, and political problems in the contemporary United States. Like community civics courses, POD courses shifted the goal of citizenship education away from transfer of information about structure and function of government. Their aim was to turn students into informed citizens with the skills and information to understand existing social problems and the will to effect social reform, while community civics courses prepared students to help existing welfare programs. In his comprehensive book, *Making Sense of the Social Studies,* David Jenness says that as originally construed, POD courses did not promote "any provocative doctrine of social criticism."[37]

Educators who saw themselves as social reconstructionists felt that for too long the political and economic agendas of the propertied had been deliberately and unapologetically embedded in school curricula. Persuaded by the socioeconomic analysis of Charles and Mary Beard and "new" historians, such as James Harvey Robinson, they wanted social studies curriculum to acknowledge the existence of racial and economic tensions in American society and to prepare students to understand the sociopolitical and economic conditions of their contemporary world. Because the nazi, fascist, and communist states of Europe and Asia already were unambiguously using their education systems to further their specific political and social agendas, George Counts boldly asserted that democratic schools should unflinchingly indoctrinate students to work actively for democratic social reforms.[38] Counts wanted teachers to become agents of social change and build a society to benefit working-class interests. This posed a particular dilemma for the U.S., with its doctrinal commitment to freedom of speech and local, school board control of schools. As already noted, Rugg and others who shared Counts' critique of authoritarian regimes believed that indoctrination of students was antithetical to an open democratic society. Instead, they supported the introduction of open debate of controversial issues into the social studies curriculum on the grounds that "there is no other way by which the democratic principle of consent can be carried on than the way of parliamentary discussion of contemporary issues and problems."[39]

Curriculum Reform in Virginia's Black Education System

During the long armistice, the urge to revise curriculum spread beyond school districts. In 1931, Virginia embarked upon a statewide curriculum reform viewed as radical and democratic.[40] The new State Superintendent of Instruction, Sidney Hall, consciously tried to further a social reform agenda. Hall wrote guiding generalizations for the curriculum reform, such as: "Individuals and powerful minorities have always sought to control and to subjugate," and "The present social order is not fixed and Permanent. Man continues to modify it in search for justice and freedom."[41] In 1936, the Virginia State Department of Education called for curriculum with "special adaptations" for Negro children. This angered African American educators who saw this as an effort to dumb down the curriculum, based on the fallacy that Blacks were less intelligent than Whites. An Advisory Committee was formed under the direction of Doxey Wilkerson, then director of the high school program at Virginia State College, a Black institution. This committee followed the state's procedures for curriculum revision to the letter, but produced a totally unexpected result—a call for "special adaptations" for Black and White students to study the same curriculum, focused on political problems, racial stereotypes, health problems, economics, crime, and delinquency. They also suggested a program of study for all secondary schools remarkably similar to what today might be termed an Afrocentric curriculum:

> African-American history and music; studies of voting and nonvoting patterns in the black community . . . of African-American educators, scientists and inventors; studies of black poetry, religion, and folk life; readings on village life in Africa, the colonization of Africa; . . . slavery and its consequences in Virginia during the 1930s.[42]

Members of the Virginia State Advisory Committee worked with classroom teachers to develop units incorporating this material into curriculum to be used by all students. By the end of the thirties, there were

> over 200 African-American study groups in 42 counties . . . that had begun to discuss, among a wide-ranging set of problems and issues, civic participation, an idea antithetical within a segregated society and apparently so odious to certain local officials that the State Department had the study groups and conferences cancelled.[43]

Encouraged by the writings of prominent African American intellectuals such as DuBois and Carter G. Woodson, the ideas of social reconstructionism, and their work in curriculum revision, Black educators organized politically.[44] Among other efforts, they began a campaign for equal salaries for Virginia teachers of both races with equal qualifications. The development of a sense of agency among Virginia's African American educators can be attributed, at least in part, to the marriage of scientific curriculum-making procedures published in the 26th Yearbook and their response to Counts' version of social reconstructionism.

The Rugg Social Science Curriculum

As any student of the thirties is aware, conflict was rife throughout American society. Labor unrest increased. The Roosevelt New Deal was accused of being fascist, for restricting the operation of business through the National Recovery Administration, and socialist, for bringing electricity to rural areas through the Tennessee Valley Authority. Americans were reading novels critical of the American way of life, such as *Main Street* and *Babbitt* during the twenties and *The Grapes of Wrath* during the thirties; but many still wanted the schools to teach their children love of country and respect for traditional American values through familiar history texts and lessons similar to their own. During this period, textbooks representing new scholarship in history, economics, and sociology came under attack.[45] The 14-volume series of social science textbooks, *Man and His Changing Environment,* authored by Harold Rugg, went from being the best-selling texts ever published (despite the economic crises of the Depression) to being the target of simultaneous attacks by such stalwart guardians of the social order as the Hearst newspaper chain, the owner of *Forbes* magazine, the Daughters of the Confederacy, and the National Association of Manufacturers. Though millions of children used the Rugg materials without public controversy for nearly 20 years, by 1941, the books had suffered public burning and were banned from use in many school districts.[46] The history of the Rugg social science curriculum raises the uncomfortable possibility that tensions between the democratic ideal of "popular sovereignty" and the practical need for academic expertise in public education may be inevitable.

Raised in a working-class New England family, Harold Ordway Rugg earned a doctorate in engineering before studying educational psychology. He assisted the psychologist E. L. Thorndike in the administration of intelligence tests to soldiers during World War I. These tests revealed a large number of adult illiterates. Instead of concluding that public education was inadequate, psychologists posited that a large proportion of adults were developmentally incapable of advanced abstract reasoning. The I.Q. tests reinforced educators' and the public's support for differentiated curricula, including materials for the intellectually gifted. In his book, *The New Technology,* Rugg wrote that "universal understanding of political and social issues was unlikely in a complex industrial society"; democracy would depend on "a well-informed articulate minority" to lead their fellow citizens in making decisions at the ballot box.[47]

In 1920, Rugg was hired as Director of Research for the private Lincoln School, operated as a "laboratory school" of Teachers College. In 1921, he started work on a new social science curriculum for the junior high school with his sociologist brother, Earle, and a group of graduate students and teachers associated with the school. From 1921 to 1929, the team wrote and published three series of experimental social science pamphlets incorporating many tenets of progressive educational thought, including: the importance of learning through doing; individual self-expression, and creativity; Dewey's ideas about problem-solving and the relationship between education and democracy; aspects of Mary and Charles Beard's critical, class-based analysis of U.S. history and James Harvey Robinson's "new history"; and Rugg's strong bias that education and society both required advance planning to work efficiently.

The social science curriculum implemented Rugg's ideas about curriculum reform. The materials eliminated what Rugg saw as the artificial divisions between subject matters and successfully integrated content from history, geography, sociology, political science and economics; this approach angered disciplinary specialists at the university and confused teachers accustomed to teaching a specific subject such as history. To select the content, graduate students culled a list of selected important scholarly books for key generalizations about American society. Rugg wanted students to learn to think like social scientists; the materials were designed to prompt analysis, inference from data, judgments about the worth of evidence, and skill in making valid generalizations, or conclusions. The Rugg curriculum de-emphasized acquisition of isolated facts in favor of helping students develop their own warranted generalizations about topics of study. This was a stark departure from the norm.

After 16 years of work, including three years of "field trials" in 375 schools, the materials were revised into a best-selling series of textbooks, *Man and His Changing Society*.[48] This was the first large-scale systematic effort to ground curriculum revision in "tested" responses of students and teachers. The 14 volumes in the series presented "an integration of the chief trends of [democratic-industrial] culture, the factors that produced them, and the current problems that emerged."[49] Each volume was accompanied by a student workbook and a teacher's guide.

For Rugg, the main goal of social studies in all grades was to assist children "[t]o value and evaluate evidence, examine both sides of a question and to understand the social world in which they live."[50] He saw the "problem of [citizen] consent" to public policy as key because democracy is "postulated . . . [upon] building . . . common understanding." He knew that

> . . . the concepts that people use in communicating with one other carry great divergencies of meaning. For example, no two people mean the same thing by such concepts as democracy, capitalism, imperialism, Communism. . . . When, therefore, a political situation arises involving these ideas, each one will select his own personal meanings with which to respond to it. Hence the consequent difficulty of building solidarity of point of view, of securing universal "consent," and of producing joint action.[51]

Rugg's curriculum was organized around "open forum" discussion of controversial ideas, to produce a society of informed citizens able to provide guidance to their elected representatives, a symbolic way of demonstrating democratic consent. Although students were expected to research and analyze contemporary social problems, they were not expected to devise solutions.

The Rugg Social Science Course was important for several reasons. It was innovative, integrated several social science disciplines, valued creativity, and required student involvement in contemporary and historical controversial social and economic issues. The first curricula designed specifically for use in the thousands of new junior high schools, they deliberately applied progressive educational theory to practice. They rejected parts of the traditional story of U.S. history and incorporated material on the socialist party, Black history, women's history, and Native American cultures and crafts.

Rugg is credited with originating and conducting the first systematic research-based evaluation of curriculum materials. The preface to the 1931 edition of *A History of American Government and Culture* describes the field testing for that textbook; a similar process was used with all the materials in the series. The trials for that book involved more than 100 schools in 40 states. Students used more than 600,000 copies of the experimental pamphlets between 1922 and 1929 and the Rugg team read 50,000 written pupil tests. More than 1,000 teachers used these pamphlets and suggested revisions in small-group "round table" conferences. Although social studies educator Murry R. Nelson faults him for trying to make the materials "teacher proof," Rugg wrote that Lincoln School teachers asked him to demonstrate the new methods of teaching in the pamphlets. He thus concluded other teachers would need written guides.

It is important not to overstate the scientific nature of the field studies. Rugg was the sole author for all versions of the curriculum. For the initial series, he wrote a new experimental pamphlet every two months. The Lincoln School team was gathering and analyzing data from one edition while Rugg was writing the next. Despite Harold Rugg's critique of such tests, his brother Earle wrote short-answer, fact-based tests for each edition of the materials, often while standing at the printer's. Two researchers who studied the social science pamphlets, Murry Nelson and Peter Carbone, both question how systematic the field evaluations actually were, given the short turn-around time.

The Texts Themselves

The Social Science pamphlets depart from school norms in many ways; they stress intellectual abstraction, feeling, and creative self-expression more than retention of facts. The first seventh grade pamphlet, *Town and City Life,* is typical of the other materials in its approach to content and student activities. After reading about five generations of one family's history from 1750 to 1920, students are directed to conduct a town survey and construct a community exhibit from their findings. Study of each aspect of community infrastructure (e.g., the water supply, food distribution, health care) is followed by a student activity involving traditional research (in the library, on a field trip, writing for information) and/or novel methods (a survey or a score card rating their own community). The pamphlets use charts, graphs, photographs (unusual in textbooks of the time), and political cartoons to engage students in data analysis, interpretation, and critical thinking. The text emphasizes the main concept (called a "cue concept") of interdependence in terms of farm and city.[52] Students are advised: "We hope that before you complete your junior high social studies, you will be able to explain: how it has come about that each part of the world depends upon other parts of the world, and that injury to one part affects the whole world."[53]

U.S. history was, and is, a staple of the eighth grade curriculum. Following the emphasis of historians Mary and Charles Beard, the Rugg course incorporated aspects of economic critique and social history, with a focus on culture, daily life, and problems of the period.[54] Rugg discusses social class, even in colonial America. The founding fathers are presented as property owners who wrote a document to preserve their privileges; students are told that only three per cent of the population was permitted to vote. He blames technology and increasing industrialization for centralizing power and increasing advantage for the wealthy, especially after 1870. The Depression is presented as a result of capitalists' excessive greed and self-interest at the expense of their fellow men.

The first eighth grade history pamphlet contrasts photos of U.S. contemporary life with a written description of Native American life in 1492. The way of life and crafts of several Indian peoples are described, implicitly asserting that Indians had a life and history that predated the arrival of Europeans. The ninth grade materials devote an entire chapter to problems in the banking and credit system of the thirties; students are asked whether they think these problems can be fixed.

The curriculum reflects the contradictions and prejudices of the time: It is the presence of "colored people" especially Negroes, that "cause" what was then called "the Race Problem." Persistent visible differences inhibit the "melting" of these races and immigrants from southern European countries into the general population. However, Rugg also discusses intermarriage and the possibility of blended-race children. The evils of the slave trade are discussed; children are told Negroes did not come willingly, unlike other immigrants. However, as the materials were revised, the description of White plantation overseers as cruel and harsh (with a few decent men among them) was replaced with text depicting most slaves as well-taken-care-of and happy, with kind masters and only occasional cruel overseers. The books call U.S. acquisition of foreign territory imperialism. With rhetoric close to that of twenty-first century preservationists, wasteful use of natural resources such as coal, water, and forests, is strongly condemned.

The Theoretical Base of Rugg's Curriculum Practice

Dewey described a "learning environment" as one that drew out each student's potential for growth. The teacher provided an educative experience in which students actively participated, thereby reconstructing previously held ideas and feelings in light of their newly emerging understandings. Children needed knowledge of the accumulated adult wisdom to date and practical skills, but the prime task of democratic education was to support the growth of children's abilities to participate in democratic social groups.[55] Rugg equated ideal government with education. I believe the town meeting was his model—an educative open forum in which people learned about social problems and came to agreement about solutions through discussion.

Rugg was familiar with the writings of psychologist William James and philosophers Charles Peirce and John Dewey. In *American Life and the School Curriculum*, Rugg noted that both James and Peirce stressed the idea that "meaning is built up through *active experience*." Quoting James, he wrote, "Experience is never yours merely as it comes to you, facts are never mere data, they are data to which you *respond*, your experience is constantly transformed by your *deeds*. . . . The simplest process, the most elaborate scientific theory, illustrates how man never really finds, he always cooperates in creating his world."[56]

Rugg clearly believed that reality was a social construction. He was aware of the impact of perspective in shaping perception, writing:

> The purposes of education . . . are discovered by thought and feeling. They are personal, subjective, and individual. . . . The setting up of goals, therefore, is a matter of . . . the best judgments we can find. It is however, a matter of judgment framed by minds confronted by a particular social order. The judgment of the great minds of the meditative Orient, for example, will be very unlike that of the intellectual leaders of the industrial Occident.[57]

This sense of the relativity of values was unusual for his time. His efforts to assist students in understanding the concepts of perspective, tolerant understanding, and the interdependence of modern nations generated antagonism from conservative groups, who believed the schools should teach that American values were (and ought to be) universals.

Students should analyze "local problems and issues, and the connections underlying them" because "A valid program of education must be constructed directly from the life of the people."[58] Persons "of the deepest feeling . . . on the frontier of creative thought" should provide guidance for the curriculum maker's judgments.[59] These "frontier thinkers" included artists and intellectuals, but not necessarily academic specialists. Rugg's list of the "greatest" frontier thinkers, who sensed "the meaning of the startling changes . . . revealing themselves in industrial culture," included Thorstein Veblen, Charles A. Beard, John Dewey, Randolph Bourne, Van Wyck Brooks (a founder of the magazine *Seven Arts*), and Waldo Frank. Their writings inspired his critique of *The New Technology*, the ideas and activities presented in his textbooks, and his beliefs about social reform. It is possible that his association with a group of artists, including the photographer Alfred Stieglitz, solidified his conviction that artistic self-expression was a fundamental element of human personality. In his writings and curriculum materials, Rugg made a point of suggesting ways for school to nurture and support children's experience with many forms of art as an integral part of their social education.[60]

Individual integrity was important. Even educators with a subject matter focus felt the schools should help students to achieve "integration" so they would be good, contributing citizens with worthwhile personal and community lives. The implicit idea is a kind of social utilitarian calculus: a good, healthy, democratic society is a collection of some large number of happy, well-integrated personalities who know how to cooperate in a democratic way. However, few worried about the impact of Americanization on the personality integration of immigrant children or Native American students, who were required to reject elements of their family's culture to succeed in school.

Though trained as an educational psychologist, Rugg faulted the standardized testing movement because " measure of the product or the growth of one individual was assumed to be those of other individuals, rather than his own capacity for production or growth." He criticized the "widespread use" of external measurement norms for contributing "to the setting up of false standards within the school as well as to the enhancement of the lack of integrity in the individual and to the widespread development of a climate of hypocrisy in the social order."[61] The social science curriculum contained many student activities, such as research projects, analysis and drawing of political cartoons, and creation of skits, that could not be evaluated through traditional tests. Progressive educators felt that many of the new student activities required different kinds of evaluation instruments, such as observation, teacher record-keeping, and evaluation of students' research and other projects. Although some of these methods were becoming standard fare in elementary classrooms, secondary teachers typically had no experience with such methods of evaluation. Teachers, parents, and students were unaccustomed to grades based on learning activities that, unlike traditional short answer tests, had no clearly right or wrong answers. In this regard, the curriculum created some of the same discomfort as the "new social studies" materials of the 1960s.

The Problem of Consent Revisited

Rugg's materials incorporated critical questioning of the distribution of power and privilege during the 1920s, before a structural analysis of capitalism had permeated the public media. The critique became common in the thirties, when millions of ordinary citizens support Roosevelt's efforts to try to end the Depression. It is clear from the texts, however, that Rugg does not support FDR's measures to fix the Depression. For example, a section on critical thinking directs teachers to guide students to see whether it was the case, as the President claimed, that the NRA and other measures were responsible for reducing unemployment.

At a time when the U.S. was becoming increasingly isolationist in outlook, Rugg believed that students needed more study of the rest of the world, particularly post-revolutionary Russia and modern China and Japan, a novel idea at the time. Social interdependence, among individuals and among nations, was a key theme, with a stress on the significance of international trade and institutions such as the World Court and the League of Nations. Rugg also supported the study of comparative political systems (still a rare experience for students today).

Most significantly, however, the Rugg course of study focused on problems in American society and departed from the laudatory idealized version of the founding fathers and their design of the Constitution. Rugg often presented his opinion as fact, as when he wrote in the *Pupil's Workbook* to *The Conquest of America:*

> Who is the criminal? The man who exceeds the speed limit in his automobile?. . . . The man who drinks strong alcoholic beverages?. . . who steals $1000 from the bank?. . . who murders his enemy? The man who charges too high a price for food, rent, or clothing?. . . who advertises his product falsely?. . . who forces his laborers to work twelve hours per day at starvation wages?[62]

Much influenced by the Turner thesis, Rugg believed that the philosophy of competition and rugged individualism that permitted Americans successfully to establish communities on the western frontier had been perverted during the period of intense industrialization. His texts criticize the excesses of capitalist greed, but they also praise the science and consequences of technological advances. Though the consistent harping on the sins of big business seems strident today, it is important to remember that President Roosevelt himself offered a similar critique through his first two terms. Rather than viewing the Rugg Social Science Course as purveying an incipient socialism, it is more accurate to see it as a response to the Great Depression that presents ideas about regulation and government intervention that lost favor as the U.S. geared up for war.

Although these were the most popular textbooks ever published (an estimated five million pupils used the materials), and earned hundreds of thousands of dollars during the Depression, by 1938, conservative groups had mounted a strong attack, charging Rugg with lack of patriotism and subversive efforts to introduce socialism into public schools. In some states, the books were actually burned. Many Americans did not want public school curricula to focus on social problems, or to challenge the school history they had learned. Business groups were angered at the way the Rugg series portrayed them. Several critics did not believe students should study different points of view; instead, they wanted one "correct" version of issues, history, and American life.[63] Controversial issues were the heart of the Social Science Course, but school boards and administrators did not want controversy in their own backyards. Rugg's materials introduced democratic consent as a key issue and supported the idea that a small group of informed citizens should shape the opinion of the majority. Ironically, a conservative minority's refusal to consent to his view that controversial issues were the heart of the curriculum decided the fate of his textbooks.

Notes

1. Harold O. Rugg, *American Life and the School Curriculum: Next Steps Towards Schools of Living* (Boston: Ginn & Company, 1936), 303.
2. Ibid., 265.
3. Wilfred Carr and Anthony Harnett, *Education and the Struggle for Democracy: The Politics of Educational Ideas* (Philadelphia: Open University Press, 1996), 53, credit journalist

Walter Lippmann with popularizing the idea that most American voters were "politically ill informed, indifferent and apathetic" in two books, *Public Opinion* (New York: Free Press, 1922) and *The Phantom Public* (New York: Macmillan, 1925). In *The Social and Educational Thought of Harold Rugg* (Durham, NC: Duke University Press, 1977), Peter Carbone says Rugg was influenced by Lippmann's ideas.

4. Herbert M. Kliebard, *The Struggle for the American Curriculum, 1893–1958* (New York: Routledge, 1992).

5. Harold Rugg, *The Great Technology: Social Chaos and the Public Mind* (New York: John Day, 1933), 401–408, as discussed in William B. Stanley, *Curriculum for Utopia: Reconstructionism and Critical Pedagogy in the Postmodern Era* (Albany: SUNY Press, 1992), 12–13. The description of social reconstructionism in this section is drawn primarily from Stanley.

6. M. Hunt and Lawrence Metcalf, *Teaching High School Social Studies,* 2nd ed. (New York: Harper & Row, 1968), 278, as quoted in Stanley, 4. See also Richard J. Altenbaugh, *Historical Dictionary of American Education* (Westport, CT: Greenwood Press: 1999), 342–343.

7. George S. Counts, *The American Road to Culture: A Social Interpretation of Education in the United States* (New York: John Day, 1930); George S. Counts, *Dare the Schools Build A New Social Order?* (New York: John Day, 1932).

8. Guy M. Whipple, ed., *The Foundations and Technique of Curriculum Construction: Part I, Curriculum-Making, Past and Present* (Bloomington, Illinois: Public School Publishing Company, 1926). 26th Yearbook of the National Society for the Study of Education. Hereafter cited as 26th Yearbook. Prepared under Rugg's direction.

9. Contributors included a "who's who" of curriculum experts, among them William C. Bagley, Franklin Bobbitt, Werrett W. Charters, George S. Counts, Ernest Horn, Charles H. Judd, William H. Kilpatrick, and Harold O. Rugg. To differentiate between their "scientific" approach to curriculum revision based on research data, and traditional subjective approaches based on personal value judgments, the Yearbook contributors described their recommendations as "objective."

10. "The Foundations of Curriculum-Making, A Composite Statement of the Society's Committee on Curriculum-Making," 14–15, 26th Yearbook, Part II.

11. Ibid, 13–19. Franklin Bobbitt's text, *How to Make a Curriculum* (Boston: Houghton-Mifflin, 1924) laid out the principles of scientific curriculum design.

12. The term "supervisor" referred to subject matter experts with authority over the subject content in the curriculum, not those who supervise and assess teaching.

13. The first junior high schools opened in 1910; by 1930, there were 4000. Rugg's social science texts were among the first commercially available materials developed specifically for use at this level.

14. See W. F. Connell, *A History of Education in the Twentieth Century World* (New York: Teachers College Press, 1980).

15. George S. Counts, 148, "Current Practices in Curriculum-Making in Public High Schools," 26th Yearbook, Part I, 135–162.

16. Rubén Donato has described one community in southern Colorado where Hispanics held visible positions of power in politics and the schools. The social context and the curriculum supported the cultural and family experience of Hispano students as normative, rather than a deviation from Anglo ways. In this, the town of San Luis clearly was an exception to regional and national norms. See "'No One Here to Put Us Down': Hispano Education in a Southern Colorado Community, 1920–1963" in *Reconstructing*

the Common Good in Education: Coping with Intractable American Dilemmas, eds. Larry Cuban and Dorothy Shipps (Stanford: Stanford University Press, 2000), 68–81.

17. Northern industrialists and philanthropies funded the General Education Board. Quaker Anna T. Jeanes set up the Jeanes Foundation in 1907 with a $1,000,000 donation to "encourage the rudimentary education of Colored people residing in rural districts"; funds were dispensed by the General Education Board. Jeanes Supervising Industrial Teachers were "paid an average of $45 per month for seven months and were expected to encourage industrial education and community involvement in rural public schools." See Valinda Littlefield, 132, "'To Do the Next Needed Thing': Jeanes Teachers in the Southern United States 1908–34," in *Telling Women's Lives: Narrative Inquiries in the History of Women's Education,* eds. Kathleen Weiler and Sue Middleton (Philadelphia: Open University Press, 1999), 130–146. Also see Karen L. Riley, "'A Toilet in the Middle of the Court House Square': The Summer Teaching Institute of 1915 and the Influence of Booker T. Washington on Negro Teacher Education in Alabama," *Education and Culture* XVIII:1 (spring 2002): 2–9.

18. James Anderson, 292, "Northern Foundations and the Shaping of Southern Black Rural Education, 1902–1935," 287–312 in *The Social History of American Education,* eds. B. E. McClellan and W. J. Reese (Urbana: University of Illinois Press, 1988) says Du-Bois told Merle Curti in the 1930s that there was "a provable correlation between the migration of Northern capital to the South for industry and industrial education."

19. Ibid, 307.

20. Ibid, 295. In *Whose America? Culture Wars in the Public Schools* (Cambridge, MA: Harvard University Press, 2002), 32–54, historian Jonathan Zimmerman notes that during the 1930s, many White Southern school boards supported elective Black history courses that aimed to develop "race pride" for their Black school systems only. But African-American students who took these courses also were required to take the standard U.S. history course, where textbooks ignored minority contributions and regarded slaves and Indians as having received appropriate treatment.

21. In *Their Highest Potential: An African American School Community in the Segregated South* (Chapel Hill: The University of North Carolina Press, 1996), Vanessa Siddle Walker notes that the Caswell County (North Carolina) Training School was able to maintain both academic and vocational (industrial) courses during this period.

22. George A. Works, 173, "Progressive Practices in Making State and Rural Courses of Study," in 26th Yearbook, Part I, 163–185.

23. Ibid, 175.

24. *Independent School District vs. Salvatierra,* 33 S.W. 2d. 790 (Texas Civ. App,m 4th Dist., 1930). See Guadalupe San Miguel, Jr., "The Struggle against Separate and Unequal Schools: Middle Class Mexican Americans and the Desegregation Campaign in Texas, 1929–1947," 333–349, in McClellan and Reese. Texas desegregated schools in 1949.

25. Harold Rugg, 11, "The School Curriculum and the Drama of American Life," 3–16, in 26th Yearbook, Part I.

26. Agnes de Lima, *Our Enemy The Child* (New York: New Republic, Inc., 1925).

27. "High grade living" was a frequently touted aim for pupils' adult lives. See Franklin Bobbitt, "The Orientation of the Curriculum-Maker," 26th Yearbook, Part II, 41–55.

28. For an overview of the Eight Year Study, directed by Ralph Tyler and social studies educator Hilda Taba, see Kliebard, 213–222 and Daniel Tanner and Laurel Tanner, *Curriculum Development, Theory into Practice,* 3rd ed. (Englewood Cliffs, NJ: Prentice-Hall, Inc., 1995), 126–131; 229–234.

29. Courses in "community civics" were ensconced in the curriculum by 1915 most often at the elementary level and the ninth grade. They focused on a pupil's role in supporting the community's welfare (and the government's role in that endeavor), along with emphasis on sound moral values and good behavior. See Julie A. Reuben, "Beyond Politics: Community Civics and the Redefinition of Citizenship in the Progressive Era," *History of Education Quarterly* 37:4 (1997): 399–420. These courses also featured a change in instructional methods, away from pupil recitation to more hands-on (if equally teacher-directed) activities. However, the high school curriculum was slow to change; the typical pattern was to add courses without dropping old ones. Thus, J. K. Flanders of the State Normal School in Oswego, New York, found an increase in laws requiring the teaching of patriotism and a course in "civics" or "citizenship" of unspecified content. (See "Curriculum-Making by the State Legislatures," 26th Yearbook, Part I, 407–423). After World War I, the schools required increased teaching of cooperation as a social necessity along with more focus on patriotism.

30. See Frances FitzGerald, *America Revised: History Schoolbooks in the Twentieth Century* (Boston: Little, Brown, 1979).

31. John L. Rury, 239, "Vocationalism for Home and Work: Women's Education in the United States, 1880–1930," 233–356, in McClellan and Reese.

32. Flanders, 422.

33. Harold Rugg, 6, "Introduction, An Adventure in Understanding," 26th Yearbook, Part II, 1–8. Emphasis in original.

34. Bagley, 33, "Supplementary Statement," 29–40, in 26th Yearbook, Part II. Emphasis in original. The California Curriculum Study showed a high correlation between retention in grade (failure) and mobility, with two thirds of the state's children attending school in two or more communities before the eighth grade, one half going to schools in three or four different communities, and one fourth attending school in more than four different locales. Similar patterns existed across the nation.

35. See their chapters in the Yearbook, already cited. Counts especially wanted to end the practice of having teachers write curriculum at the end of an already full workday.

36. Larry Cuban, 384, "The Persistence of Reform in American Schools," in *American Teachers: Histories of a Profession at Work,* ed. Donald Warren (New York: Macmillan, 1989), 370–392.

37. David Jenness, *Making Sense of Social Studies* (New York: Macmillan Publishing Company, 1990), 77.

38. Counts, *Dare The Schools Build A New Social Order?*

39. Rugg, *American Life and the School Curriculum,* 299.

40. Connell, *History of Education,* 290–91.

41. Michael E. James, "Southern Progressivism During the Great Depression: Virginia and African-American Social Reconstruction," in *Social Reconstruction Through Education: The Philosophy, History and Curricula of a Radical Ideal,* ed. Michael E. James (Norwood, NJ: Ablex Publishing Corporation, 1995), 109–138, at 120.

42. Ibid, 128.

43. Ibid.

44. Woodson, best known today for his 1933 manifesto *The Mis-Education of the Negro* (reissued in 1990 by Africa World Press), was founder of the Association for the Study of Negro Life and History. According to Zimmerman, 42, Woodson also wrote "textbooks for special 'Negro history' courses in all-black schools."

45. See Zimmerman, 55–80, for a succinct account of these conflicts.

46. Good sources for the history of the controversy over the Rugg textbooks and discussion of their content include Kliebard, FitzGerald, Zimmerman, and Elmer A. Winters, "Man and His Changing Society: The Textbooks of Harold Rugg," *History of Education Quarterly* 7, no. 4 (1967): 493–514. Rugg also discusses the conflict at length in his autobiography, *That Men May Understand: An American in the Long Armistice* (New York: Doubleday, Doran and Co., Inc., 1941).

47. Harold Rugg, *The Great Technology*, 199–201, as cited by Peter Carbone, Jr. and Virginia Wilson, "Harold Rugg's Social Reconstructionism," 58–88, in James.

48. The figure is from a telephone conversation with Peter Carbone, February 16, 2002.

49. Preface to textbook series, p. v.

50. Murry R. Nelson, "Building A Science of Society: The Social Studies and Harold O. Rugg," (Ph. D. diss., Stanford University, 1975), 93.

51. Rugg, *American Life and the School Curriculum*, 287–288.

52. Interdependence was one of the key concepts in several of the pamphlets. The idea that the post-World War I world required more interdependence among nations was frequently cited by opponents of the series as a "collectivist" (communist) fallacy.

53. Social Studies Pamphlet, vol I, 3, 35 as quoted in Nelson, 113.

54. See Margaret Smith Crocco, "Forceful Yet Forgotten: Mary Ritter Beard and the Writing of History," *The History Teacher* 1, no. 1 (1997): 9–31. Crocco says Mary Beard pioneered inclusion of culture in study of American history.

55. John Dewey, *Democracy and Education: An Introduction to the Philosophy of Education* (New York: Macmillan, 1916).

56. Rugg, *American Life and the School Curriculum*, 229. Emphasis in original.

57. Ibid, 202–203.

58. Ibid, 9.

59. Ibid, 203.

60. Rugg's ideas about art, and his sense of indebtedness to the works of frontier thinkers and his personal association with many of them, are evident in all the books he wrote for adults. See especially, Rugg and Ann Shumaker, *The Child-Centered School: An Appraisal of the New Education* (Yonkers, NY: World Book, 1928), his autobiography, *That Men May Understand,* and Carbone, *The Social and Educational Thought of Harold Rugg.*

61. Rugg, *American Life and the School Curriculum*, 205.

62. This rather heavy-handed approach is visible in remarks directed at students in many of the *Workbooks*. This quote is drawn from Virginia Wilson, "Harold Rugg's Social and Educational Philosophy as Reflected in His Textbook Series, 'Man and His Changing Society,'" (Ph.D. diss. Duke University, 1975). Also see Nelson.

63. Zimmerman presents quotations from the criticism of many individuals. Rugg's autobiography, *That Men May Understand,* describes the attacks in detail. He believed that many of his accusers, especially those who spoke at school board meetings in various cities, had never read the texts they were condemning. It is obvious from reading the curriculum materials themselves that Rugg was correct, as several critics make claims about language and ideas that do not appear in the curriculum.

3

CIVIC HANDS UPON THE LAND: DIVERSE PATTERNS OF SOCIAL EDUCATION IN THE CIVILIAN CONSERVATION CORPS AND ITS ANALOGUES 1933–1942

I have moments of real terror when I think we may be losing this generation. We have got to bring these young people into the active life of the community and make them feel they are necessary.

ELEANOR ROOSEVELT[1]

Depression-era America was not only a crisis for adults suddenly facing economic hardships, it was a disaster for many millions of young people as well. The financial crisis led to shorter school terms, school closings, and a greatly reduced teacher force. For millions of American students, schooling became an unaffordable luxury. Worries about "losing this generation," prompted almost immediate action on the part of the incoming Roosevelt administration and led to the creation of the Civilian Conservation Corps. By the end of its lifespan in 1942, this program included almost 2.5 million young men in thousands of camps who worked on countless more thousands of wilderness and rural conservation projects. Many also received an education, both experientially and in direct instruction.

This chapter depicts that educational experience and its meaning as social education. Social education, according to Margaret Smith Crocco, includes learning about democracy and citizenship "in settings beyond the school."[2] Social education to Crocco is designed to equip learners with enhanced ability to live "effectively in a democracy."[3] Since the CCC, by definition, dealt with youth no longer in the K-12 setting, social education, rather than the traditional classroom oriented social studies, is most applicable.

Because the CCC was really not one program but several (one for white young men, a segregated experience with a modified educational plan for African-American men, and a completely different program for Native Americans called CCC-ID or Indian Division), and because women were excluded, this is a complex story. The issue is further compounded by the fact that clear tensions existed over the nature of social education to be offered in the CCC.

After briefly describing the background conditions leading to the creation of the CCC. I will outline some fundamental qualities and dynamics in the education program that applied mostly to white enrollees. I will then describe some experiences of African-Americans, and selected Native American tribes. While there was no CCC for women, I have included a section on their CCC-like camp experiences because these were created as a direct analogue and because their approach to education was both instructive and creative. Finally, I will summarize by considering all of these in light of important curriculum movements of the era.

My intention is to demonstrate that the CCC, a massive temporary employment program affecting millions of young men and its analogue affecting thousands of young women, was the setting for a richly complex and instructive battle over the kind of social education Depression-era America was prepared to support. Three curriculum movements, social efficiency, vocationalism and life adjustment, and core elements of the 1918 Cardinal Principles of Secondary Education[4] were powerful in the CCC especially, and evident in the women's programs. Together, they formed a strategy that represented the ideas of the Army and, to a lesser extent, the Roosevelt Administration.

The original concepts of education and civic vision in the CCC was a blend of narrow vocationalism (learning to use the tools involved in a single project), social efficiency (finding one's place in the economic order and learning just what one needs to fulfill the obligations of that place) and life adjustment (learning how to be dependable, a good worker, obedient and reasonably content with one's lot). With time, and the infusion of cooperation from the Office of Education, these deepened into programs supported by educational advisors. In the CCC, these ideas were in early conflict with an attempt at social reconstructionism, in the form of social criticism. This proved too controversial and was suppressed. Unlike their male counterparts, the women's camp projects were a premeditated blend of all of these movements including social reconstructionism. While the women's program was somewhat more open to a critical social perspective, what prevailed in the men's program was a social education dominated by finding maintaining employment, fitting in with community members, starting a family and learning to use leisure time constructively.

Facing a Crisis for America's Youth

In his study of Depression era runaway teens, Errol L. Uys estimates that there were 250,000 young men and women riding boxcars during the depths of the Depression.[5] "The director of the American Youth Commission estimated that during the Depression years. 40 per cent of youth (16–24) in the whole country were neither gainfully employed nor in school. In 1932, at least a third of a million children had their education interrupted because local school districts lacked the funds to keep schools operating."[6]

Obviously, the image of hundreds of thousands of angry, desperate unemployed young people was threatening and required immediate attention. In response, one of President Franklin Roosevelt's first acts was to propose a relief program for unemployed young men. By late spring, 1933, FDR had initiated the CCC along with nine other "alphabet soup" programs that became the heart of his 100 Days response to the Depression. Historian Calvin Gower described the general structure of this program: "The Department of Labor enrolled the young men; the Department of War using regular and reserve Army officers supervised the CCC camps; the Departments of the Interior and Agriculture organized and oversaw the conservation work which the enrollees performed."[7] In an economic crisis, this division of management was deemed necessary. Each department, especially the Army, had expertise that could speed along the establishment of the CCC. What came along as well was an incompatible merging of cultures and political perspectives that cast a shadow upon the character of social education offered by the CCC.

Early Educational Work in the CCC: Two Perspectives at Odds

The first signs of an explicit educational program in the CCC appeared in April 1933 and took the form of learning about forestry and possible extension courses. These were very limited additions to CCC projects and were intended to supplement, not supplant the physical work of enrollees. By May 1933 W. Frank Persons, the Department of Labor's representative on the CCC advisory board proposed a more formalized plan entitled, "Suggestions for Educational and Vocational Counselors for Forest Camps." This idea included hiring unemployed teachers to take on the work of instruction but stopped short of formal classes.[8]

Describing the spirit of education in the early CCC, historian Leslie Lacy credits the work of Guy B. Arthur of the Department of the Interior and Lt. Colonel Sidney Bingham of the Department of War. According to Lacy both understood the power of connecting enrollees to projects that had a clear meaning as well as demonstrable usefulness to the community over time.[9] This faith in the experiential nature of CCC education in general had meaning for its impact on social education as well. By understanding the economic, historic, and community context of their work, enrollees would better understand their role in the constellation of social forces surrounding them and find their place. The goal of these War Department officials was almost always to maintain a pragmatic, if narrow, interpretation of education. Hands-on outdoors work would prevail, in their minds, over bookish study organized by, "long haired men and short haired women" educators.

There was another side to this debate. The conflict between the Army and CCC head Robert Fechner on one side and the educators on the other side came to a head with the publication and suggested distribution in CCC camps of William Ogburn's book, "You and the Machine" in 1934. Ogburn, who had been director of President Hoover's committee on social trends, warned that "the government, the family and the church are behind the times. The machine seems to be their master. The machine produced a factory system which produced a class of factory worker and wealth was distributed unequally between these classes."[10]

Fechner argued against the book and eventually banned its distribution. "It is my feeling that it is not a desirable publication of Emergency Conservation Work. Instead of developing a healthy questioning attitude, it seems to me that the booklet will induce a philosophy of despair. In addition to a discouraged feeling it also seems to me it might induce a desire to destroy our present economic and political structures which are held to be responsible for the present conditions. I feel that we would also lay ourselves open to the charge of becoming propagandists for unemployment and old age insurance."[11] Although Fechner's suppression of the book in November 1934 was upheld, it was criticized by noted educators of the time such as J. W. Crabtree, secretary of the National Education Association, and Charles Judd, Dean of the University of Chicago's School of Education.

The "You and the Machine" conflict was not an isolated event. Liberal journals like the *New Republic* and the *Nation* were banned from CCC libraries and educational advisers were given pamphlets that helped them to steer clear of controversy. There was also the question of dealing with outsiders coming into the camps. Here the issue surrounded so-called communist agitators in the camps. In these cases, it appears that the Army discharged enrollees who had even come in contact with such people with the logic that these enrollees had become somehow contaminated.[12] The CCC may have been designed to save a generation from the worst of American capitalism's disasters, but these young men were not encouraged to question the fundamental economic assumptions undergirding the social order itself. While it may be tempting to view Fechner's response as repressive, it is also possible that he understood the limits of the CCC's political boundaries.

Literacy Education

Literacy education became an important element in CCC formal education programs since many came to the corps with only rudimentary reading skills. The literacy program combined reading and writing skills with a strong dose of a particular vision of citizenship education. One challenge for the literacy project was to provide enrollees with appropriate reading texts. Eventually, a series known as "Camp Life

Readers" was adopted. These books not only help us understand the reading program, they are also a useful lens through which to see some underlying social values.

Arlene Barry, examining the potential for modeling new literacy programs after the CCC example, considered the dual messages in the *Camp Life* series of readers. First, there was the declared purpose of enhancing literacy among a group with profound needs. Allied with this was a hidden curriculum.[13] These implied goals are just as potent as the stated curriculum and involve inculcating values and attitudes.[14] In the case of the CCC, the hidden curriculum aimed at teaching the need for stable lives,[15] patriotism, group cooperation,[16] and the need for guiding rules of behavior in a complex society.[17]

"After You Leave Camp," the story ending the second reader and workbook, again reveals many of the CCC's desired values for enrollees. Like all other stories, it is accompanied by a line drawing. Like all others, the drawing is a pleasant one, in the countryside like most of the companion pieces. In this case there appears a smiling couple, mother holding a small child on her lap as she sits in an Adirondack chair in a field beyond a neatly built, but modest home. Standing to her right is father, in a jacket, vest and tie. The child smiles and waves at us as we read:

> Your camp experiences will be of value to you during the remainder of your life. Many of the things you learn in camp will carry over into your private life. You will use many of these things after you are married and have a family. You might train your children by some of the standards that you learned while at camp.
>
> Have you ever thought of these many things that you learn in camp? We may list a few of them. You learn to live and get along with your fellowman. You learn the value of a well-ordered life. You learn the value of cleanliness. You learn the value of well balanced meals. You learn the value of good health. You learn the value of exercise. You learn to give first aid to the sick and injured. You learn the value of the worthy use of leisure time. You learn the value of thrift. You learn the value of safety. These are only a few things. Can you think of others? Write them on the lines below.[18]

The values associated with this example are obvious. Hard work, competition, family life, marriage, and the "well ordered life," are themes found in many pages of this CCC reader series. The values of the 1918 *Cardinal Principles of Secondary Education* is an important dimension of these texts as well, such as civic duty and health.

Critical analysis of the American economic order seemed possible for a short time, but this bent in social education proved no match for a more traditional philosophy of training enrollee to fit into the existing order. CCC education would grow over the years and tensions between the Army and the Interior Department's Office of Education would remain fixed. But the thrust of social education in the camps was established along the lines of traditional patriotism and support for the existing social order. In marked contrast to the social reconstructionist ideals for educators like Harold Rugg,[19] CCC enrollees did not normally engage in solving social problems. They confined their work to the immediate challenges of their construction project and the social problems of displaced, poverty-stricken young men needing to find a place in the world beyond their time of enrollment.

While the New Deal programs opened doors for people of color and women, American society was still a place of very limited possibilities for these groups. It will come as no surprise that the CCC programs for African Americans and Native Americans varied markedly from those for white men and that women were completely excluded. Yet, a basic understanding of the CCC programs developed for the first two groups, and the alternative program designed for women is essential if we are to see the CCC in the context of its era.

African American Experiences in the CCC

For most African Americans, conditions in the CCC reflected conditions in the country in general; there was an official condoning of separate but equal treatment on the surface and an actual experience of separate and unequal treatment. Even with restrictions in enrollment and segregated camps, however, the CCC provided a useful experience to hundreds of thousands of African American men from 1933 to 1942.

Like the whites in the CCC, vocational education was a dominant theme but in this case, with race-specific socialization. Harold W. Oxley, National Director of CCC education working out of the Office of Education in the Department of the Interior, spoke about career education in the CCC for African Americans. "In an effort to prepare Negro youth for employment, camp advisers are training them for those types of jobs which they will be most likely to enter. Vocational classes afford them instruction in auto mechanics, chauffeuring, cooking, table work, mess management, personal service, laundering, pressing, shoe repairing, barbering, clerical work, painting and farming."[20] Fifty-two percent or 15,210 of African American enrollees were in vocational education. Historian Olen Cole noted that there were similar patterns in the educational programs offered to white and African American CCC enrollees in California. One important exception was the fact that whites were not taught such skills as cooking and serving while all camps for African Americans offered such courses. Cole concludes that this shows an intention to train African American men in what were then called Negro jobs. Such stereotyped social reproduction clearly had its own hidden curriculum as well as a likely acknowledgement of the limited career possibilities in a pre–civil rights America.[21]

Culture and citizenship through character education was stressed. Education Director Oxley stated in 1937, "By means of a well rounded program of academic, vocational and citizenship training and experience, each of the 186 CCC Negro companies is attempting to do its part in developing a more self-sustaining, self-reliant and intelligent Negro youth."[22] Cultural education among the African American enrollees included arts and crafts groups, music organizations, dramatic clubs, and newspapers. Citizenship was taught through discussion debating clubs, honors societies, and camp publications. Chaplains also spoke to enrollees. As in all CCC education programs, the constructive use of leisure time was an important topic in classes, again resonating with the *Cardinal Principles of Secondary Education*.[23]

In much the same way that the CCC aimed at shaping young white men, it soon took into account similar social expectations when defining programs for African Americans. On one side, the glaring racial stereotypes stand out graphically. Just as disturbing is the fact that for many, even these aspirations were beyond their reach.

CCC Experiences from the Perspective of Two Native American Tribes

Poverty among Native Americans at the time of the Depression was severe. The Meriam Commission reported in its voluminous independent study of 1928 that 46.8 percent of American Indians lived on a per capita income of $100 to $200 per year while only 2.2 percent received incomes of over $500 per year.[24] In addition to the stunning levels of poverty, reservations were in need of conservation work ranging from erosion control to forestation and upgrading grazing lands. There was some movement to include Native Americans in the regular CCC but objections by such influential people as Interior Secretary Harold Ickes helped initiate the concept of a separate program, based on the belief that Native Americans would want to live with their families and work on their own lands. In April 1933 FDR agreed and what became known as the CCC–Indian Division (CCC-ID) was established. Funds to start and run the CCC on reservations were timely since recent cuts had in the Indian Service appropriations had just taken place. The CCC revenue earmarked for Indian reservations made up more than the difference and promoted projects that otherwise might have taken many years to fund.[25]

The development of educational programs in the CCC–Indian Division was slow and reflected the national debate over the role of formal classes, if any in the CCC. Thus, the competition between project completion and resources, in terms of time and dollars, for education classes, existed on the reservations just as it did in the camps administered by the Army.[26] Adding to this was a perception that working on the projects, learning to earn money, and cooperate in a group were educative tasks. One argument not found in those debates was the idea that the enrollee's minimal or non-existent educational background was reason enough not to attempt a formal education program. Whereas the mainstream CCC had enrollees with a range of school experiences, the case of Native Americans was far more skewed toward the lower end.

Lakota and Oglala in the CCC-ID

Formal education programs held at Pine Ridge and Rosebud reservations were generally outside of the CCC-ID framework but deserve mention since they were organized by the Office of Indian Affairs, the same agency that orchestrated the CCC-ID and since the CCC-ID was often more community-based than the mainstream CCC. These programs mixed white, middle-class values with some attention to sustaining the Native American community on the reservation.

Historian Thomas Biolsi explained, "Thus, the objectives of adult education on Pine Ridge included inculcating among the Oglala an understanding of the 'intelligent expenditure of funds,' an 'appreciation of property,'"—in general, "economic intelligence." Other goals were facilitated "cooperating with members of groups and with public officials," "racial harmony," and "public spirit." Also on the list were goals directly linked to the Cardinal Principles of Secondary Education such as fostering, "family pride and personal pride in assuming family responsibilities," as well as an appreciation of American Indian culture, "moral obligations," and the "worthy use of leisure time," in short, character development.[27]

Education for adults at the Rosebud reservation took on a self-help character that focused on subsistence farming, animal husbandry and personal diet.[28] Tribal officials joined agency staff and local community members in organizing and presenting at meetings. Topics at Rosebud included, "development policy, the tribal constitutions and law and order codes, livestock management, health, music, arithmetic, writing for newspapers, spelling, Lakota language, and Lakota crafts, music and dance."[29]

Native Alaskan Participation

Much of CCC-ID social education for Native Alaskans centered on saving and preserving totem poles. While it appears that some missionaries and the Bureau of Indian Affairs had misgivings about the Totem poles and their restoration, the record of Native Alaskans in the CCC is clear. As one official justified this cultural work, "Certainly there is a high educational and recreational value in the opportunity to view these poles in their natural surroundings and the same is true of the interesting Indian graves in similar isolated situations."[30] From 1938 to 1940 there were twenty-one totem pole restoration projects. These took place in eight of the fifty-six Native villages that had CCC projects and included shipping a 56-foot tall pole to Seattle. Because of their importance to Native Alaskans, totem pole restoration projects met the original CCC education criteria described earlier. Like other successful projects, this work had deep meaning for participants and their community.

Although varied, these two examples of CCC-ID education continue the pattern of social education that blended local circumstances with values from the society outside of the reservations. There was, if anything, more sensitivity to local culture shown in the CCC-ID.

Education Experiences in Women's Camps
Patterned after the CCC

The problems faced by the unemployed men at the start of the New Deal received immediate attention as we have seen and became a powerful rationale for establishing the CCC in the first place. The same cannot be said in the case of unemployed women. Estimates show between two and four million unemployed women or women searching for work in the first days of the Roosevelt administration. There are also figures of 140,000 homeless women at that time, "wandering the streets and railroad sidings of America."[31] Yet the turbulent activity in Washington in the spring of 1933 saw no organized attempt to alleviate their condition.

In large measure, Eleanor Roosevelt became a leader and focal point in the movement to create something like the programs that existed for men. Beyond meetings to raise awareness, Mrs. Roosevelt went to work to get at least one camp for women established. At Bear Mountain State Park, midway between New York and Hyde Park, the first such camp was opened in June 1933 called Camp Tera, after New York State's Temporary Emergency Relief Administration.

Opening up one experimental camp was a first step but the need of unemployed girls and women vastly dwarfed this first effort. Growing from the early days at Camp Tera, a small system of varied programs developed. These projects were decentralized, unlike the CCC but followed federal guidelines. While some derided the concept as "She-She-She," important curricular themes such as worker education stand out and the picture of social education in women's camps emerged.

Perhaps the strongest advocate for these programs was Hilda Worthington Smith, former dean of Bryn Mawr College and founder of that institution's Summer School for Working Women. Smith's role in the Roosevelt administration was head of worker education projects at the Emergency Education Program. In an October 1933 letter to Marian Dickerman, head of the Todhunter School in New York, Smith described a general plan for helping unemployed women. "We are hoping to plan non-residential schools and residential schools, both in the cities and in the suburbs for unemployed women to combine relief with an educational program this winter. The schools would be of different types, according to age group and various occupations."[32] She later shared her vision of education in a future women's program: "The educational program would combine general education, including what we have called worker's education, vocational opportunities in nearby cities and health education."[33]

In a 1934 article in *Progressive Education,* Smith offered a definition of worker education. "In the broad interpretation of the term, workers' education offers to men and women workers in industry, business, commerce, domestic service and other occupations, an opportunity to train themselves in clear thinking through the study of those questions closely related to their daily lives as workers and as citizens. Its primary purpose is to stimulate an active and continued interest in the economic problems of our times and to develop a sense of responsibility for their solution."[34]

Smith described her vision of education as an integral element in workers' education. "Current industrial and social problems of daily concern to workers" from their own experience was of central importance. The social sciences were to take center stage in the movement. "Classes in economics, economic history, government, legislation, community problems, the history of the labor movement, current industrial situations, international affairs, social psychology, and other allied subjects are of great interest to those workers who are confused by changing industrial conditions, and who seek to understand their own responsibilities as workers and as citizens."[35]

This example typifies the mixed approach found in the women's programs. Training for employment was often linked to stereotypical jobs at the time, much like the pattern for African-American men in the CCC. General health education, again like the CCC existed in most women's projects. Unlike the CCC, there was also an emphasis on critical social and economic conditions. Equally different from the CCC, Smith described a flexible system of programs meant for women with many different needs.

By assuring a staff with diverse perspectives, including workers' education, instruction in social sciences, English, health education, vocational counseling, and a house director to train women in home economics, the women's program built-in a specific range of priorities into the curricular design of the camps. Again, unlike the CCC, when and educational advisor might not be able to teach in an area of expertise, the women's program planned for focus among several areas. The CCC achieved diversity through such approaches as correspondence courses, the women's program concentrated on diversity of programs at the camp itself. Finally, the CCC seems to have allowed for greater personal choice in education, to participate or not and to decide on what to learn and when, the women's program was more oriented toward whole group participation.

The CCC and Its Analogues in Context

It is fitting, therefore, for the themes of civics to be equally complex. I will conclude this chapter by offering an analysis of the social education in the CCC and related women's programs in two ways. First, I will consider the relevance of the CCC and women's camp experiences in light of important curricular movements of the era. These include social efficiency, vocationalism, social reconstructionism or social meliorism, and the life-adjustment movement. Second, I will examine the subtext or hidden curriculum of the camp experiences and their possible meaning for social education.

While the social efficiency movement was in part the product of such writers as Fredrick Taylor[36] early in the last century and applied at first to raising productivity in industry, other writers such as Franklin Bobbitt[37] made a clear connection to curriculum planning. A key issue for proponents of this movement was directing students to the kind of training that would prepare them for their likely role in society, rather than concentrate on the developmental needs of learners or their desires to grow in creativity. The programs of the CCC and women's programs did have this element in educational planning as well. When planners described the need for young people to take their place in "the army of wage earners" the question was one of the individual fitting into a social-economic construct. This was also evident when Army officers talked about the CCC as a place for poor boys who needed to learn to make a living, "not how to make a rug." Looked at from the social efficiency point of view, the fact that there were separate camps for different groups—white men, African-American men, Native American men and women—says something about the segregated nature of the culture at one level and also something about the clear, though unequal, pathways within that economic order as well. The camps' emphasis on training for likely jobs meant reinforcing stereotypical training, in correspondence courses and direct experiences for many under-privileged white men and women, African Americans, Native Americans.

The vocational education movement, which was geared towards educating for specific trades and occupations in the economy is hardly new. Kliebard points out that Benjamin Franklin's academy, later to become the University of Pennsylvania, was one early example of this kind of curricular design.[38] The emphasis on vocationalism in the public schools, however, became a potent force in the first decades of the twentieth century, supported by state education commissioners such as David Snedden[39] and included such famous debates as those between Booker T. Washington[40] and W. E. B. DuBois.[41] The proponents of vocationalism supported learning for jobs in the industrial economy through hands-on experience, often through apprenticeships. By the time that the U.S. entered World War I, the federal government was formally involved in supporting these programs of job training.

The camps' focus on learning on the spot, from such experiences as the construction lessons was of clear importance. In Utah, enrollees were told that their work in truck driving, caterpillar operation, and cooking would prepare them for work in the world outside of the CCC. The relevance of the capital equipment to learning was a useful sales tool for those wanting to attract new enrollees, recalling the description of such equipment as better than in the finest voc-tech schools. Vocationalism is also evident in the fact that about one third of the correspondence courses fell into this category. Camp training in photography, cooking, and radio mechanics was an additional example of vocationalism. Again, it is worth remembering that vocational training for African Americans, women, and Native Americans had a distinct character, often aimed at fitting the individual into stereotyped jobs.

While the life adjustment curriculum movement came to full bloom as the CCC period was coming to a close, it is important to note that the federal work projects like CCC were used a models. The emphasis for the life adjustment advocates was one of encouraging specific work habits and the skills needed to sustain employment, balanced by family life and community participation. Guidance programs in the camps are an example of the life adjustment curriculum in action. This was a serious allocation of time since about one quarter to one third of the typical educational advisor's time was spent in guidance and counseling.

For African Americans, the life adjustment themes may have been even more clearly pronounced. It appears that the educational advisors in African American camps may have been more proactive in guiding enrollees to courses and "meeting the young man's problems" than in other CCC camps. Further, Oxley had specific goals for African Americans in the camps. His aspiration for "a more self-sustaining and intelligent Negro youth,"[42] was a kind of life adjustment issue also heavy with imagery and judgment. Character education was a high priority in African American camps and included citizenship lectures and sermons from area clergy.

There was an early but unsuccessful attempt to infuse the three curriculum movements above (social efficiency, vocationalism, and life adjustment) with a strong dose of social reconstructionism, very much in line with the ideas in Harold Rugg's social studies textbook series,[43] Charles Beard's work on the Commission for the Social Studies in the Schools,[44] and social criticism of George S. Counts throughout the 1920s and 1930s.[45] However, the limits of social reconstructionism in the CCC became clear as we have seen.

Yet the goal of all of the CCC programs and the women's equivalents was to help young people in a time of crisis to find some place in society and may also be viewed as an attempt at actual social reconstructionism on a large, sustained scale. Smith's description of worker education is one articulation of many of the social reconstructionist's curriculum goals. Eleanor Roosevelt's desire not to lose a generation of young people and her goal of developing an "active life of the community," for youth is another. The struggle to include African Americans in the CCC, to develop at least some kind of program for women and to extend the CCC to Native Americans were other examples of social problem solving in action. Contextualizing meaning for the work projects in their "economic value to the people" considering "what change the project would make in local activities," is also a point of view friendly to social reconstructionism.

Conclusion

The story of the CCC and its counterpart for women is complex and the lessons of social education require thoughtful analysis. There was not one CCC, but several. There was not one education plan with an integrated curriculum philosophy, but contending ideals, rarely in balance. Social efficiency, vocationalism, and life adjustment certainly held a leading position while elements of reconstructionism managed to survive. Just like its varied organizational structures, the CCC was at times confusing and at other times remarkably creative. Some lessons in social education were limited and even negative, while others were dynamic and idealistic. These probably reflect the varied currents of the men and women who created this most unusual system of relief for unemployed young people. It would be, perhaps, too easy to criticize the programs for their clear inadequacies. It seems to me that these resulted from conflicting social visions. What is revealed in this study is the contending of those visions for supremacy. The result was a complex brand of social education, emphasizing traditional values and roles for white and African American men and modified white cultural values for Native Americans. For the women's programs, the mixture was richer since social criticism was more consistently combined with training. Returning to Crocco's definition of social education, it cannot be reasonably denied that the CCC and its analogue for women was a powerful way to transmit democracy and citizenship *as they existed in Depression-era America*.

But dwelling on the shortcomings and compromises that ended up being social education in of the CCC and women's programs might mean misunderstanding the source of the CCC itself. FDR's New Deal was, in a sense, a series of cascading programs aimed at stemming an economic and social crisis before the society itself unraveled. That strategy may have meant the evolution of a new social order in a generation or so. It did not mean the creation of immediate social and economic revolution. It was a case of liberal not radical government at work. Social critics like Lewis Mumford condemned this strategy as nothing but, "aimless experiment, sporadic patchwork, a total indifference to guiding principles . . . an uncritical drift along the lines of least resistance, namely the restoration of capitalism."[46] While this may be a harsh analysis, it appears that in the CCC's case, many of the underlying inequities of American life were meant to be challenged by attrition, not direct confrontation. The possibility that this may have been as far as the majority of Americans wished to go in the 1930s is, perhaps, the most powerful lesson of the entire study.

Notes

1. Olen Cole Jr., *The African American Experience in the Civilian Conservation Corps*. (Gainesville, FL: University of Florida Press, 1999), 9.
2. Margaret Smith Crocco and O. L. Davis Jr., eds., *"Bending the Future to Their Will": Civic Women, Social Education and Democracy*. (Lanham, MD: Rowman & Littlefield Publishers, Inc., 1999), 1.
3. Ibid.
4. Commission on the Reorganization of Secondary Education of the National Education Association 1918 Cardinal Principals of Secondary Education. Washington, DC: U.S. Printing Office.
5. Errol Lincoln Uys, *Riding the Rails: Teenagers on the Move During the Great Depression* (New York: TV Books, 1999).
6. Internet site: http://newdeal.feri.org/cccmem/cccmem01.htm 1999.
7. Calvin W. Gower, "Conservatism, Censorship, and Controversy in the CCC, 1930's," *Journalism Quarterly* 52 (Summer 1975), 277.
8. Ibid.
9. Leslie A. Lacy, *The Soil Soldiers: The Civilian Conservation Corps in the Great Depression* (Radnor, PA: Chilton, 1976), 38–39.
10. Gower, "Conservatism, Censorship, and Controversy in the CCC, 1930's," 280.
11. Ibid.
12. Ibid.
13. Arlene Barry, "Is the Civilian Conservation Corps of the 1930's a 1990's Approach to Dropouts and Illiteracy?" *Journal of Adolescent and Adult Literacy* 42 (May 1999), 651.

14. Michael W. Apple, *Ideology and Curriculum* (London: Routledge, 1979).
15. Peter Earp," Curriculum Content in the Civilian Conservation Corps Camps of Illinois" (Unpublished Master's Thesis, Colorado State College, 1937).
16. United States Civilian Conservation Corps, *Camp Life Reader and Work Book: Language Usage Series,* No. 1 (Washington, DC: U.S. Office of Education 1939), 44.
17. Ibid.
18. United States Civilian Conservation Corps, *Camp Life Reader and Work Book: Language Usage Series,* No. 2 (Washington, DC: U.S. Office of Education 1939).
19. Joseph Watras, "Debating the Curriculum: Social Studies or History, 1892–1937," *The Social Studies* (November–December 2002), 93, 247–248.
20. Howard W. Oxley, "Meeting the Problems of the Negro Enrollees," *School Life* 22 (January 1937), 145.
21. Cole, *The African American Experience in the Civilian Conservation Corps,* 50. See also James D. Anderson, *The Education of Blacks in the South, 1860–1935* (Chapel Hill: University of North Carolina Press, 1988).
22. Oxley, "Meeting the Problems of Negro Enrollees," 155.
23. Ibid 155.
24. Donald L. Parman, "The Indian and the Civilian Conservation Corps, " *Pacific Historical Review* 15 (February 1971): 39.
25. Donald L. Parman, *The Navajos and the New Deal* (New Haven: Yale University Press, 1976).
26. Parman, "The Indian and the Civilian Conservation Corps."
27. Thomas Biolsi, *Organizing the Lakota* (Tucson, AR: The University of Arizona Press, 1971), 121.
28. Ibid, 121.
29. Ibid, 122.
30. Connor Sorenson, *Alaska Native Participation in the Civilian Conservation Corps.* Alaska Historical Commission Studies in History No. 206 (ERIC Document Reproduction Service No. ED294702, 1986), 19.
31. Blanche Wiesen Cook, *Eleanor Roosevelt* (New York: Viking , 1999), 85.
32. Hilda W. Smith to Miriam Dickerman 10 October, 1933. File 70 Hilda Worthington Smith Papers, Franklin D. Roosevelt Library, Hyde Park, New York.
33. Ibid.
34. Hilda W. Smith, "Workers' Education and the Federal Government," *Progressive Education* (April–May 1934): 240.
35. Ibid.
36. Frederick W. Taylor, *The Principles of Scientific Management* (New York: Harper Brothers, 1911).
37. Franklin Bobbitt, *The Curriculum* (Boston: Houghton-Mifflin, 1918).
38. Herbert M. Kliebard *The Struggle for the American Curriculum, 1893–1958* (Boston: Routledge & Kegan Paul, 1986).
39. David Snedden, "Vocational Education," *The New Republic* 3 (1915), 40–42.
40. Booker T. Washington, *Tuskegee and Its People: Their Ideals and Achievements* (New York: D. Appleton, 1905).
41. W. E. B. DuBois, *The Negro Artisan* (Atlanta, GA: Atlanta University Press, 1902).
42. Oxley, "Meeting the Problems of Negro Enrollees," 155.
43. Harold O. Rugg, *Man and his Changing Society. The Rugg Social Science Series of the Elementary School Course,* Vols. 1–6 (Boston: Ginn, 1929–1932).

44. The American Historical Association, *Conclusions and Recommendations of the Commission on the Social Studies* (New York: Charles Scribners Sons, 1934).

45. George S. Counts, *Dare the Schools Build a New Social Order?* (New York: John Day, 1932).

46. Richard H. Pells, *Radical Visions and American Dreams* (New York: Harper & Row, 1973) 84.

4

Yoon K. Pak

TEACHING FOR INTERCULTURAL UNDERSTANDING IN THE SOCIAL STUDIES: A TEACHER'S PERSPECTIVE IN THE 1940S

Peering through the historical looking glass into everyday classroom culture and teachers' thoughts on pedagogical concerns is fraught with challenges and limitations. Aside from teachers' journals and oral histories—both providing invaluable sources—we have yet to fully capture the complexities of the type of world in which the teacher was subsumed.[1] While prominent educational theorists and philosophers have lent their views on education, we still have very little in relation to everyday teachers' views of incorporating educational theory with practice.[2] Whereas previous research in the history of education focused more on the institutional aspects of schooling, there exists an increased attention to the larger notions of who taught and for what purposes. Drawing on a series of short stories written by a middle-school teacher in the 1940s, this chapter addresses the influence of intercultural education theory, in particular the democratic citizenship notion of *e pluribus unum,* to the development of intercultural relationships in the classroom. Also included in this chapter is a discussion of the national Service Bureau for Intercultural Education organization and its original leader, Rachel Davis Du-Bois, in the development of curriculum materials on the contributions of racial and ethnic groups to American life. Even though Ella Evanson, the teacher, and Davis DuBois probably never met in person, I attempt to connect how DuBois' ideas through the Service Bureau paralleled the ways in which Evanson approached the development of intercultural relationships. These female educators on the opposite ends of the coastal United States worked in their separate and distinct spheres to achieve similar aims.

Ella Evanson held a view of her students that came as a white woman teaching in one of the most racially and ethnically diverse neighborhoods in Seattle before World War II. Evanson's stories reveal the importance of how a more culturally relevant pedagogy not only enhanced the traditional curriculum but also aided in the development of more caring relationships between the teacher and her students.[3] That academic achievement was inextricably linked to the incorporation of the lived experiences of students was a central feature of her stories. Congruent to the larger progressive reforms during the 1940s, the teacher's stories also tell of the centrality of a cultural democracy that characterized the extension of constitutional democracy in its extension to the application of race and culture group relations.[4] In other words, democracy demanded an understanding of how various religious, racial, ethnic, and socio-economic groups contributed to the building of a national identity. Bruno Lasker, an educator and regular contributor to the *Intercultural Education News,* explained in further detail that: "The Concept of American [cultural] democracy, then does not imply the superiority of one imported way of life over others, one national heritage over others, of one racial strain over others. Nor does it mean that all who inhabit this great country must as quickly as possible be made alike in their thinking in their beliefs, in their tastes. It means, rather, that in the diversity of their heritage they shall recognize the diversity of life itself where it is fullest and most vigorous."[5] Intercultural education, therefore, sought to incorporate cultural democracy at the core of its aims in classroom instruction, particularly in the social studies, by paying specific attention to racial, religious, ethnic, and socioeconomic group conflicts.[6]

While Evanson advances and broadens the scope of what it means to be an American through her stories, she also perpetuates certain racial and ethnic stereotypes of the students she describes. To be sure, a "generous read" of the teacher is worth employing. Contradictions are an inherent part of all of our lives, and to dismiss the teacher wholly on the basis of racial naiveté risks losing the larger, contextual portrait of teaching in the 1940s. Also, to consider the limits of the teacher's shortsightedness borders on a presentist critique of a historical moment. In many ways, the paradoxical views of race and ethnicity during the progressive era—critiquing the biological basis of race while at the same time perpetuating certain stereotypes—was also one of the constraints of intercultural education in the 1930s to 1950s. The mainly white teaching force still delivered a version of intercultural education aimed at assimilation to the larger, mainstream society. Yet, I would maintain that there were those social experiments aimed at genuinely attempting to understand the diverse population of students and how the various cultures of students would enhance the educational experiences of all, including the teachers themselves. Again, that is the central aim of this chapter, to investigate how Ella Evanson incorporated examples of intercultural understanding in her classroom through her stories about her students. Distinguishing her stories as examples, rather than as exemplars, highlights how the advances in progressive education were still limited in scope.

Ella Evanson, Progressive Teacher

Evanson's arrival to the Pacific Northwest's premier city occurred at a time when the post-Depression and pre–World War II migration into the area increased dramatically. Like many young cities along the West Coast, Seattle's defense industry proved to be a most welcome economic relief to the long-time residents and new inhabitants coming from all parts of the United States. Midwesterners and Southerners made up the bulk of those seeking new opportunities. Likewise, Evanson's new home in Seattle was a far cry from her native state of North Dakota. Perhaps eager to experience a world beyond the prairie lands of the Midwest, and to satisfy her sense of travel and adventure, she saw teaching as one of those few professions available to women seeking independence.

What is little known about the life of Evanson is revealed in a *Seattle Times* newspaper article that featured her collection of students' letters and farewell messages on the bombing of Pearl Harbor and the Japanese American incarceration three decades after the devastating events. As an English and Social Studies teacher at Washington School in the 1940s, she saved what would later become critical evidence for beginning to understand how wartime events affected Japanese American students.[7] Her teaching career began in her native state of North Dakota before heading east during World War I to work for the government. Afterwards she reached the opposite end of the coast to the Pacific Northwest and earned a Washington State teaching certificate at Bellingham's Normal School, now Western Washington University. She taught for a year in Everett, the site of a well-known naval base, commuting on the interurban nearly sixty miles roundtrip daily from Seattle. Evanson managed to secure a position closer to home at B. F. Day Elementary School in Seattle before transferring to Washington School in 1928 where she remained until her retirement in 1956. Seeking further adventures abroad as a retiree, Evanson boarded a freighter that covered the vast expanse of the Pacific and several destinations around the world lasting for more than a year. Her penchant for travel extended several more years before finally settling down at a home for retired teachers in Seattle. After having lived what was for Evanson a fulfilling life, she passed away on January 1986 at the age of eighty-eight.[8]

Context for Social Change

The time period in which Evanson taught was a moment of great change and innovation in education. The national and international events of the Great Depression and the United States' entrance into World War II catapulted schools to act as agents of social change. The westward migration of people from all parts of the country to the West Coast, seeking employment in economically destitute times, further heightened the intense ethnic and racial relationships already pre-existent. Scores of publications by the National Education Association and prominent educators redirected the efforts of schools nationwide toward understanding the meaning of a democracy in a changing society.[9] The language of religious and racial tolerance against the backdrop of Nazism abroad became the rally cry of promoting democracy. Despite nativist organizations' attempts to limit the scope of Americanism, much like what occurred during the First World War, the overseas treatment of Jews based on a "racial" argument was hard to ignore at home. How could we espouse equal treatment under the law and still live within a system of *de facto* and *de jure* segregation?

Minority groups, particularly African Americans, had raised this very question since the early days of the Republic, but it wasn't until the Harlem and Detroit race riots in the 1930s and 1940s that educators began to take notice. Just what would education for equality look like? What would be some strategies for teaching to the nation's motto, *e pluribus unum*? Educational historian Jonathan Zimmerman provides an account of the cultural and religious wars in the schools ranging from what type of social studies texts to use in the classrooms to the question of how, and if, to broach the existence of God.[10] Certainly the answers would not be easy to come by, but there was at least increased motivation by national and local school officials to begin to address this issue.

Curriculum for Intercultural Education

Pioneer educator Rachel Davis DuBois initially conceived the idea of intercultural education in 1924 as a Quaker teacher in a New Jersey high school after witnessing racial discrimination in her school. Using that incident as a way to bridge her experience with her doctoral work, she investigated and tested techniques to combat prejudicial behaviors in youth. The results of her efforts have earned her the distinction of having begun an "ethnic studies" approach in the public schools.[11] In 1934 DuBois organized the Service Bureau for Human Relations, the forerunner to the Service Bureau for Intercultural Education that officially became a committee of the Progressive Education Association in 1935. The Service Bureau for Intercultural Education was the major educational organization to develop and disseminate the latest social scientific research on intercultural education.

Going beyond tolerance, a word she despised, DuBois aimed to change the attitudes of the way people thought about various immigrant and racial minority groups. A typical pedagogical tool she would employ would be to ask students, mostly teacher education students, if they ever came into contact with African Americans, for example, and were aware of the various cultural contributions of Negroes to American life. Generally the response would yield total silence as students in her classes rarely met anyone outside their race.[12] The results of her doctoral work at New York University, in conducting a systematic study of behaviors and attitudes of students toward prejudice reduction, led DuBois to integrate curriculum materials that emphasized the contributions of different racial and immigrant groups. To those who criticized her method, she defended her approach as one that best reflected the ways in which *all* groups of Americans shared in the development of a democratic society. And as such, one group did not hold precedence, or superior status above others.

The curriculum units DuBois developed would be considered innovative and challenging, even through present-day eyes. From 1933 to 1936 she formulated classroom materials related to Negro, Chinese, Japanese, and Jews focusing on subjects such as American History, Literature, Music, Art, Economics, and Science.[13] In the fall of 1938 DuBois became the educational director for the national award-winning radio program sponsored by CBS, "Americans All, Immigrants All," where several million people, in the course of twenty-six Sunday afternoons, heard the contributions of various racial and nationality groups to the social, economic, and political development of the United States.[14] The scripts of the program were also disseminated to the major urban school districts across the country, which most likely included the Seattle Public Schools. The curriculum materials DuBois devised in the early 1930s became the basis for the content of the radio programs that featured one ethnic or racial group each Sunday. Sample titles of the radio programs were: "Orientals in the United States," "The Negro in the United States," "Jews in the United States," and "Irish in the United States."

Some of the curriculum units are worth highlighting as these early classroom units were also adapted for the publication and development of workshops for teacher educators all across the United States by DuBois and others involved the Service Bureau for Intercultural Education. Further, the topics of group discussion within these subjects dealt with countering the prevailing norms of what and who constituted an American and challenging the very notions of democratic citizenship. In that light, these sets of curriculum units parallel the ideas embedded in the stories of Ella Evanson in the early 1940s. In investigating the Reconstruction Period in American history, DuBois consciously chose the intellectual scholarship by Carter G. Woodson, Booker T. Washington, and W. E. B. DuBois with the objective: 1) to show that some Negroes after the Civil War were fit and able to take part in local and national government; and 2) to show the part the Negro played in the period after the Civil War."[15] An excerpt by Woodson from *The Negro in Our History* further accentuates the message DuBois wished to impart to students: "The charge that all Negro officers were illiterates, ignorant of the science of government, cannot be sustained. Some of them had undergone considerable training and had experienced sufficient mental development to be able to discharge their duties with honor."[16] In her "Suggested Class Situation," DuBois included a potentially controversial idea when studying the problems of democracy. W. E. B. DuBois' *The Negro Citizen* served as the backdrop to critically analyze the meaning of "a system of color in the United States based on a legal and customary race distinction and discriminations having to do with separation in travel, in schools, in public accommodations, in residence and in family relations."[17] Incorporating the works by prominent African American scholars bolstered DuBois' approach toward a curriculum that considered minority perspectives. More importantly, her units reveal a perspective that goes beyond the generic cultural contributions approach toward a means to understanding the complex face of democracy and citizenship by raising issues rarely discussed in the public schools.

The legal and constitutional questions of citizenship in the classroom units also extended to the "Yellow Problem," popularly referred to in the media when discussing the Chinese and Japanese immigrants in the United States. DuBois wrote a fact sheet entitled "Some Rules of Immigration and Citizenship," to provide background information on who was eligible for citizenship based on the 1790 limit to naturalization based on "free white persons" and the subsequent amendment made after the Civil War to include "persons of African descent." The limitations of citizenship for Asian residents, and in some respects implicitly questioning the basis of exclusionary policies, were introduced through her brief discussion of the Chinese Exclusion Act of 1882 as well as the 1924 Immigration Act.

The classroom materials on Japan, particularly framed for English and history, aimed to have students consider further problems of democracy in relation to Asian immigrants. DuBois outlined the general objectives: 1) to make students appreciate the desirability of Japanese as neighbors and citizens; and 2) to influence them to take a fair attitude toward the feeling of Japanese on the Exclusion Act. In particular, attitudes to be counteracted rested on Japanese being "tricky, unassimilable, generally inferior and general undesirable as citizens." Such notions were quite advanced for the time as throughout the West Coast numerous anti-Asiatic leagues heightened the general public fears about the yellow peril and the threat to democracy if the Japanese, in particular, would be considered for citizenship.[18] Resting on the argument that they, regardless of their legal status in the United States, would forever remain loyal to the emperor of Japan perpetuated the notion that Japanese (and most other Asian immigrants) would remain unassimilable and unfit as citizens.

To counter the idea of Asians as unfit for citizenship and undesirable, the story of Lue Gim Gong, a pioneer Chinese American who invented a new breed of oranges in Florida, was featured in one of DuBois' curriculum projects.[19] Naturalized in the U.S. prior to the 1882 Exclusion law, Lue Gim Gong created a new type of orange, known as the Lue Gim Gong Orange, that earned him the Wilder medal awarded by the United States Department of Agriculture. Gong, a pomologist and plant breeder, developed a hardier brand of oranges that was able to resist cold and remain unchanged on the tree after it had ripened for up to two years. Revealing his humble, honest, and Christian character, Gong represented what was best about Asian immigrants and that his allegiance to the United States was unquestioned.

While no individual stories of American success were highlighted in the section on the Japanese, DuBois included references by authors who were sympathetic to the Japanese American communities in California, and their economic contribution to the agricultural industry. The message of Japanese as hardworking, persevering, and potential model citizens[20] (even though the second-generation were citizens by birth) served to underscore to students the viability of extending citizenship to Asians.

Typifying what was termed "the incidental approach" to intercultural education, DuBois wrote extensive materials speaking to the benefit of such an approach. An example of her method is worth quoting at length:

> How many of our young people know that the first man to lose his life in the Revolution was a Negro—Crispus Attucks—and that the celebration of his birthday was our first national holiday? Or that the first successful operation on the human heart was performed by a Negro physician, Dr. Williams of Chicago? How many know that the man who did most in financing the Revolution, Haym Salomon, the Philadelphia Jew who gave his whole fortune, died a poor man; and that never has there been even a monument erected to his memory?
>
> These and many more interesting facts could be woven incidentally into our classroom work without harming either the College Boards or Regents Exams.[21]

Further, pointing to the aim of progressive education in integrating the social studies around important issues or problems, DuBois saw the classroom as a "natural unit for planned situations and discussions—a sociological laboratory as it were—when general conclusions will be drawn by the group."[22] Expounding on John Dewey's vision of democratic living as a mode of associated living, the exposure of various religious and racial minority groups, with appropriate factual information, would become a place to deliberate on issues of social and moral import in the classroom; to discuss the promise and possibilities of equality under the law.

The national publication, *Intercultural Education News,* which was the sounding board of the Service Bureau, and where DuBois played a prominent role in the earlier published volumes as its Educational Director, reported on the use of the incidental method by classroom teachers throughout the United States. In one article a teacher educator from Girard College in Philadelphia wrote: "What is more natural than to draw upon their [the students'] varied cultural backgrounds for the enrichment of our experiences in schools and out of it? The word foreign does not connote inferier [sic] to us but suggests, rather, an opportunity to widen our horizons."[23] In addition, writing assignments drawing upon the "emotional life of the child," to overcome, especially amongst immigrant students, feelings of inferiority of one's ethnic heritage and to maintain a sense of equality among all students was emphasized.

The Seattle Public Schools and Intercultural Education

Similarly, the Seattle Public Schools maintained a long tradition of progressive education established by its first Superintendent, Frank B. Cooper.[24] Bryce Nelson's study of the Seattle Public Schools maintains that it was far superior to other schools in promoting progressive education, which was tremendously aided by the liberal local politics at the time. Pak's study on the Seattle schools' approach to democratic citizenship education reveals an underlying current of deepening human relations based on an intercultural model as expressed in the main social studies text used by the schools, *Living for Today, Learning for Tomorrow.*[25] Although having always existed in a progressive tradition, the Seattle Public Schools formally adopted an intercultural education policy in 1942. The seven primary principles on which the district's policy rested were:

1. That educators take a positive leadership role in maintaining the democratic way of life in school and community and that we offer in our conduct exemplification of that belief
2. That there be a concerted effort to build broader understanding and a deeper appreciation of the contributions every individual and every group can make to a richer democratic life
3. That emphasis upon the contributions of all segments of our population be specifically included in the curricula at all grade levels and in all areas of study
4. That the academic and social life of the school provide equal opportunities for all its citizens
5. That the school not only discourage but make a conscious effort to ban the use of names, terms, and jokes which tend to promote misunderstandings
6. That schools groups work cooperatively with those public and private agencies which have as their purpose the fostering of democratic practices in American education
7. That the right to prepare in school for vocational competence and the right to earn in occupational life be based upon the individual's interests, abilities, aptitudes, and skills.[26]

In addition the district conducted workshops led by national intercultural educators such as Stewart Cole and officers within the National Association for the Advancement of Colored People. The teaching staff, as part of their in-service programs, attended workshops on intercultural education at the University of Chicago, Stanford University, Reed College, and the University of Washington. Throughout the 1940s the public schools in Seattle carried forth the aims of intercultural education as one of their major curricular goals in guiding the general education program.[27] The overarching goals of: respect for humanity, social justice, social understanding, critical judgment, tolerance, world citizenship, and devotion to democracy would not only reflect their general curriculum but that of the whole conduct of the district.[28] The national intercultural education reforms initiated by Rachel Davis DuBois and others in the Service Bureau for Intercultural Education, as well as the local efforts instituted by the Seattle Public Schools, surely influenced the work of lay teachers, including Ella Evanson.

Intercultural Education through Social Relationships

The school where Evanson taught was situated in one of the most diverse neighborhoods in the city, even to this day. Additionally, the principal, Arthur Sears, equally aimed to provide an atmosphere where students of all different backgrounds learned to appreciate one's heritage as well as others. Bringing in the home culture of the students as a way to integrate learning in the social studies and English became a common feature of the school's pedagogy.[29]

Evanson's portrayal of a cultural democracy plays a central role in her stories about her students. While no evidence is found directly linking Rachel Davis DuBois to Evanson, the tone of the stories Evanson writes expresses the type of democracy DuBois often published. They suggest a teacher who genuinely cared about developing relationships with her students beyond the confines of the classroom walls.[30] And within the context of that came an effort to implement more non-traditional forms of teaching that paralleled the progressive and intercultural framework. Above all it seemed as if Evanson's curiosity about the lives of her students provided a pathway for her to develop a more heightened sense of diversity, thereby being transformed herself by what her students brought to the class.

Six short stories written in the 1940s comprise Evanson's collection. They were based on the actual lives of her students at Washington School and their representation reveals the ethnically diverse classroom in which Evanson taught. Interestingly enough, however, all the stories were based on her male students: "The Little Professor" based on a Japanese American; "Ming Chin and the Baby Panda" about a Chinese American; "With Liberty and Justice for all" about a Jewish American; "Honest Abe," about an African American; "Greek John" about a Greek American; and "Juvenile Delinquency" based on a European American. Reflecting the voice of an educator, there contains a strong didactic tone in the stories with an emphasis on revealing the melting pot ideal of America combined with a strong desire for citizenship. With the exception of the last story, all of the subtitles contain a hyphenated American identity.

The stories reveal a human face to understanding the racialized ways in which her students were perhaps perceived by mainstream culture. Evanson consistently emphasized the notion of equal opportunity of all students, pride and loyalty to America, the sameness of humanity versus a distinction based on racial inferiority, and the claiming of an American identity regardless of race. She describes her class as an "audience suggesting America's melting pot" with its "multi-colored faces."[31] And that she worked in every way to imbibe in her students the motto of Washington School often reiterated by Principal Sears: "One Race, the Human Race, One Nationality, American."[32] The characters and the school she writes about were all real but bear pseudonyms in the stories.

"With Liberty and Justice for All"

One of the stories most representative of that view was about Meyer, a German-Jew who immigrated to Seattle with his mother and grandmother in the 1930s.[33] The Jewish population in Seattle, though small numerically in comparison to the larger cities such as New York, had a close-knit network of community leaders and activists who provided much-needed services to its newly arriving immigrants. The Jewish Settlement House run by the Council of Jewish Women, for example, provided various services for easier acculturation into American life, while providing the cultural and religious link to their respective heritage.[34]

Evanson's depiction of Meyer concerns his ambivalence toward adopting America as his new home, "Of course America is fine, but is so different from my old home. How can I be loyal and love a strange land? I must! I do wish to, but how can I?" Little is revealed about the exact nature of Meyer's personal history other than the flashbacks he and his grandmother had about the "Fatherland." Meyer's grandmother is engrossed by a fear that "they" were coming to take her away. The specter and terror of Nazism haunted her every move. Even Meyer would recollect of his experiences at the Hamburg School for Jews where with "the bare schoolrooms, frightened teachers, and meager opportunities" the "new regime had reduced his race."[35] The only reference to Meyer's father, "He was loyal to the fatherland to the last," perhaps was an allusion to his murder at a death camp in Germany. Despite the lingering nightmares of his homeland, Meyer did not know quite how to reconcile his ambivalence and divided loyalties until it came time for him to graduate from the eighth grade.

The graduation ceremony at Washington School came to resemble the epitome of a "melting pot" America. A Chinese American girl gave a speech on democracy and equal opportunities, Principal Sears reiterated the oneness of everyone's identity, and as the voice of Meyer continues: "There's Abe, the Negro drummer. I like him. He helped me find my way about the school the first day when everything was so confusing. There's Frederico, the Filipino, and Tony, the Italian. Some of them are Spanish, Italian, Turkish, Chinese. No! Not Spanish, Italian, Turkish, Chinese, but all American!" In realizing the opportunities now available to him in America, Meyer enthusiastically recited the Pledge of Allegiance along with his classmates reveling in his newfound American identity. The school's goal of teaching an understanding of a unified political identity while maintaining one's ethnic identity underscores Evanson's portrayal of a school that promoted cultural democracy.

"Greek John"

Living in a democracy also came with presumptions of "looking American." In writing about an eighteen year-old Greek man who enrolls in her class to gain English competency, not an uncommon practice in the schools of Seattle's diverse neighborhoods, "Greek John" captures the attention of his fellow eighth-grade classmates with his shaved head. When asked about his bald head and what he looked like with a full head of hair, John (the ever quintessential "American" name) showed a photograph of his days in Greece with a thick coat of black hair. As Evanson writes:

The picture showed a handsome young man with heavy black hair that rose straight into the air, adding several inches in height to his stocky size. At first sight, it did look unnatural, resembling the black bearskin busby worn by the guards at Buckingham Palace. Though interesting and attractive to others, to John his hair was the badge of a foreigner, and his first step in his Americanization was to eliminate that mark.[36]

John was determined to erase any markers bearing his foreign identity. To sociological theorists[37] studying the impact of immigrants at the time, the choice of foregoing one's old culture in favor of a new one marked the usual transition from immigrant to citizen. In many ways, it was a necessary step, in the researchers' views, towards the process of structural assimilation. Yet in this story, it is Greek John's life experiences that provides for a fruitful and fulfilling experience for the rest of the class. Evanson seemed eager for all students to share their stories, seeing the value in such an exchange. Otherwise, little would be known about what Greek John lived through and how his experiences brought the rest of the class closer to what seemed a distant place.

Greek John, as he soon was called, had had an adventurous life. Born in Greece, an orphan at eleven, he went to sea, and his ship had taken him to every important port in the world. He had a smattering of many languages, and in his two years in Spain, he had gained a good knowledge of Spanish. Although he lacked the power to express himself in good English, his face would kindle with excitement whenever a familiar place was mentioned in any of the classes, and he would dash to the wall map and point it out waving his hands excitedly. The class would be quite impressed, though they understood little except his much repeated sentence, "When I learn English, I tell you."

While Greek John was not yet able to articulate his excitement in English, Evanson recounts how his knowledge of Spanish helped him communicate with the children of Spanish refugees, as well as the little bit of German and Latin that she was able to speak with him. As such, the class resembled an amalgam of various tongues, "And so it was that a class recitation sounded more like a recitation in foreign languages than a class in English or history." That kind of diversity added to the curriculum, through Greek John's presence, first-hand knowledge about the architecture of the Parthenon, bombings in Barcelona and London, and submarine attacks at sea. Keying into what would make for an engaged pedagogical experience, Evanson felt at ease to have the class learn from each other, initiated by their curiosities derived from class discussions. Clearly, while Greek John's goal to assimilate was foremost in his mind, his cultural background and knowledge facilitated a more progressive and intercultural exchange to take place.

"The Little Professor"

The desire towards assimilation in light of being deemed "unassimilable" has been one of the devastating stereotypes affecting Asian Americans. The Naturalization

Act of 1790, the Chinese Exclusion Act, The Gentlemen's Agreement, and the 1924 Immigration Act are examples of laws that curtailed Asian American civic participation and entry into the United States. In urban areas such as Seattle where the history of Asian Americans extended as far back as the mid-nineteenth century, the children of the pioneering immigrants witnessed various forms of prejudice and structural racism inflicted against their parents. The constant reminder of their "foreign" status and their questionable loyalty branded them inferior. The more sensitive educators of these Asian American children became attuned to the first generation immigrant's struggle for citizenship and humanity through the stories of their students. Evanson was one of those teachers.

Her stories depicting the lives of Toji and Ming-Chin reflect the nature of becoming "all-American" in the face of governmental policies distinguishing them as different and unassimilable. The story of Toji is particularly telling as it takes place during World War II, when Toji and his Nisei classmates were forcibly evacuated into concentration camps. Regarded as a genius among his classmates and Evanson, Toji aspired to become an inventor, a scientist with a pedigree from the Massachusetts Institute of Technology. He carried a pocket sketchbook containing more than fifty meticulously hand-drawn ideas for inventions. Toji was equally drawn to his Shinto religion, where his parents were ministers of the Shinto church in Seattle. Evanson writes of her attendance at one of the church's annual Harvest Festivals where Toji acted as interpreter during the ceremony. Through this interaction with Toji and his family beyond the confines of the school, she began to see more of what his life entailed and reveals, "Miss Brown, now understood many things which had puzzled her. She saw the training Toji had been getting in interpreting both language and religion . . ."[38]

Evanson reveals the sad irony during the war, especially for Toji:

> As Toji climbed the stairs on Monday morning, his newly-acquired brisk walk was gone. He heard the school orchestra practicing "O Come All Ye Faithful, Joyful and Triumphant," but to Toji the song was a mockery. A whole world had crashed for him. Last night the F.B.I. had taken his father. He sat down to write his English assignment, but he could not concentrate on it. His thoughts were occupied with questions about the future. "What will happen to my father? Will we be safe in the blackouts? Will the boys let me play baseball in the spring? Do they suspect me of being a fifth columnist?"[39]

With the impending incarceration looming in his future, Toji assumed responsibility for handling his family's affairs and looking after his mother. Evanson realized the extent to which schooling became a secondary feature to his life now. In a sense her depiction of Toji reflects her anger and confusion, especially in light of her belief in the oneness of America with an all-inclusive citizenship, regardless of race. Her sentiment was revealed in a final dialogue sequence between Toji and a classmate, "'It's a gyp,' wailed Chin. You are as much American as I am.'"[40] The story of the "Little Professor" reveals the stark reality of racism and the powerlessness of the teachers, principals, and schools to overturn governmental orders. In spite of that reality, however, Evanson provides a multi-layered view of a young American boy who possessed loyalty to his home—the United States—like everyone else.

Evanson seemed to have a great fondness for Toji. Her description of the Harvest Festival and various aspects of the Shinto religion provide almost an ethnographic portrait. Her vivid details and explanations for certain ceremonial gestures, as if written by someone who possessed a good deal of knowledge of Shintoism, contain a great deal of respect and reverence for its symbolisms. Evanson's relationship with Toji and his family clearly extended outside the boundaries of the school. This became particularly acute during the war, just prior to his incarceration. The immediate arrest of Toji's father by the FBI disrupted any semblance of normalcy, to state the least. His stress and anxiety was clearly visible in his mannerisms in the months following the bombing of Pearl Harbor and whatever assistance Evanson provided was revealed in a letter written by Toji's father, who was at the time interned in Fort Missoula, Montana, to Evanson expressing his gratitude for her help in ensuring that his sons received a proper education despite the major disruptions caused by the war.

"Ming Chin and the Baby Giant Panda"

Again, the desire for citizenship and for building a permanent life in the United States is reflected in the story of "Ming Chin and the Baby Giant Panda." Another telling feature of this story is that Evanson provides in greater detail the context and content of her pedagogy in describing how her class helped to bring Ming Chin's father from China to the United States. In what started out as a class project to help fund the delivery of a baby panda bear from China to the United States,[41] the project soon developed as a source of curriculum planning on geography, international relations, immigration, and zoology.

According to Evanson, Ming Chin worked every morning in his brother's laundromat before school to help save money for his father's ticket to the United States. Ming's father remained in China to take care of his ailing grandfather. Having been a professor of zoology in Hong Kong, Ming's father planned on coming to the United States to pursue graduate study. But one student's remark, " 'Anyway, how can your father come here? I thought the United States wouldn't let any more Chinese enter.' James was remembering his history,"[42] shows how Evanson taught aspects of immigration policies in her social studies and history classes on the more exclusive practices by the United States.

Witnessing Ming's dwindling hopes of bringing his father to the U.S., as he could never seem to save enough money, Evanson initiated contacts with friends at the Woodland Park Zoo to have Ming's father accompany the baby panda that was now set to arrive in Seattle. The whole class became focused on Ming's father and the panda, and as a result centered lessons on learning about the fate of panda bears through geography, science, history, and international relations. Through

Ming's family situation, "China, instead of a remote spot on the globe became to the class a real place absorbing all interest. They were especially fascinated by the zigzag airplane views of the Burma Road."[43] Rather than ignoring Ming's despondent countenance over whether or not he'd ever see his father again, Evanson encouraged Ming to talk about his situation in class:

> Miss Brown, realizing Ming Chin's loneliness, found a way to unlock his tense lips.
> "Ming, I'd like to hear about your home in China. How long since you left? What does your father do?"
> The class suddenly stopped. They had keen ears for stories. A look of happiness changed the handsome face of the fourteen-year-old boy, and though he spoke timidly in a low voice, not one of the forty interested listeners missed a word.

Evanson's recounting of Ming's personal story was really emblematic of how the interaction between the teacher and students provided a means for intercultural relationships to develop. The primacy of relationships afforded a classroom environment in which an integrated curriculum, incorporating the lived realities of students, became an integral feature for the study of social studies. As a result, social studies truly reflected the study of social relations across cultures.

Methodological Issues

The "actual" accounts in the lives of the teacher's students appear overly dramatized, to be sure. Yet they still provide a view of Evanson as a teacher who promoted the ideals of interculturalism by working to adopt aspects of her students' lives into the school curriculum. Without appearing to wholeheartedly defend Evanson, the stories she wrote are clearly indicative of the kind of person she was. She was eager to learn about her students' complex lives. She knew that for some, their racialized identities were at the core of how the outside world judged them. Evanson also knew, however, that the boys she wrote about were typical boys living an everyday American life. The fact that her students were culturally and racially diverse added to the strength of her belief in equality.

Still problematic, however, is her representation of her students. For example, the selection of "Toji" for the Japanese American student is very close to the name of one of the Generals of Japan during the war, Tojo, who was the target of hatred amongst Americans during World War II. Was Evanson aware of this fact upon the time of her writing this short story? Or was she herself operating under a stereotype to which she was unaware? If so, what does this then say about the depth of her intercultural awareness?

In writing about "Honest Abe," the African American student, Evanson appears to be almost obsessive about the color of Abe's face, in spite of her expressed desire to be race-less and colorblind. She describes Abe in the following manner: "His skin was the exact color of the bitter-sweet chocolate . . . ;" "[H]is little black-brown face;" "little colored Abe;" with the "curly black head." Having been elected by the class to deliver flowers and letters to a classmate hospitalized after being hit by a car (the "Juvenile Delinquent" of the last of Evanson's stories), Abe missed the hospital visitation hours due to having stayed after school to complete his math homework. Faced with the choice of telling the truth (that being under 14 years of age he could not visit his friend at the designated time of three o'clock), versus telling a lie to see his friend at four o'clock (telling the nurse that he was indeed 14 and that his short stature was due to his father being a midget), Honest Abe elected to tell the truth. As it turned out, the truth enabled him to bypass hospital regulations and he was able to save the day after all.

Evanson's depiction of Abe's story, in that he is an honest and moral individual, makes one question if the stereotype of African Americans were one of dishonesty and immorality. As Evanson was attempting to dispel certain stereotypes about her Asian American students, perhaps she was doing the same for Abe. In addition, the choice of calling the student "Honest Abe," after Abraham Lincoln is also telling.

Her construction of race is both radical and typical. It is radical in the sense that her views reflect the influence of Franz Boas' work in anthropology and education on dismantling the biological basis of race, thus eliminating for the first time that racial characteristics were rooted in biology.[44] The notion of race was only applicable to the human race, thereby eliminating the racial characteristics that demarcated the boundaries to which racial and ethnic minorities could not enter. Thus to proclaim everyone as an American regardless of race was radical for the time; especially given a history that delimited people to attain full citizenship on the basis of race.

Yet however, Evanson's construction of race was also typical. Her steadfast belief in the colorblind theory worked in tangent with the larger assumptions about the process of immigrant assimilation; that the second generation would forsake their old heritage for a new American one. Evanson does not critique nor analyze the meaning of a new American identity other than providing a positive spin that being an American would afford anyone new and equal opportunities. She knew that in the case of Toji, however, that what the government was doing was at best questionable. Yet with the ultimate aim of achieving success in America, her stories reveal the pattern at the time of broadcasting "successful" immigrant stories, much akin to the popular radio broadcast series, "Americans All, Immigrants All," directed by Rachel Davis DuBois. In that sense, her stories can be construed as templates for others to follow.

Rarely is the study of social issues in the classrooms a perfect venture. Even Ella Evanson's views of what constitutes a democratic ideal contained limits in capturing the mosaic of America that is often described presently. Yet, the intercultural classrooms portrayed provide today's educators with a glimpse of the pedagogical processes that occurred in attempting to fully recognize students' diversity. The incidental method that was popular in classrooms in the 1930s and 1940s provided the means to incorporate those identities of students often deemed inferior in mainstream society.

On the national front, female progressive educators such as Rachel Davis Du-Bois sought to change the traditional system of schooling by aiming to demonstrate the importance of intercultural understanding. Rather than choosing to invoke a more white, patriarchal view of curriculum design, she asked the experts such as W. E. B. DuBois as to how best to learn about the various contributions of African Americans and the legal limits that inhibited their full civic participatory powers. The passion with which she desired to change the role of schooling, in general, and the study of social issues, in particular, was met with resistance by some of the leaders within the Service Bureau for Intercultural Education. Led more perhaps by sexism, the critics of DuBois charged that her methods were oriented too much to the classroom context, lacking intellectual rigor. When analyzing the curriculum units on intercultural education, however, it becomes evident that DuBois was meticulous in seeking factual evidence and including the very voices of people who were deemed marginal.

In a similar vein, the theories of an intercultural classroom DuBois devised became an actual lived reality in the classroom where Ella Evanson taught. Even though these two women probably never met, it becomes apparent how the larger, theoretical work of educators such as DuBois became enacted in classrooms clear across the country. Evanson's sensitivity of the diversity that surrounded her became a critical learning environment where students' voices mattered. To her, social studies *necessitated* a direct relationship to the experiences of her students otherwise, schooling had no relevance to life. All the more important, the school environment in which she taught welcomed intercultural education predicated under progressive ideologies. The principal's reiteration of the importance of learning from the cultural backgrounds of students paved the way for teachers such as Ella Evanson to do the kind of work that she desired. Echoing what other principals such as Leonard Covello conducted in the New York City public schools, Principal Sears of Washington School and Ella Evanson attempted to model democratic ideals in their school and classroom.

Notes

1. Some of the more prominent works in this area include: Larry Cuban, *How Teachers Taught: Constancy and Change in American Classrooms, 1890–1980* (New York: Longman, 1984); Polly Welts Kaufman, *Women Teachers on the Frontier* (New Haven: Yale University Press, 1984); Kate Rousmaniere, *City Teachers: Teaching and School Reform in Historical Perspective* (New York: Teachers College Press 1997); Vanessa Siddle Walker, *Their Highest Potential: An African American School Community in the Segregated South* (Chapel Hill: University of North Carolina Press, 1996); and Kathleen Weiler, *Country Schoolwomen: Teaching in Rural California, 1850–1950* (Stanford: Stanford University Press, 1998).

2. The dearth of research in the history of education that relates to teaching is more fully explained in William J. Reese, "What History Teaches About the Impact of Educational Research on Practice," in *Review of Research in Education,* eds. Asghar Iran-Nejad

and P. David Pearson (Washington, DC: American Educational Research Association, 1999), Vol. 24, pp. 1–19.

3. Some of the current debates centering on the academic efficacy of the Progressive era in education is most voiced by Diane Ravitch, *Left Back: A Century of Failed School Reforms* (New York: Simon and Schuster, 2000).

4. William E. Vickery and Stewart G. Cole, *Intercultural Education in American Schools: Proposed Objectives and Methods* (New York: Harper & Brothers Publishers, 1943), 34.

5. Bruno Lasker, "What is Cultural Democracy? A Little Homily," *Intercultural Education News* 2, no. 2 (1941), 6.

6. Vickery and Cole, *Intercultural Education in American Schools*, 148.

7. This is discussed at length in Yoon K. Pak, *"Wherever I Go I Will Always Be a Loyal American": Seattle's Japanese American Schoolchildren during World War II* (New York: Routledge/Falmer, 2002).

8. Personal Communication, Seattle Retired Teachers' Association, 22 October 1996.

9. Special issues devoted to education for democracy during wartime were prevalent in the early 1940s.

10. Jonathan Zimmerman, *Whose America? Culture Wars in the Public Schools* (Cambridge, MA: Harvard University Press, 2002). Zimmerman's book lays a foundation for understanding the national competing interests in the deliverance of various school policies on controversial matters. However, there is limited discussion on the influence of the intercultural education movement.

11. A thorough biography of Rachel Davis DuBois and her role in the Service Bureau for Intercultural Education can be found in Nicholas Montalto, *A History of the Intercultural Educational Movement, 1924–1941* (New York: Garland Publishing, Inc., 1982). DuBois's role as a feminist activist can be also found in O. L. Davis Jr., "Rachel Davis DuBois: Intercultural Education Pioneer," in *"Bending the Future to Their Will": Civic Women, Social Education, and Democracy*, eds. Margaret Smith Crocco and O. L. Davis, Jr. (Lanham, MD: Rowman and Littlefield Publishers, Inc., 1999), 169–184.

12. Rachel Davis DuBois with Corann Okorodudu, *All This and Something More: Pioneering in Intercultural Education* (Bryn Mawr, Pennsylvania, 1984), 62–98.

13. Rachel Davis DuBois Papers, Immigration and History Research Center Collection 114, Box 29, Folder 11, "Service Bureau for Intercultural Education, Classroom Materials, ca. 1933–1936." Immigration History Research Center, University of Minnesota, College of Liberal Arts. Subsequent references to this collection when summarizing the curriculum units will be cited hereafter as: DuBois Papers, Folder 11, IHRC.

14. Service Bureau for Intercultural Education, *Out of the Many—One: A Plan for Intercultural Education* (New York: Service Bureau for Intercultural Education, 1939), 5.

15. DuBois Papers, Folder 11, IHRC.

16. Woodson, *The Negro in Our History*, 249–251, as quoted in the DuBois Papers, Folder 11, IHRC.

17. As quoted in the DuBois Papers, Folder 11, IHRC.

18. See for example, Ronald Takaki's *Strangers from a Different Shore* (Boston: Little, Brown, 1989).

19. The story of Lue Gim Gong was also a highlighted story in the 1938–1939 popular radio broadcast directed by DuBois, "Americans All, Immigrants All."

20. Which would later, in the 1950s and 1960s, be used against Japanese and Chinese Americans to couch them as "Model Minorities" in comparison to the plight of African Americans and Latinas/os during the Civil Rights Movement, as a further demarcation

used by mainstream media to differentiate between the "good" and "bad" minorities. As Stacy Lee reveals, the model minority is a hegemonic device further perpetuating the notion of Asian Americans existing outside the purview of citizenship, *Unraveling the "Model Minority" Stereotype: Listening to Asian American Youth* (New York: Teachers College Press, Columbia University, 1996).

21. DuBois Papers, Box 17, Folder 4, "Developing World-Minded Attitudes by Thinking, Feeling and Acting," 6, IHRC.

22. Ibid.

23. Ethel M. Duncan, "The Incidental Approach in Attitude Building," *Intercultural Education News* 1, no. 2 (1939), 1.

24. Bryce Nelson, *Good Schools: The Seattle Public School System, 1901–1930* (Seattle: University of Washington Press, 1988).

25. Pak, *Wherever I Go I Will Always Be a Loyal American*.

26. Seattle Public Schools Administrative and Service Center Memorandum, "Dr. Babcock's Report on Intercultural Education Program," 9 February 1951. Superintendent's Files, A78-4, E4-18, Box 18, "Race Problems and Religion." Seattle Public Schools' Archives and Records Management.

27. *The Curriculum: Annual Report of the Superintendent, Seattle Public Schools for the Year Ending June 30, 1946* (Seattle: Office of the Superintendent, Seattle Public Schools, 1946).

28. *The Seattle Educational Bulletin,* October 1939, 2.

29. This is expounded further in Chapter 4 of Pak, *Wherever I Go I Will Always Be a Loyal American,* 73–93.

30. There are scores of examples in the teacher's papers that suggests how she sustained caring relationships with her students. In particular are the letters from her Japanese American students written to her on the eve of the incarceration and afterwards at a detention camp in Puyallup, Washington. The evidence reveals that she corresponded regularly with her former students and sent them books whenever possible. She kept up correspondence with one former student well into the 1970s.

31. Evanson, "Honest Abe," Unpublished manuscript. Ella Evanson Papers, Accession No. 2402, University of Washington's Manuscripts and Archives Division. All of Evanson's stories are included in this archival collection.

32. Ibid.

33. In 1940, the total German population in Seattle was around 3,500. Source: Richard C. Berner, *Seattle 1900–1920: From Boomtown, Urban Turbulence, to Restoration* (Seattle: Charles Press, 1991), 373.

34. Council of Jewish Women, University of Washington Manuscripts and Archives, Accession No. 2089-29.

35. Evanson, "With Liberty and Justice for All," Unpublished manuscript.

36. Evanson, "Greek John," Unpublished Manuscript.

37. The work of sociologist Robert Park at the University of Chicago in the early part of the twentieth century exemplifies this model of assimilation. A comprehensive study of the impact of the University of Chicago's Sociology department, spearheaded by Parks is found in Henry Yu's *Thinking Orientals: Migration, Contact, and Exoticism in Modern America* (New York: Oxford University Press, 2001).

38. Evanson, "Little Professor," Unpublished manuscript.

39. Ibid.

40. Ibid.

41. Personal communication with the Woodland Park Zoo in Seattle, WA, revealed that in 1939 a baby giant panda arrived in Seattle en route to St. Louis, a monumental event in the zoo's history. Email communication, August 2002.
42. Evanson, "Ming Chin and the Baby Panda," Unpublished manuscript.
43. Ibid.
44. Examples of the Boasian influence can be found in Audrey Smedley *Race in North America: Origin and Evolution of a Worldview* (Boulder: Westview Press, 1999), 297–303; and Ivan Hannaford *Race: The History of an Idea in the West* (Baltimore: Johns Hopkins University Press, 1996), 371–372, among others.

5

Benjamin M. Jacobs

JEWISH EDUCATION FOR INTELLIGENT CITIZENSHIP IN THE AMERICAN JEWISH COMMUNITY, 1910–1940

This study broadly considers the ways in which American Jewish education developed along the lines of progressive education and social education in the early part of the twentieth century (1910–1940), and focuses especially on the roots, aims, and practices of one key component of the Jewish school curriculum—the teaching of Jewish history and civilization.[1] My main argument is that the American Jewish education enterprise was consciously directed towards supplementing and complementing, and not supplanting or contradicting, American public education during this period. As we shall see, just as American educators conceived of citizenship education as one of the primary purposes of public schooling, so too did progressive Jewish educators conceive of Jewish education as education for intelligent citizenship in the American Jewish community. Just as American educators regarded social education as a centerpiece of the public school curriculum, so too did Jewish educators place emphasis on the teaching of Jewish history and civilization in Jewish schools. Just as the progressive conceptions of "socialization" and the "new history" provided the foundations for social studies instruction, so too did they underpin Jewish history instruction. Finally, just as progressive American educators hoped to meliorate American society through the schools, so too did progressive Jewish educators hope to use Jewish schools as vehicles through which to reconstruct American Jewish society. Indeed, in the minds of progressive Jewish educators, the ultimate purpose of Jewish education was not merely to transmit knowledge of the past, but also to shape the American Jewish community of the future. In this way, Jewish education could be at the forefront of American Jewry's self-conscious adjustment to their surroundings.

Worlds Apart?: Public vs. Parochial Schooling for America's Immigrant Jews

Most of the two million Jews who immigrated to the United States at the turn of the twentieth century brought with them a deep appreciation of Old World traditions. Seeking to retain ties to Jewish customs, culture, and society, and afraid of the real or perceived threat of anti-Semitism, they typically settled in ethnic Jewish neighborhoods, affiliated with Jewish-run social welfare organizations, worked in Jewish-owned businesses, and sustained or created a variety of religious and cultural institutions. However, some powerful New World forces threatened the long-term viability of the Jewish community in America.

First, American society put strong demands on immigrants to assimilate. Settlement houses, public schools, political machines, and other civic institutions aimed to ensure that new immigrants would abandon their distinctiveness in favor of rapid acculturation into the prevailing Anglo-Protestant middle-class national culture. Second, a gulf inevitably developed between immigrant parents, who clung to old folkways, and their children, who yearned to take advantage of the new and open cultural environment. As a result, the traditional Jewish home, which had long been a pivotal setting for religious identification, lost much of its influence on the rising generation. Third, and most important, the inherently liberal, individuating, and pluralistic nature of American society allowed Jews the freedom to choose how outwardly "Jewish" and/or "American" they wanted to be.[2] In fact, beyond feeling the pressure to acculturate, most Jews felt a genuine and powerful desire to do so. America's free society would allow them to shift from a life of inner existence, oriented by religious tradition and restraint, to a life of boundless existence, oriented by universal rights and opportunities. Thus, American Jewry's greatest prospect for maintaining continuity was to find ways to balance the prerogatives of American citizenship and opportunity with the responsibilities of preserving Jewish tradition and communal distinctiveness.

In this context, it is not surprising that American Jews had a difficult time determining how best to educate their children. In the Old World—particularly Eastern Europe—Jews were isolated from the surrounding population due to political, economic, and social restrictions, and often proscribed from state-sponsored schools. Thus, the education of Jewish youth was almost exclusively the province of the Jewish community. Given that most Eastern European Jews lived in a distinctively Jewish environment in which all matters of life were regulated by religious law, their schools naturally placed a heavy emphasis on teaching and learning Judaic studies—Torah (Hebrew bible), Talmud (rabbinical canon), Hebrew language, Jewish history, ritual, and prayer—so as to inculcate in children an unwavering commitment to Jewish traditions, doctrines, and practices, and thereby ensure the community's survival. Secular education and vocational training, if available, were viewed by and large as supplementary educational pursuits. Conversely, in America, where public education was universal and compulsory, Jewish schooling essentially became superfluous for all but those who sought a traditional religious education.

The overwhelming majority of Jewish immigrants embraced the free public school system because it offered children the chance to learn English, associate with their non-Jewish neighbors, and gain the tools necessary to become responsible and productive American citizens.[3] However, public schooling also had its drawbacks. In the process of Americanizing students, teachers often denigrated Old World customs. Furthermore, the schools were either completely secularized, or they promoted an American nationalist identity that linked social mobility with a nonsectarian but essentially Christian ethic of public piety. The paradoxical nature of public schooling—which could be beneficial to Jewish individuals, as it empowered them to achieve social, economic, and political status in American society, but detrimental to the Jewish community, as it broke down bonds between children and their social and religious group—presented American Jewry with a crisis of adjustment that needed to be addressed. Would Jews throw themselves headlong into American society, or would they struggle to retain their Jewish identity despite their environment?

Some staunch traditionalists tried to combat the effects of Americanization in the public schools by sending their children to *heders* (elementary religious schools), Talmud Torahs (community-sponsored Hebrew schools), or all-day *yeshivas* (talmudical academies), which taught the traditional Jewish canon exclusively. Others sent their children to so-called "radical" Jewish schools, which were organized for Yiddish, Zionist, and/or socialist instruction, and also represented a rejection of the public schools. Still others were so intent on having their children succeed in America that they were hardly concerned with providing for a Jewish education at all. In fact, attendance rates at Jewish schools confirmed that, at any given time, the vast majority of immigrant children were not receiving any Jewish instruction.

Between those who refused to Americanize and those who were anxious to Americanize was a significant group of Jews who felt that the future of American Judaism depended on adapting to the American environment while preserving that which they considered to be most essential to their religious and cultural identity. Hence, they sought the best of both the American and Jewish educational worlds; they established supplementary religious schools, such as Hebrew weekday schools and congregational Sunday schools, which would allow children to receive a Jewish education at night or on weekends while reaping the benefits of public education during the day. Moreover, they endeavored to make the Jewish school system perfectly compatible with the public school system, mainly by applying to Jewish education the progressive ideas that were influencing American education in the early twentieth century.[4]

Drawing on the progressivist notion of educational efficiency, Jewish educators sought to modernize the curriculum, instruction, administration, and organization of Jewish schools by improving teacher training, writing new textbooks, experimenting with innovative teaching methods, implementing systems of educational measurement, and standardizing school management. Drawing on developmentalism, Jewish educators designed their curricula with the needs and interests of children in mind, and developed activities-based projects to teach subject matter. Drawing on social reconstructionism, Jewish educators argued that the Jewish schools were the main vehicles through which Jewish society could be transformed so that it could thrive and be creative in America.[5] Overall, progressive Jewish educators hoped that by adjusting Jewish education to the American environment, they would bring about a genuine synthesis between American and Jewish life. Dare the Jewish schools build a new social order?

American Jewish Education in the Early Twentieth Century: Problems and Progress

By all accounts, the status of American Jewish education at the turn of the century was dismal. The first problem was that attendance rates at Jewish schools were poor (in 1910, only approximately 21 percent of elementary school-aged Jewish children in New York City were enrolled), and drop out was significant (at most Talmud Torahs, student exodus exceeded influx).[6] The new immigrants' eagerness to enter the middle-class meant that most children attended public schools in the mornings and then took jobs in the afternoons, evenings, or on weekends, in lieu of attending Jewish supplementary schools. The lure of recreational life on the street also took its toll on Jewish school attendance. As the writer Irving Howe bluntly put it, "the pupils resent the *heder* as a theft of time that might be better used playing stickball."[7]

The second problem was that curriculum and instruction in the Jewish schools were completely inadequate. In the first community survey of Jewish education in New York City (1909), Mordecai M. Kaplan and Bernard Cronson described a *heder* as a school conducted "for the sole purpose of eking out [for the teachers] some sort of livelihood which they failed to obtain by any other means." The instruction "seldom goes beyond the reading of the prayer book, and the teaching of a few blessings by rote. . . . Each pupil, not knowing when he is needed, straggles in at random, and waits for his turn to come, in the meantime entertaining himself with all sorts of mischief." In the Talmud Torahs, claimed Kaplan and Cronson, "neither the aim nor the curriculum is carried out in practice," "the teaching is found to be very poor," and "the discipline is poor."[8] Remarkably, these second-rate schools were considered the best of those surveyed. Clearly, concluded the researchers, sweeping reform of the Jewish school system was necessary if the community was to provide an adequate education for its children.

The establishment of the New York Bureau of Jewish Education (1910) marked the beginning of the modern era of American Jewish education. The Bureau was charged with training teachers and administrators, organizing the school system, developing original curricula, publishing educational materials, and operating experimental schools that could serve as models for future development. Given the tasks at hand, it was auspicious that Samson Benderly, the former head of a laboratory-style progressive Jewish school, was appointed as the Bureau's director. Benderly was an outspoken critic of Jews who favored abandoning the public school for the all-day parochial school, as Catholics had. Such a move not only would hamper opportunities for Jews to integrate comfortably into American society, he argued, it also would suggest that Jews willingly isolated themselves from the surrounding culture and were thus un-American and undemocratic. Instead, Benderly wholly supported attendance at public schools as a means of involving Jews fully in the American educative process. At the same time, he viewed public schooling as only one prong of a two-pronged educative process for American Jews that necessarily included Jewish schooling. For Benderly, Jewish adjustment to the American environment was not to be regarded as a one-sided endeavor, such that Jews would accept American social values but, in the process, lose their own group character, and offer society nothing in return. Rather, the entire raison d'être of Jewish education was the development of a normalized Jewish life in harmony with American civilization, such that American Jews would realize their maximum self-fulfillment as Americans and as Jews. Put differently, Jewish education was to be a process by which the personality of the individual Jew and the strength of the Jewish group would be enhanced, while, concomitantly, the responsibilities of Jews to American society would be emphasized. In this way, Jewish education, like public education, would be a process of Americanization and an expression of American democracy.

In Benderly's view, the professionalization of Jewish schools could come only through the development of a supplementary Jewish school system that was truly complementary to the public school system. "One of the first functions of the modern Jewish educator," he claimed, "is to discover the laws, habits, and practices which regulate the American environment, and to plan and build accordingly."[9] Modeling Jewish schools on public schools would ensure a harmonizing of educational aims and outcomes; more practically, it would provide a smooth transition from one educational setting to another. With an abiding faith in the principles of progressive education—which called for teachers to be (1) attuned to the needs, interests, and capabilities of children, (2) skilled in the science of curriculum development, (3) knowledgeable in subject matter, (4) experienced in modern instructional methods, and (5) trained in school management—Benderly recruited a young and enthusiastic cadre of American-educated Jewish men and women, instructed them in Judaic subjects, progressive pedagogy, and educational administration, and sent them to work in the Bureau's experimental progressive Jewish schools.[10]

Many of the so-called "Benderly Boys" also attended the Teachers Institute at the Jewish Theological Seminary (T.I.). The teacher training program at T.I. called for students to earn a Bachelor of Jewish Pedagogy, which included rigorous course work in Jewish studies, and a Bachelor of Science in Education at Teachers College, Columbia University (T.C.), which included a heavy dose of progressive philosophy and pedagogy. Among the ideas emanating from T.C. that would eventually make their way into the progressive Jewish education literature were John Dewey's thoughts on experience and education, socialization, the individual and the community, the school as a social institution, democracy and education, social reform, and progress; William Heard Kilpatrick's "project method" for tying the curriculum to the experience of the child; E. L. Thorndike's theories on educational psychology, measurement, and testing; and, Harold Rugg's integrative, problems-based social studies curricula. The impact of the T.C. progressives on the Benderly Boys was so great, claims the historian Arthur A. Goren, that in a sense, "the young professionals of the Bureau replaced scriptural authority with Dewey's educational philosophy."[11]

The project of modernizing American Jewish education required not only a fresh perspective on pedagogy, curriculum, and educational philosophy, but also a fundamental reconsideration of the purposes of Jewish schooling. Mordecai M. Kaplan, a prominent Jewish scholar who served as head of T.I., provided the Benderly Boys with a set of guiding principles for Jewish education in America that emerged from his newly formulated "Reconstructionist" philosophy of Judaism. The most important aspect of Kaplan's Reconstructionism vis-à-vis Jewish education was his ground-breaking idea that Judaism is not merely a religion, but rather a civilization, or a way of life, which incorporates folkways, religious beliefs, culture, language, history, art, music, customs, ethics, education, and above all, a sense of peoplehood. To be a Jew involves choosing to belong to the Jewish community, to believe in the Jewish religion, and to participate in Jewish life. In Kaplan's scheme, choice is paramount—he was a pragmatist, functionalist, and modernist who felt that Judaism must constantly evolve in order to meet the needs of its adherents in any time or place. In America, where democracy and pluralism allow Jews to live simultaneously in two civilizations (American and Jewish), Jews should draw the best from both cultural environments, so that the community can evolve and progress while retaining that which is essential to its identity. Moreover, he argued, because liberty, freedom, and individualism are elemental to the American social environment, individual Jews should be allowed to decide for themselves which elements of Jewish life they want to accept, based on their own social conditions and interests. Consequently, it was inappropriate for Jewish schools to teach the traditional Judaic studies canon for its own sake, for that would stifle individual creativity. Instead, Kaplan believed that the schools should encourage students to think independently and evaluate Jewish culture critically. At the same time, Jewish educators needed to be strongly committed to transmitting the spiritual and historical heritage to the next generation so that future citizens of the community would willingly lead a Jewish way of life.

For Kaplan, the aim of Jewish education should be to "cultivate in the child that power of *social imagination* whereby he might be enabled to live over in his own soul the most fruitful and ennobling experiences of Israel, past, present and future." In other words, Jewish education should inspire in children the desire and capacity to use Jewish history, religion, and civilization as incentive for personal and communal conduct. It should also bring children into practical relation with American society: "Unless, by means of it, our children will make better citizens of the state, unless it will fit them spiritually for the larger world in which they must live, unless it will give them worth and character, it cannot endure."[12] For this reason, Kaplan hoped that democratic values such as freedom, equality, and mutual understanding would permeate the entire Jewish school curriculum, alongside traditional Jewish values. Overall, claimed Kaplan, Jewish education in America should be directed towards (1) fostering a loyalty to the Jewish community and an ability to participate in Jewish life; (2) conditioning habits of ethical conduct, religious observance, and cultural creativity; (3) imparting knowledge of the Hebrew language, Jewish history, Jewish texts, and Jewish rituals and beliefs; (4) inculcating ideals of justice, tolerance, and open-mindedness that could be applied in interactions with Jews as well as people of other groups, races, and faiths; and (5) providing training in the tools of reflective thinking and decision-making that would enable students to confront contemporary Jewish problems appropriately.[13] Once children learn the ideals, habits, and attitudes of American Jewry, concluded Kaplan, they should be able to participate intelligently and effectively in both Jewish and American communal life.

Conceived in this way, American Jewish education was, in essence, a total program of social education — that is to say, it was a system of education for intelligent citizenship in the American Jewish community. Hence, it seemed perfectly complementary to public education, which had also defined its goals in terms of citizenship education, particularly via the social studies curriculum. Given that progressive Jewish educators wanted to follow American models, it is not surprising that they would pay considerable attention to the role of Jewish history instruction in the education of American Jews.

The Teaching of Jewish History and Civilization in American Jewish Schools, 1920s–1930s

In 1917–1918, Leo Honor wrote a landmark series of articles on the teaching of Jewish history for *The Jewish Teacher*, a magazine for progressive Jewish educators, which enunciated the ways in which Kaplan's idea of "social imagination" could be developed in the Jewish schools. For Honor, the focus of Jewish history education needed to shift from the past to the present, for history is important "only in so far as the knowledge of the past will *function* in our own lives."[14] The notion that Jewish history is functional represented a fundamental departure from the traditional methods of teaching the subject. Previously, claimed Honor, Jewish history curricula were packed with facts, events, names, and dates, and the aim of teaching Jewish history was to convert students into storehouses of information. Moreover, the scope of Jewish history instruction was generally limited to the biblical period, there was a strong tendency toward teaching legends, and emphasis was placed on the relationship between history and theology. However, Jewish history treated functionally implied that the true aim of teaching history in the schools was to prepare Jewish children for the struggle of adjustment that confronted them in America.

In order to develop Jewish historical-mindedness, argued Honor, the aims of teaching Jewish history needed to progress in three directions: first, give students the ability to interpret contemporary Jewish life in light of Jewish history; second, develop within students an emotional appreciation of Jewish ideals, hopes, and struggles through history; and finally, make students aware of the fact that Jewish ideals are compatible with American ideals and American life. Most important, it was the function of the Jewish history teacher "to transmit the social habits of the group, so that the community of the past may not be broken," and, at the same time, to make students "aware that progress is attained through conscious adjustment of our inheritance from the past, to the currents and forces at work in the present."[15]

In terms of the scope and sequence of the curriculum, Honor suggested that Jewish history be taught in cycles. This way, the whole of Jewish history would be covered several times over, each time from a different and progressively more intensive point of view. Further, the varying needs and maturity levels of the students could be met appropriately throughout the course of study. In the first cycle, for elementary school, the purpose was to arouse in the students an emotional consciousness of belonging to the Jewish people, and a general interest in their historical struggles and achievements. In the second cycle, for middle school, the aim was to have students learn about the historic movements and schools of Jewish thought that represent the adjustments Jews have made in times of crisis. The ultimate lesson students should learn is that Jews have maintained their continuity through change—that is, that Jews have always adjusted to their environment without relinquishing their inner strength. The third cycle, intended for high school, was designed to give students the tools necessary to understand Jewish society as it exists contemporarily, to discover the historic forces that have brought about existing conditions, and to prepare the students for service to the Jewish community as intelligent citizens. The final cycle, for high school and college students, was a "Jewish problems" course in which students would be encouraged to develop their own social philosophy of Jewish life.

In developing the aims and curricula for Jewish history education, Honor was not only influenced by Kaplan, he also drew heavily on the principles of the "new history," a progressive interpretation of the nature and study of history articulated by James Harvey Robinson (Honor's mentor at Columbia) and others. According to the "new historians," history is continuous and progressive, and all historical antecedents must serve as means to the end of helping us understand ourselves, our community, and the problems and prospects of society today. The implication of the "new history" for the teaching of Jewish history, in Honor's view, was that students should develop an understanding of the dual processes of change and continuity in the Jewish past, so that they can devise intelligent solutions for the problems of their own day.

The National Education Association's (N.E.A.) seminal *1916 Report on the Social Studies in Secondary Schools* also seems to have been a major influence on Honor. To the N.E.A., the ultimate purpose of teaching history was citizenship education. By this they meant that students should be encouraged to understand problems of vital importance to both society as a whole and to the pupils themselves, and they should develop the intelligence, will, and responsibility necessary to participate in the promotion of the social good. This way, social studies education would serve a broad social purpose—it would ensure that democracy would be sustained, and even improved, by intelligent citizens who had a sense of justice, a loyalty to the nation, and a commitment to the prospect of social betterment. Among the N.E.A.'s recommendations reflected in Honor's curriculum are that history education is elemental to citizenship education, history should be taught in cycles, and the apex of the curriculum should be a problems-based course about the contemporary Jewish community much like the N.E.A.'s "Problems of Democracy" course.

By being the first to provide a theoretical and practical direction for Jewish history education, Honor made a significant and lasting contribution to the development of the American Jewish school curriculum. In the next few decades (1920s and 1930s), progressive Jewish educators continued Honor's work, outlining the aims, methods, and content of Jewish history courses, experimenting with curricula, and generally advocating an increase in the prominence of Jewish history instruction in the schools.[16] As can be expected, they had diverse opinions on what type of curriculum would be best: some focused on teaching Jewish history chronologically or in cycles, while others proposed a problems-centered approach; some suggested special projects and activities, while others recommended the source method of history instruction; and so on. Although it would be unfeasible to examine each of these curriculum models in depth here, a number of significant trends and exemplary proposals are worth noting.

First, Jewish history educational reformers set out to create a cache of new instructional materials that could be considered on a par with those found in general education. Many articles on the teaching of Jewish history that appeared in *Jewish Education* (the journal of record for American Jewish education) made specific mention of the influence of the "new history," the social studies, Deweyan thought, and progressive pedagogy on the Jewish history curriculum. Textbook writers began incorporating sociology, geography, economics, and politics into their historical narratives; they offered a critical rather than a moralistic viewpoint; they covered a cross-section of Jewish society, rather than focusing on heroes and elites; they placed emphasis on problems and controversies in community life; and, they consciously related Jewish historical experiences to the contemporary experiences of American Jewish children.[17] One typical "new Jewish history" writer, Mordecai Soloff, consciously drew on Rugg's social studies textbooks as templates for his series *When the Jewish People Was Young, How the Jewish People Grew Up,* and

How the Jewish People Live Today. Like Rugg, Soloff selected content based on how "functional" it was in terms of both history and education: Can it help the child understand any phase of modern Jewish life? Can it help the child realize that Judaism today is the result of a long and continuous process of evolution? Can it help the child participate in Jewish life?[18]

Progressive pedagogy also made its way into the Jewish history curriculum, particularly in terms of instructional methods. Inspired by Kilpatrick's "project method," several Jewish educators designed history projects that aimed to engage learners in purposeful activities and experiences. Representative of these endeavors was Abraham Segal's newspaper project, in which middle school students wrote news items, editorials, cartoons, advertisements, and letters to the editor, as if their newspaper was being published in the time period they were studying (Late Antiquity). Segal's aim was to have the students "like Jewish history and make it their own intellectual and emotional property." After six months of experimentation with the project, he claimed that the children found it more interesting and enjoyable than any formal type of lesson, especially because they were learning by doing. What made the project most valuable, in Segal's view, was that it helped to make history "close and vital" to the students, as they were able to describe and pass judgments on issues and events that happened yesterday, but from the perspective of their sensibilities today.[19]

Some teachers proposed a fusion of the traditional Judaic studies subjects into a Jewish-style social studies curriculum, while others preferred to teach Jewish history as an academic discipline. Exemplifying the fusionist approach was Harry Comins' "Jewish life" course—also inspired by Rugg—which called for an integration of Hebrew, bible, Jewish history, ceremonials, and the assembly program into topical units that would be taught through inquiry, art, and dramatics. To Comins, the advantage of an integrated curriculum was that "the child will be engaged simply in studying Jewish life instead of artificially isolated and abstracted aspects of that life [i.e., the disciplines]."[20] By contrast, Jacob Golub's "laboratory method" for the Chicago Sunday schools transformed the middle and high school history classroom into a "laboratory where historical problems are solved" using the methods of professional historians. Golub established stringent criteria for the selection of subject matter: facts had to "meet the test of scientific critical history"; materials had to be "broad enough in scope to include the treatment of social, economic, and generally cultural aspects of Jewish society, in addition to the military, political, or religious"; the story of "the Jewish people" had to be related, "not merely the account of lives of prominent Jews"; and students should be able to understand chronology, cause and effect, and comparison and contrast. At the same time, Golub insisted that Jewish history had to be presented in such a way that students could develop an appreciation for their cultural heritage. In terms of instructional method, Golub proposed problem-solving and critical thinking exercises. In addition, he argued, "good method" must make subject matter concrete by providing illustrative anecdotes, slides, maps, and diagrams, and, it must allow students to produce historical documents themselves, such as essays, journals, and illustrations.[21]

Of all the approaches to Jewish history curriculum design, the problems-based method gained the most adherents. In fact, almost all Jewish history programs documented in Jewish education journals at the time were purportedly grounded on the historical and contemporary problems of the Jewish people. That so many educators were compelled by the problems-based approach suggests that Jewish history education was, in their minds, more about citizenship education and social education than it was about teaching the Jewish past. For example, Abraham Segal and Solomon Grayzel developed a "retrogressive" approach to teaching Jewish history to upper grades, whereby an inquiry would begin with some question or topic that troubles the student, "and then, *beginning with the child, with his own time and place, we must trace back with him only as far as necessary,* the story of that question in Jewish life."[22] Roland Gittelsohn developed a "Modern Jewish Problems" course for Jewish high schools—ostensibly modeled after the "Problems of Democracy" courses in the public schools—that addressed such issues as, "What keeps Jews together? Why remain Jews? Does charity end at home? Are Jews really hated? What can we do about it?"[23] Robert Kahn's course in Jewish decision-making had high school students addressing such problems as, "Under what type of government will the Jews be best off?," "In the light of the increase in state philanthropy, shall we continue our own specifically Jewish agencies?" and "Shall the Jews voluntarily restrict their own entrance into certain crowded professions?"[24] Emanuel Gamoran's problems-based approach entailed students engaging in Jewish values clarification exercises. In his scheme, "survival" values are those related directly to group preservation, such as keeping the Sabbath, supporting Palestine, and commemorating Jewish lifecycle events, while "humanistic" values are those of general social worth, such as justice, charity, and social responsibility, which are central to Americanism and also inherent in many Jewish customs and activities. For Gamoran, it is these sets of values, rather than the traditional subject matter, which should serve as the organizing principles for the curriculum of the Jewish school.[25]

Some of the Jewish problems-based courses were more bent on social meliorism. Ben Edidin, head of the Buffalo Bureau of Jewish Education, suggested that the "basic aim of Jewish community education ought to be social reconstruction, that is the construction of a more democratic, a better co-ordinated, and more effectively functioning Jewish community." Edidin was likely invoking here the American Historical Committee's Commission on the Social Studies, which issued a series of reports in the 1930s claiming that it was up to the schools to be the vanguard of social reform by instilling in children a progressive outlook and a deep commitment to democratic ideals. In Edidin's view, it was irresponsible for Jewish schools to leave it to the public schools to advocate social reconstruction alone. Rather, Jewish education should aim foremost to instill in children a sense of meaning and purpose as vital members of a minority community dedicated to the realization of social justice for American society in general. Claiming that "the young must be shown the shortcomings of the present order and imbued with a passion for changing it," he placed great emphasis on acquiring skills through direct action in the community. Not only would Jewish students gain first-hand experience "in initiating, planning, executing and evaluating [Jewish] community undertakings," they would also work with non-Jewish institutions "for furthering good will and understanding between Jews and non-Jews." In the end, Edidin hoped students would learn that "the improvement of the Jewish community also furthers improvement of the general community, and that general social progress also affects the Jewish group."[26]

A final noteworthy area of interest for progressive Jewish educators was the historical and contemporary experience of the Jews in Palestine. Given the great concern among Jewish educators in adjusting Jewish children to the American environment, the emphasis on the Land of Israel and the Zionist movement seems incongruous. Yet, by and large, American Jews saw little conflict between loyalty to Zionism and loyalty to America.[27] This was due in part to the fact that the Zionist movement aimed not only to establish a Jewish homeland and restore national sovereignty, but, more broadly, to enhance Jewish political, spiritual, and cultural life the world over through the reconstitution of the Jewish people as a powerful and creative nation. In the Zionists' view, the most crucial step in strengthening Jewish peoplehood was raising ethnic consciousness among Jews worldwide. The homeland would serve as a focal point for the renascence of Jewish life, and its strength and spirit would radiate throughout the Diaspora; but, the nation's survival would also depend on Jews serving as its advocates and benefactors wherever they resided. American Jews thus could turn to Zionism for ethnic identification, reaffirm a sense of solidarity with Jews throughout the Diaspora, and wholeheartedly support the building up of a Jewish homeland in Palestine, but continue to live as loyal (albeit ethnically proud) citizens of the United States. As translated into the Zionist curriculum, this meant that as much emphasis was usually placed on promoting Jewish culture in America as it was on endorsing the national center in Palestine.[28] Indeed, the teaching of Zionism was often the main vehicle for incorporating into the school curriculum activities such as Jewish art, songs, dances, and dramatics, as well as projects such as pro-Zionist penny drives, expos, and assemblies.

Despite the apparent resolve of progressive Jewish educators to teach about Palestine and Zionism, a heated controversy developed at the twelfth National Council for Jewish Education (N.C.J.E.) conference in 1937 regarding the Jewish civilization curriculum. The debate over "the next step in Jewish education" brought to light an ideological rift between those council members who were "American-centered" and those who were "Palestine-centered." Speaking for the first group, Emanuel Gamoran rearticulated the principles of progressive Jewish education: education is socialization, most American Jewish children will live in America as adults, so the primary purpose of Jewish education must be to prepare them to live a real Jewish life in America. Jacob Golub, representing the Palestine-centered group, claimed that the tide of assimilation engulfing American Jewry, combined with the anti-Semitism manifesting itself in Germany and elsewhere, proved that Jewish existence in the Diaspora is precarious and temporary. Therefore, "progressive methods of teaching . . . are of secondary importance" to a curriculum based on making "Palestine and Hebrew living realities for our pupils."[29] In the conference minutes, T.I. registrar Samuel Dinin lamented that it was impossible to get down to a discussion of the "next steps" in American Jewish education because of the split among council members regarding the future of the American Jewish community itself. The progressive movement in Jewish education had reached an impasse.

Social Education and American Jewish Education in Historical Perspective

The debate at the N.C.J.E. conference highlights some of the difficulties progressive Jewish educators—and American Jews in general—faced time and again in balancing the dual goals of autonomy and accommodation on the American scene. As an ethnic minority striving to retain their distinctiveness within a society that tended towards homogenization, American Jews had no choice but to put their faith in the idea that participatory democracy depends on cultural pluralism. In the minds of the cultural pluralists, America was not a melting pot that melded all of its sub-groups into one uniform "American" type. Rather, Jews (and other minorities) were entitled to develop themselves culturally, so that democratic society could in fact support the full growth and free interaction of all individuals and groups, and thereby become even more democratic. For Benderly, Kaplan, and their disciples, preparing Jewish children to live lives as Jews in American society meant providing them with equal parts of identification (Jewish education) and acculturation (American education), so that they could understand and accept their responsibilities as citizens of both civilizations. To this end, progressive Jewish educators embraced social education—which, in this volume, we take to mean teaching and learning about how individuals understand social, political, economic, and cultural circumstances, past and present, and the implications of these understandings on the development of future citizens—as one of the primary purposes of Jewish education in America. A child going through the two-pronged Jewish educative process would ostensibly gain a deep appreciation of American history, culture, society, and citizenship in the public schools, and of Jewish history, culture, society, and citizenship in the supplementary Jewish schools. The product of this educative process was not to be the American type or the Jewish type per se, but the "American Jewish" type.

Despite these intentions, progressive Jewish educators were never fully able to reconcile the particularistic nature of Jewish education with the universalistic nature of public education. After all, even if the Jewish schools did inculcate broad American values (e.g. religious tolerance and social justice) that could reinforce lessons learned in the public schools, they also transmitted uniquely Jewish values (e.g. ethnic pride and Zionism) that seemed to challenge the notion that being a good Jew was the same as being a good American. Moreover, in light of immigration restrictions, quota systems, nativism, religious fundamentalism, and other social, political, and economic forces at work in the 1920s and 1930s, American society was not becoming more pluralistic, egalitarian, or democratic. In fact, like other minorities, Jews were generally being kept at arm's length. Judaism and Americanism may have been harmonized in Kaplan's theory, but they were not in reality. Ultimately, the success of social education in Jewish schools did not depend on the ability of the schools to bring about a new social order within the American Jewish community, but on a new social order being able to support the progressive character of the schools. And if that new social order was not thoroughly realized, then the enterprise was destined to flounder.

Yet, the progressive movement in Jewish education did have a notable impact on the future of American Jewish schools and society. By reaching out into general education in order to rationalize their pedagogical approaches, and by amalgamating instructional methods, content, and values from both the Jewish and American contexts, progressive Jewish educators forever changed the face of Jewish education as it would be delivered in the modern world. For two thousand years, Jewish children learned their tradition mostly by rote. Now, the Jewish heritage would be presented not as a set of abstract principles, but as a way of life. Emphasis would be placed on active Jewish learning, through projects, activities, problem solving, and decision-making. Most importantly, Jewish education would now aim towards the total socialization of Jewish children into the ideals, attitudes, and habits of the American Jewish community, based on the premise that the community depends on intelligent citizenship and active participation in order to sustain itself.

While the process of borrowing and adapting from American education in order to create American Jewish education may have been fairly one-sided, American schools and society did gain a significant benefit in return. Because the supplementary Jewish school system was intent on being complementary rather than contradictory to the public school system, it allowed public schools to progress relatively unhindered by the interests and concerns of an increasingly influential minority group. In other words, if the success of the Jewish schools depended on the success of the public schools, the success of the public schools (particularly in large urban areas such as New York City where most Jews were concentrated) may have been impossible without the support of the Jewish community.[30] This is not to say that American Jewry abstained from getting involved in public education policy; in fact, they were staunch defenders of the separation of church and state in the schools on one hand, and active promoters of Hebrew language instruction in urban public schools on the other. Still, it might be the case that the social education project carried out in American schools in the first part of the twentieth century may have been altered in some way had American Jews galvanized in opposition to it. Instead, citizenship education in the public schools was championed by the majority of American Jews as a crucial element of the larger Jewish educative process in America.

In the final analysis, it is difficult to determine how successful the progressive Jewish education movement was in achieving its ambitious goals. Were the schools transmitting an adequate knowledge of the Jewish heritage and an ability to solve contemporary Jewish problems? Were they conveying a sense of loyalty and responsibility to both the American and the Jewish community? Were they inspiring a commitment to participate in Jewish life? Were they successfully inculcating ideals of justice, tolerance, and open-mindedness? Did the Jewish schools genuinely change American Jewish society? Scant evidence on the outcomes of progressive Jewish education prevents us from accurately assessing its effects on the rising generation of American Jewry.

Nevertheless, progressive Jewish educators can certainly be credited with making Jewish schools a genuine product of the American environment. Indeed, a significant aspect of the story of Jewish adjustment to American society is the story of the progressive Jewish educators themselves, for they embodied the ideal of the integrated American Jew they hoped to create through the schools—that is, someone who is steeped in the Jewish community and at home in American society. As the historian Deborah Dash Moore points out, it was the ability of second generation Jews such as the Benderly Boys to recast available American institutions into instruments of self-perpetuation that marks their important contribution to American Jewish history.[31] Since their time, Jewish schools in the mainstream have been consonant with American schools and a far cry from the Eastern European *heder*. In fact, the American Jewish education enterprise is flourishing nowadays, due in no small part to the foundations laid by this talented group of educational philosophers, practitioners, and prognosticators. To be sure, much can still be learned from their example. Old ideas and practices would naturally have to be fitted to the particular needs and challenges of the contemporary American Jewish community. But, only after knowing what happened in the past can there be informed progress in the future.

Notes

1. I am grateful to Margaret Smith Crocco and Stephen J. Thornton of Teachers College, Columbia University, Robert Chazan of New York University, and Michael Stanislawski of Columbia University, for comments on earlier versions of this paper.
2. It is important to note that the Jewish community was not monolithic in character: among them were Ashkenazim and Sephardim, Westerners and Easterners, Orthodox and Reform, traditionalists and secularists, and so on. Hence, even within the Jewish community, adjustment to America had a variety of different meanings and forms.
3. Deborah Dash Moore, *At Home in America: Second Generation New York Jews* (New York: Columbia University Press, 1981), 90–95.
4. A caveat: there has long been much contention in education circles regarding how "progressive education" should be defined. Herbert M. Kliebard's *The Struggle for the American Curriculum, 1893–1958*, 2nd ed. (New York: Routledge, 1995), provides an excellent summary of the scholarly debate. For the purposes of this study, it should be noted that progressive education—as it was understood by Jewish educators—primarily involved Deweyan educational philosophy, child-centered instruction, and/or a commitment to social reform through the schools.
5. See Samuel Dinin, *Judaism in a Changing Civilization* (New York: Teachers College Bureau of Publications, 1933), 198–212.

6. Israel S. Chipkin, *Twenty-five Years of Jewish Education in the United States* (New York: Jewish Education Association of New York City, 1937), 40.

7. Irving Howe, *World of Our Fathers* (New York: Schocken Books, 1976), 201.

8. Mordecai M. Kaplan and Bernard Cronson, "Report of Committee on Jewish Education of the Kehillah Presented at its First Annual Convention, New York, February 27, 1910," in *Jewish Education in the United States: A Documentary History*, ed. Lloyd P. Gartner (New York: Teachers College Press, 1969), 118–126.

9. Samson Benderly, "The Next Decade in Jewish Education," *Jewish Education* 4 (1932): 14–17, 62.

10. Alexander M. Dushkin, "The Personality of Samson Benderly—His Life and Influence," *Jewish Education* 20 (1949): 9–10. The "Benderly Boys"—among them Dushkin, Leo Honor, Jacob Golub, Samuel Dinin, Emanuel Gamoran, and A.P. Schoolman, as well as Devorah Lapson, Rebecca Brickner, and Libbie Berkson—would all assume prominent positions as directors of Jewish education bureaus and national organizations, instructors at teachers colleges and seminaries, school principals, and curriculum writers. It should be noted that, to date, perilously little research has been done on the Benderly women. This would be a valuable area for further study.

11. Arthur Goren, *New York Jews and the Quest for Community* (New York: Columbia University Press, 1970), 119.

12. Kaplan, "The Function of the Jewish Religious School," *The Jewish Teacher* 1 (1916): 5–12. Kaplan's emphasis.

13. See Kaplan, *Judaism as a Civilization* (New York: Macmillan Company, 1934; reprint Philadelphia: Jewish Publication Society, 1981), 505–507.

14. Leo L. Honor, "The Teaching of Jewish History," *The Jewish Teacher* 1 (1917): 113–118; emphasis in the original.

15. Ibid.

16. *Jewish Education* was published beginning in 1929 by the National Council for Jewish Education. At least eighteen articles were written between 1929 and 1940 that addressed Jewish history or Jewish current events instruction specifically, while several more articles about Jewish education in general addressed Jewish history instruction as part of the larger school program. Also, the N.C.J.E. dedicated a significant portion of their Fifth Annual Conference (held in New York City, June 21–25, 1930) to a discussion of Jewish history education.

17. See Joshua Starr, "Some Current Issues in the Teaching of Jewish History," *Jewish Education* 4 (1932): 104–109.

18. Mordecai Soloff, "Jewish History in the Intermediate Grades," *The Jewish Teacher* 4 (1936): 1–9.

19. Abraham Segal, "A Jewish History Project," *Jewish Education* 5 (1933): 45–52.

20. Harry L. Comins, "An Integrated Curriculum for the Jewish School," *Jewish Education* 4 (1932): 93–110.

21. Jacob Golub, "Some Experiments in the Jewish Sunday Schools of Chicago," *Jewish Education* 1 (1929): 34–43.

22. Abraham Segal, "A Retrogressive Approach in Teaching Jewish History," *Jewish Education* 6 (1934): 23–30. My emphasis.

23. Roland B. Gittelsohn, "Modern Jewish Problems," *The Jewish Teacher* 3 (1935): 18–23.

24. Robert I. Kahn, "A Problem Approach to the Teaching of Jewish History," *Jewish Education* 7 (1935): 51–54.

25. Emanuel Gamoran, *Changing Conceptions in Jewish Education, Book Two: Principles of the Jewish Curriculum in America* (New York: Macmillan, 1924).

26. Ben M. Edidin, "Aims of Teaching Jewish Community Life," *Jewish Education* 7 (1935): 101–106.

27. See Naomi W. Cohen, *American Jews and the Zionist Idea* (New York: Ktav Publishing, 1975), 14–50.

28. See Dushkin and Honor, "Aims and Activities of Jewish Educational Organizations in America," *Jewish Education* 5 (1933): 136–146. Instruction in Modern Hebrew was also a cornerstone of the curriculum.

29. Dinin, "Proceedings of the 12th Annual Conference of the N.C.J.E.," *Jewish Education* 9 (1937): 87–94.

30. See Paula S. Fass, *Outside In: Minorities and the Transformation of American Education* (New York: Oxford University Press, 1989), for an analogous argument regarding Catholic education in the twentieth century.

31. Moore, 9.

FROM ASSIMILATION TO CULTURAL PLURALISM: THE PTA AND CIVIC EDUCATION, 1900–1950

In 1933, social studies scholar Bessie Louise Pierce produced her second book on the part played by voluntary associations in shaping civic education. Applying the observations of Alexis de Tocqueville to public education, she argued that civic associations "constantly spring into life in America to meet the exigency of the hour, and which sometimes exercise, while they last, a profound influence in amalgamating public opinion and in promoting both civil and political programs."[1] In her meticulously documented work, Pierce demonstrates the widespread influence of voluntary associations in promoting patriotism, loyalty, and citizenship by holding essay contests, donating American flags, and even writing high school history texts. For example, by 1931, the Veterans of Foreign Wars had distributed nearly four million copies of its pamphlet, "Etiquette of the Stars and Stripes," and promoted its motto "One flag, one language, one country" in schools around the nation.[2] Pierce's research, which she began during the Americanization fervor of the post–World War I years, reveals the efforts of voluntary associations in preserving a nativist version of American ideals.[3]

The deluge of immigrants on American shores prior to the 1920s resulted in civic education programs that called for the assimilation of these strangers into American ways. Civic education under this educational regime was characterized by teaching loyalty and social cohesion through pledges and loyalty oaths, patriotic songs, marches, and salutes, and English lessons.[4] As Jeffrey Mirel argues, the goal of assimilation was to teach immigrants to espouse American political values and to work toward the ideal of the Anglo-Saxon, Protestant vision of citizenship.[5] However, Michael R. Olneck suggests that these efforts were largely ineffective in practice, though they hold symbolic implications for the educational researcher because such civic education endeavors depicted identity, recognized status, and expressed and sanctioned the normative orthodoxy of dominant social groups.[6]

After the 1920s, educational leaders as well as members of voluntary associations brought about a new vision of civic education that began to embrace Horace Kallen's notion of cultural pluralism.[7] With immigration quotas in place, the onset of the Depression, and a proliferation of ethnic cultural groups and associations, civic education began to be transformed in an effort to "incorporate at last minority and disadvantaged groups that had long been 'outsiders' to the mainstream of American political and educational life."[8] Moreover, the threat of totalitarianism in Europe prompted educational leaders to develop civic education programs that highlighted the differences between totalitarianism and democracy. In particular these programs were engineered to teach "how democratic governments and societies dealt with ethnic and religious minorities."[9] Yet, no one version of cultural pluralism won out, as theory was interpreted and applied in different settings to suit any number of agendas.[10] Nonetheless, what Nicholas Montalto terms the "New Pluralism" of the mid-1930s had, in educational circles, become "intensive and widespread."[11] Social studies texts of this era by George Counts and Harold Rugg document this shift toward pluralism. Likewise, Rachel Davis DuBois created her theory of intercultural education during these years to teach about ethnic and racial difference and promote cultural understanding.[12] Also, an NCSS Bulletin on intercultural understanding in the 1940s by Hilda Taba and William Van Til was a best seller.[13]

This chapter examines the shift from assimilation to cultural pluralism outside the realm of professional educators, in a major voluntary education organization, the National Parent-Teacher Association (PTA). Interestingly, among the many groups studied by Bessie Louise Pierce in the early twentieth century, the PTA was not among them. Since Pierce produced her scholarship, voluntary associations have remained under-researched in the history of education and, when investigated, are portrayed typically as "ignorant hordes who were clamoring at the schoolhouse gates."[14] This examination of PTA civic education activities builds on research undertaken on Americanization and reveals the wider public's interest in civic education in the first half of the twentieth century. It reveals the attempts by white, middle-class women to assimilate working-class and racially and ethnically diverse women and children according to middle-class, white, Protestant ideals. Additionally, it shows how, as the shift to cultural pluralism transpired, the PTA began to reckon with its own racial segregationist policies. Therefore, this chapter reveals the complex nature of civic education programs as well as their implementation by different racial groups, since the PTA was segregated and its two associations dealt with civic education in different ways. In short, the PTA's emphasis on tolerance and understanding of other cultures after 1930 found its greatest challenge in its own segregationist policies. Therefore, this chapter argues that various interpretations of and approaches to civic education found expression among volunteers and lay activists, who added their voices to discussion of the education of the civic polity.

The Origins of the PTA

Extensive structural changes characterized public education during the Progressive era as newly forming administrative hierarchies helped consolidate rural schools and reconfigure urban school districts. Likewise, social service programs, such as school lunch programs, safe playgrounds, and medical inspections, became part of the mission of public schools. The transformed school curriculum stood out among these sweeping changes. Between 1890 and 1920, the school curriculum was reworked from an emphasis on liberal arts to efficiency and functionality that included differentiated courses of study at the high school level, the replication of the junior high school around the United States, and the widespread implementation of vocational curricula.[15]

Citizens reacted to the bureaucratization of public education and the professionalization of teaching by organizing home-school groups and school improvement societies in urban and rural regions around the country.[16] William J. Reese argues that parent-teacher groups, mainly comprised of women, played a role in mending the fissure between the average citizen and educational institutions that were becoming increasingly centralized and under the purview of professionals.[17] Women's organizing parent-teacher groups was an extension of their municipal housekeeping, for which they sought to improve the health and sanitary conditions of municipalities, including the public schools.[18] African American teachers and clubwomen in the South undertook similar, yet separate, efforts on behalf of public education. Out of this grassroots activism in the late nineteenth century emerged several women's national associations, one of which would become a leader among the national voluntary associations to address the growing gap between school and home, the National PTA.

In 1897, a group of elite, white women in Washington, DC, convened the first National Congress of Mothers (NCM), the precursor to the National Parent-Teacher Association (PTA), to address poverty, rising immigration, and the adverse effects of industrialization on children and society. Over the first three decades of the twentieth century, PTA organizers focused on education for motherhood and home-school cooperation as they worked to unite numerous mothers' clubs, women's clubs, and school improvement societies under their leadership. After the well-publicized first National Congress meeting, state units were formed in the ensuing years to complete the federated structure by 1926 with 49 state and territory associations. In 1924 the association changed its name to the National Congress of Parents and Teachers, after two decades of success in influencing national legislation such as mothers' pensions and the Sheppard-Towner Maternity and Infancy Act, which provided health education for expectant mothers and women with young children.[19] By 1930, the PTA had over one million members and had become a household name due to its far-reaching networks and publications. Given the high profile of the association, virtually no school was untouched by the involvement of a local women's club or parent-teacher association, though membership in the National PTA remained largely white and middle class well into the twentieth century.

Reflecting the interest among African American teachers and community members in the South, the National Congress of Colored Parents and Teachers (NCCPT)—the segregated branch of the PTA—was organized in 1926. The founding of the organization represented the uniting of local and state units that had been organized around the South since the 1890s. Its purpose was to "function only in those states where separate schools for the races were maintained."[20] Though the membership of the association lagged behind its white counterpart, the NCCPT—or black PTA—was a visible and vocal force in public education of African American children. More politically radical than the white PTA, the black PTA worked to eradicate racism in schools and society through its local networks of associations that worked closely with other African American associations such as the National Association for the Advancement of Colored Persons (NAACP) and National Association of Teachers in Colored Schools. The black PTA built separate schools where there were none, coordinated donations of schoolbooks and other educational materials, and promoted the teaching of black history in the schools.[21] In 1970, the two segregated branches of the PTA finally merged into one (since the National PTA decided after the *Brown* decision to leave the desegregation initiatives to local and state units).

Both black and white PTAs emphasized education for parenthood, whereby each popularized and promoted various educational goals and programs to its members. Parent education was necessarily civic education for PTA leaders, as the principles of what it meant to be an American was embodied in proper parenting as an obligation of all citizens to eradicate crime, poverty, and ignorance. The PTA's approach to civic education changed over the first half of the twentieth century as it reacted to the wider political climate and to the changing needs of American society. In its early years, the PTA dedicated itself to assimilating immigrants and promoting peace, character education, and community reform as the duty of all women. This program was shaped in reaction to larger political, social, and economic forces, especially military conflicts.[22]

Civic Education for Assimilation

William J. Reese maintains that during the Progressive era women's voluntary associations "influenced every important administrative change, curricular reform, and social service established in local cities."[23] However, the scholarship by Reese and others on this topic focuses on women volunteers' social service work rather than the curriculum reforms they supported and enacted. PTA leaders, like many leaders of women's organizations of this era, believed that women should bear some, if not all, of the responsibility for the civic education of youth. The original platform of the PTA included emphases on peace, character education, and community activism that lasted until the World War I years, when Americanization efforts became the core of its program. From the outset, PTA leaders believed the home to be the place that civic education would begin, which meant passing on certain principles of peace, character education, and concern for the community. In the years prior to the Nineteenth Amendment one PTA leader argued the mother's duty was the education of her sons, since she "has almost exclusively in her hands the training of our future voters."[24] Girls, in contrast, were to be raised to be good mothers, in order to perpetuate the cycle of preparing sons for citizenship and daughters for motherhood.[25]

According to R. Freeman Butts, the Spanish-American War of 1898 "stimulated a nationalistic and even militaristic fervor and flavor in civic education" in the public schools.[26] Voluntary organizations, such as the newly formed PTA, followed suit. The second annual meeting of the Mothers' Congress was held in the weeks following the declaration of war against Spain, prompting the organization's leaders to define the meaning of patriotism for women in terms of motherhood. Speaker Mary Lowe Dickinson connected every mother's obligation to her country: "In an hour like this the Nation we love demands the highest patriotism, and the highest patriotism demands the noblest type of citizenship, and the noblest citizenship calls for the bravest manhood, and the bravest manhood comes only from the purest boyhood, and the purest boyhood is the highest gift to the Nation of the noblest type of motherhood."[27] However, the declaration of war also impelled the newly formed PTA to infuse this patriotism with a maternalist emphasis on peace. The organization had the previous year endorsed the work of the Universal Peace Union and requested that the lessons of peace be taught in home and school.[28] Thus, the PTA was among the many women's associations of this era to speak out against the war and cause controversy as a result. For example, newspapers criticized the request made by PTA president Alice Birney that the American public, "eliminate from childhood the swords and guns and caps, the toy cannon and other destructive emblems of war."[29] Even more controversial was the discussion as to whether the PTA should send condolences to the Queen of Spain regarding the high number of casualties of war from that nation. The *Washington Post* reported that the PTA leaders had contemplated doing so, noting that the organization was going too far by sympathizing with the enemy. Defending her position, one leader responded, "If we are not in sympathy with the mothers of Spain, what mothers are we in sympathy with and what are we here for?"[30]

At the turn of the twentieth century, PTA leaders believed they were best suited to lead other Americans to higher moral ground, as concerns over increasing numbers of immigrants, rising poverty, and encroaching industrialization prompted them to focus on civic education. Thus, the leaders of the Congress believed that strong character was a precondition of the good citizen. Criticizing the dearth of character education in the schools, the PTA's first president, Alice Birney, remarked in 1897 that it was important not to subordinate "character building . . . to the so-called cultivation of the mind."[31] While B. Edward McClellan argues that character and moral education during this time had to compete for a place in curriculum that was becoming increasingly crowded with coursework emphasizing skill, efficiency, and social competence, PTA women saw it differently.[32] They did not separate character education from citizenship training or the functional curriculum. For them, character development came about through manual and domestic training in addition to direct instruction in morals and manners. All of this made for the good citizen, and was one of the reasons they called so vociferously at this time for "manual, domestic, and moral training [to] be embodied in the school curriculum."[33]

Reflecting a larger discussion in public education, professional educators speaking at annual PTA meetings debated who held responsibility for civic education, and by definition, character education. Some, such as educator Henry Sabin of Iowa, supported the opinions of the PTA, that the home was primarily responsible. At the 1900 PTA meeting, Sabin spoke on the "Duties of Parents in Training Children for Citizenship." Sabin's talk reflects his nativist fears over the rapid and wide-ranging changes in demographics during this era. He confirmed the PTA's belief that "the American home must make the American citizen" by arguing:

> The obligations which rest upon every citizen to accept a public office as a bounden duty is omitted from all our text-books upon civics and is seldom mentioned in our schools or homes. . . . [The] home ought to teach many things essential to good citizenship, to which the school is a stranger.[34]

Taking the opposite position, well-known progressive educator Francis W. Parker argued that civic education was the purview of the public schools. Parker maintained that it was the school's responsibility to teach civic duty and democratic ideals, telling Mothers' Congress delegates, "[t]he ideal school is the ideal community, and an ideal community is a democracy."[35] Progressives like Parker sought to reunite the social institutions that industrialization had fractured. However, since he valued professional expertise above parent or volunteer knowledge, the schools had the responsibility to prepare citizens. This was not necessarily in conflict with PTA ideals, since the association grew out of the progressive movement and supported the professionalization of teaching as well as parent education programs.

Professional expertise notwithstanding, the PTA endeavored to work inside as well as outside the schools to promote a community-minded civic education. At its third annual meeting in 1899, the organization passed a resolution that approved the work of the League of Good Citizenship "and endorse[d] its plans for introducing to the public schools the idea of self-government, which shall prepare our youth for citizenship."[36] The organization's extensive work on behalf of civic education was noted at a meeting of the National Education Association (NEA) in 1907 by a speaker who explained "the work of the women's patriotic orders has been extended in nearly every community for the furtherance of the teaching of patriotism and knowledge of our country's history."[37] By 1908 the PTA had made a commitment to support "the effort to introduce into all schools training for the hand as well as for the head, and definite instruction in ethics and civics."[38] The sentiment continued over the years; in 1911, at the Second International Congress on Child Welfare, which the PTA hosted, civic education took a high priority among the organization's resolutions. The organization recognized the importance of "training children in the privileges and responsibilities of citizenship," so it passed a resolution to favor promoting "such civic education."[39]

PTA women defined citizenship, and hence, civic education, according to their own standards of community activism and reform, and not by the right to vote. In fact, the organization's founders refused to endorse suffrage for women because they viewed it as too divisive an issue for the mothers of the nation. As a result, the PTA promoted the ideal that "the self-respecting and self-considerate mother will be able to make the child understand that domestic relations always involve reciprocity. In fact, this understanding is one of the highest qualifications of citizenship."[40] By construing civic participation in this way, as broader than the vote or any other formal political processes, the PTA stood at the vanguard of redefining civics and citizenship education in the early twentieth century. As a result, the PTA and other women's associations inspired some of the ideas in the early social studies program devised by the NEA committee, which was called community civics.[41] Community civics included what was to become a central aim of public education by the second decade of the twentieth century, character, citizenship, and complete living.

Reese argues that by World War I the public schools began to play a significant role in national defense and preparedness.[42] Following the lead of the schools during this time, the PTA consistently promoted acts of patriotism in schools and communities, as it continued to define its role as a keeper of American values. War and immigration influenced the PTA to promote patriotism among the mothers and children of the nation in efforts to assimilate immigrants, but also to remind the white, middle-class members of the association that they needed to model American virtues. State PTA reports by June of 1918 document the extensive patriotic efforts of local associations. At the meeting of the Second District of the California Congress of Mothers and Parent-Teacher Associations, members viewed a display of educational posters that included the captions "Playgrounds help Uncle Sam by making strong, vigorous bodies, clean morals, mental alertness. These mean life, liberty, happiness." And, "Play ideals: Happiness, cleanliness, politeness, obedience to law, loyalty, fair play, honesty, courage, team play, character."[43] Mirroring English-only initiatives around the country, at the state level in California, the PTA resolved to pressure schools to discontinue the teaching of German.[44]

The national leadership of the white PTA was less concerned with school curriculum issues—unless the curriculum directly challenged American ideals—than it was with larger, social education issues relating to citizenship and responsibility to community and nation. Hannah Kent Schoff, president of the PTA in 1918, set forth the goals of the organization during the war: "The National [Parent-Teacher Association] is today the logical medium for reaching all homes, and through it every form of cooperation can be given the government at this serious struggle for world freedom in which we are engaged."[45] White leaders' lack of interest in subject matter was a reflection of the organization's attempt to leave the educational work to the expertise of professionals and provide ongoing support to parents for the civic education of their children.

War work of women's clubs in relation to education included school gardens and neighborhood centers and a curricular emphasis on home economics, "scientific food conservation," and industrial preparedness "to hasten at top speed the Americanization of our immense population."[46] In what appears to be single-minded attention to the topic, the PTA publication *Child Welfare Magazine* featured stories on "Americanization," "Education for Citizenship," and "The Kindergarten—A Vital Americanizing Agency."[47] The war affected the work of the PTA and women's clubs, as its onset prompted the PTA to disseminate pro-American propaganda to immigrants.[48] The association even created a Department of Americanization in 1918 to promote English. This policy formalized the work of local associations that, like the Tennessee Congress, had been teaching English to "foreign mothers."[49] In addition to the work that women volunteers undertook in communities, they lent support to patriotic programs in schools. In Tennessee, a local PTA reported the following: "We are having patriotic films made to be sent over the state, showing history and etiquette of the flag."[50] At this time, educational leaders praised the civic education function of local associations and supported the work of the PTA, as they noted the organization's role in implementing patriotic programs and civic education in schools and communities. In his address to the Department of Superintendence of the NEA meeting, Charles A. Wagner proclaimed, "[The PTA is] and must be the primal spring from which all streams of influence and direction in democracy flow."[51]

After the 1920s, the PTA retreated from its promotion of peace and pacifism as World War I signaled a major shift in the political climate in the United States. In some respects the PTA remained in support of the notion of peace, as indicated by PTA president Hannah Kent Schoff, who in 1918 asserted "The education that made the War shall not be the education of youth if mothers have the power to prevent it."[52] Yet, in December 1922, the PTA withdrew its affiliation with the National Council for the Prevention of War (NCPW), an anti-war organization that promoted education as a means to eradicate combat.[53] One of the largest women's organizations in the NCPW, the PTA would not tolerate accusations of communism and therefore backed away from its promotion of peace initiatives during the Red Scare years.

Working toward Tolerance

In the 1930s, the PTA continued its patriotic efforts as it took more seriously its own role as preserver of American values. It was not uncommon for local school meetings to be part business, part patriotic exhibition. A November 1934 meeting of the (white) Jamestown, New York Parent-Teacher Association included tables decorated with American flags and red, white, and blue candles, and speeches on the work of the school boy patrol and the importance of keeping dues current.[54] Throughout the 1930s, the Jamestown PTA met regularly, as its members partook in different activities. They sang the "Battle Hymn of the Republic," and they discussed "The Home's Responsibility in Developing the Fundamental Standards of Good Citizenship."[55] The emphasis on patriotism and teaching citizenship continued through the 1940s as the Jamestown PTA listened to school children sing the Star Spangled Banner and debated whether to order new dishes for its monthly meetings, given the importance of rationing and doing away with non-necessities during World War II.[56]

However, among the national leadership of the black and white PTAs and in black local parent-teacher associations of the South, the post–World War II years saw the increased attention to tolerance of other races and cultures in schools and communities. These developments came about after the 1926 founding of the National Congress of Colored Parents and Teachers in Atlanta, Georgia. After years of working through black networks, African American leaders in the South decided to affiliate with the white PTA at that time in an attempt to secure higher educational standards for black children since the white PTA had achieved a significant measure of power and national visibility.[57] Yet the white and black PTAs, two branches of one organization with separate local, state, and national officers, regarded the notion of cultural understanding from two different standpoints. The white PTA's approach to cultural tolerance and sensitivity involved looking beyond its borders to other countries and nationalities, rather than focusing on racial disparities in the United States. These efforts contrasted with those of the segregated branch of the PTA, whose members worked to undo racism in the United States. The different perspectives came together only through the intergroup relations committees initiated by the black PTA.

Beginning in the late 1930s, the official organ of the white PTA, *National Parent-Teacher,* began to run articles on tolerance and cultural understanding. For example, in a 1939 article, Annette Smith asked, "Should a democracy permit any kind of propaganda? Should it permit pleas for dictatorship, for violence, for 'race' prejudice?"[58] Though this and other articles referred to the need for tolerance, they apparently never turned the lens on the white PTA's program and what it was doing to work for equality in education and to end racial segregation. Instead, discussions of race were connected obliquely to the problems of discrimination against other nationalities.[59] Likewise, the white PTA's endorsement of curricular programs was more removed than in its hands-on approach of the past. The association promoted new curricular developments to parents and other school volunteers during this era, which included the integration of the social studies in American schools, yet it did not give any detail on the particulars of social studies or how it was defined. For example, in an article on *National Parent-Teacher,* one educator highlighted the pivotal role of parents' associations in popularizing "the equally important three S's of our day—Science, Social Studies, and Social Personalities. . . .

How much better it is to face the fact that although parents are naturally rather conservative in educational matters they will often accept ideas and suggestions from someone within their own ranks."[60]

PTA historians Harry and Bonaro Overstreet noted the association's shift toward valuing of pluralist ideals during the 1930s and 1940s as an effort to build tolerance and understanding.[61] In the 1940s, the white PTA created a committee called the World Citizenship Committee to coordinate programs that would address these ideals.[62] The association's use of the term "world citizenship" reflected a common usage of a term introduced in 1938. In *The Purposes of Education in American Democracy* educator William H. Carr argued for the importance of each citizen becoming a "cooperating member of the world community."[63] The emphasis on world citizenship was a welcome and comforting way to discuss cultural understanding for white PTA leaders who resisted any suggestion that they scrutinize their own complicity in racism and racial segregation in the United States. In 1948 PTA leaders maintained "the citizen's highest loyalty today is to the one world of humanity" and that the association's new goal was to build "character in the framework of the world," thereby extending its fifty-year focus on cultivating good citizens beyond the boundaries of the United States.[64]

Only rarely did white PTA publications refer to racism in the United States. For example, in 1943, white PTA President Minetta A. Hastings proposed that local associations work toward world citizenship by first removing "bias toward minority groups within our own borders."[65] While further research on local white PTAs is warranted, it is clear that those in less diverse areas of the U.S. did not heed this call because there was no direct pressure to do so. Instead, they perhaps were like the Jamestown PTA, which continued to serve local needs and the local white population. Yet many urban regions were diverse, which prompted educators to observe that the PTA played an important role in helping promote an understanding of difference. Edgar Dale, professor of education at Ohio State University, observed "[i]n a nation composed of people from many different lands, . . . 'the blending of all these elements into a truly American culture . . . is one of the PTA's most valuable contributions.'"[66]

The approach to cultural pluralism was different in the black PTA at the local, state, and national levels. Beginning in the late 1940s, black PTA leaders took an interest in the notion of interculturalism that had been developed by social studies scholar Rachel Davis DuBois. As a classroom teacher in New Jersey, DuBois had developed curricula in the 1920s and 1930s to cultivate sympathetic attitudes in school children toward people of other races and ethnicities, further promoting the intercultural education movement. She designed and led assemblies and lessons that highlighted the contributions of minority groups, in particular African Americans. As a Quaker and an active member of the NAACP, she was committed to improving relations between the races. In 1934 she organized the Service Bureau for Intercultural Education (SBIE) as a center for teachers. Later criticized for glorifying ethnicity and fostering divisiveness among Americans, the SBIE was wrested from her control and redirected under new leadership toward a focus on "respect for a national culture with limits to expression of cultural differences."[67] DuBois continued her work, however, by creating the Workshop for Cultural Democracy in 1941. For the rest of her long life, DuBois worked with community groups and schools implementing her "group conversation method," which involved different groups of people coming together to get to know one another in a social atmosphere and to overcome stereotypes and prejudices.[68]

DuBois found a willing audience among the officers and members of the black PTA, as well as those white members who sought racial equality. Since its founding, the black PTA embraced the principles of racial equity and understanding. Having found a social education program that articulated its hopes, the black PTA adapted the principles of intercultural education to its organizational structure and formed groups to work on racial harmony and educational equity. Beginning in the 1940s, the association successfully encouraged state and local units to form committees on intercultural relations with the white PTA leaders in Southern states.[69] A report on black parent-teacher associations published in the *Journal of Negro Education* in 1945 explains that intercultural education was a staple of the adult education programs sponsored by the association.[70] By the 1950s, DuBois had become a featured speaker at the annual meetings of the National Congress of Colored Parents and Teachers.[71] The emphasis on intergroup relations committees of the black and white PTAs did not focus solely on black-white relations, but extended into different areas, such as recognition of religious diversity. White and black PTA members used intercultural education to build bridges between Christians and Jews through its alliance with the National Conference of Christians and Jews.[72]

In northern urban communities that experienced racial conflicts, DuBois was called upon to lead group conversations to solve problems. When the conflict involved schools, DuBois favored having local PTA groups partake in the exchanges. In her memoirs DuBois recounts one such day around 1950:

> After ten weeks of working together and sharing, a mothers' group gathered in the coffee canteen of a West Side public school in Manhattan to celebrate in January's zero weather the birth of two babies on the same day—one black and one white, brought to the PTA when a month old, by their mothers. The fun of sharing old-wives' tales about birth and babies moved into a deep feeling of joy when they sang each other's lullabies, while passing the babies around the circle.[73]

With or without Rachel DuBois, the PTA's intergroup relations committees continued in the second half of the twentieth century, as the two PTAs worked toward integrating. The national leadership of the white PTA left the decision to integrate to each state organization, which resulted in the slow state-by-state desegregation of the PTA that was not completed until 1970.[74] As state PTAs tore down the racial barriers, some found the intergroup relations committees useful, like that of the Kentucky Colored Congress, which voted to continue their association "since the group could still be of great service" to African Americans in that state.[75] In the application of intercultural and intergroup relations, the PTAs—both black and white—created a pluralistic civic education program that encouraged its members to see the similarities among different groups of people while teaching them to value difference. Further research has the potential to assess the widespread impact of intercultural education among PTA groups as this chapter suggests a complex picture of resistance and harmony in its history.

Conclusion

The civic education curriculum of the PTA focused on peace, character education, and community civics in the years following the Spanish American War of 1898. By the 1920s, the PTA's assimilationist programs reached a fevered pitch with Americanization programs that included an emphasis on outward displays of patriotism and learning English. Due to changes in the political and social climate during the 1930s, the PTA continued its Americanization efforts, but through a new lens. It endeavored to promote tolerance and cultural understanding. This change in the civic education ideals and programs of the PTA played out differently in the majority white PTA, and its segregated counterpart, the National Congress of Colored Parents and Teachers, or black PTA. In its nationally distributed publications, the white PTA promoted world understanding, emphasizing the sameness of people around the globe. By contrast, the black PTA implemented intergroup relations teams to support the recognition and acceptance of differences. As a result, state-level PTAs in the South created intergroup relations committees to work toward integration and racial understanding. Such activities reveal to us the myriad ways that citizens sought to co-opt their own civic education in a diverse and ever-changing society.

Much research remains to be done on the creation and adaptation of civic education initiatives among community groups and voluntary associations in the first half of the twentieth century. Scholars of today and tomorrow need to revisit Pierce's studies on the assimilationist approaches of fraternal, military, and peace organizations. Likewise, Rachel Davis DuBois' work on group conversation that was carried out in "all sorts of places—PTAs, churches, synagogues, settlement houses, labor union halls, YMCAs and YWCAs, scouts, libraries, and hospitals," is as of yet untapped.[76] In an attempt to redress these oversights in the literature, this chapter argued that one of the major voluntary organizations of the twentieth century, the National PTA, played an influential role in promoting civic education programs as changes in civic education went from an emphasis on assimilation to ponder the concept and reality of cultural pluralism. It also argues that, as an association dedicated to bridging the gap between home and school, the PTA stands as an important link between changing approaches to civic education and the American public.

Notes

1. Bessie Louise Pierce, *Citizens' Organizations and the Civic Training of Youth* (New York: Charles Scribner's Sons, 1933), x. For a recent translation of Tocqueville's writings, see Harvey C. Mansfield and Delba Winthrop, trans., *Democracy in America* (Chicago: University of Chicago Press, 2000).

2. Pierce, *Citizens' Organizations*, 54–55.

3. See also Bessie Louise Pierce, *Public Opinion and the Teaching of History in the United States* (New York: Alfred A. Knopf, 1926).

4. R. Freeman Butts, "Historical Perspective on Citizenship Education in the United States," in *Education for Responsible Citizenship*, National Task Force on Citizenship Education (St. Louis, MO: Institute for Development of Educational Activities, 1977), 56.

5. Jeffrey Mirel, "Civic Education and Changing Definitions of American Identity, 1900–1950," *Educational Review* 54, no. 2 (2002): 145.

6. Michael R. Olneck, "Americanization and the Education of Immigrants, 1900–1925: An Analysis of Symbolic Action," *American Journal of Education* (August 1989): 399.

7. Horace Kallen, *Culture and Democracy in the United States* (New York: Arno, 1970 [1924]); Mirel, 147–48; Jonathan Zimmerman, *Whose America?: Culture Wars in the Public Schools* (Cambridge: Harvard University Press, 2002), 13.

8. Butts, 60. See also Mirel, 148 and Kathleen Weiler, "Corrine Seeds and the Avenue 21 School: Toward a Sensuous History of Citizenship Education," *Historical Studies in Education* 14, no. 2 (2002): 204. Weiler notes that in California in the 1920s, local schools allowed cultural groups—Mexicans, Japanese, and Russian—to use the schools.

9. Mirel, 149.

10. Zimmerman points out that cultural pluralism could be used to reinforce ideological conformity (p. 31). See also Nicholas V. Montalto, *A History of the Intercultural Educational Movement, 1924–1941* (New York: Garland Publishing, 1982), 285, where he argues, "such an approach may serve a variety of purposes."

11. Montalto, ix, 124.

12. For Counts and cultural pluralism, see Mirel, 149; for Rugg and pluralism, see Zimmerman, 249, footnote 9. For intercultural education, see Montalto, *A History of the Intercultural Education Movement*.

13. I thank Margaret Smith Crocco for bringing this to my attention.

14. Jonathan Zimmerman, "Storm over the Schoolhouse: Exploring Popular Influences upon the American Curriculum, 1890–1941," *Teachers College Record* 100, no. 3 (1999): 603. A notable exception is Jonathan Zimmerman, *Distilling Democracy: Alcohol Education in America's Public Schools, 1880–1925* (Lawrence: University Press of Kansas, 1999).

15. David B. Tyack, *The One Best System: A History of American Urban Education* (Cambridge, Mass.: Harvard University Press, 1974); William J. Reese, *Power and Promise of School Reform: Grassroots Movements during the Progressive Era.* (Boston: Routledge & Kegan Paul, 1986); Kenneth M. Gold, *School's In: The History of Summer Education in American Public Schools* (New York: Peter Lang Press, 2002); and Herbert M. Kliebard, *Forging the American Curriculum: Essays in Curriculum History and Theory* (NY: Routledge, 1992). See also Edward A. Krug, *The Shaping of the American High School, 1880–1920* [1964] (Madison: University of Wisconsin Press, 1969).

16. Tyack, *The One Best System;* Reese, *Power and Promise of School Reform,* xxi; and William W. Cutler III, *Parents and Schools: The 150-Year Struggle for Control in American Education* (Chicago: University of Chicago Press, 2000), 3–4.

17. William J. Reese, "Between Home and School: Organized Parents, Clubwomen, and Urban Education in the Progressive Era," *School Review* (November 1978), 3.

18. Municipal housekeeping, according to Anne Firor Scott, allowed for women's discontent with existing social and political conditions to be addressed through volunteer work in cities, towns, and rural areas as it made respectable what might have been considered "unseemly public or political activity." Scott, *Natural Allies: Women's Associations in American History* (Urbana: University of Illinois Press, 1992), 142.

19. Also known as the Federal Act for the Promotion of the Welfare and Hygiene of Maternity and Infancy, the Sheppard-Towner Act supported educational programs and free clinics for mothers beginning in 1921 but was repealed in 1929. For fuller discussions of these reforms, see Muncy; Skocpol, *Protecting Soldiers and Mothers;* and Molly Ladd-Taylor, *Mother-Work: Women, Child Welfare, and the State, 1890–1930* (Urbana: University of Illinois Press, 1994).

20. National Congress of Colored Parents and Teachers, *Coral Anniversary History* (Dover, DE: National Congress of Colored Parents and Teachers, 1961), 9.

21. Christine Woyshner, "Race, Gender, and the Early PTA: Civic Engagement and Public Education, 1897–1924," *Teachers College Record* 105, no. 3 (2002): 520–544. For a case study of PTA work in an African American community, see Vanessa Siddle Walker, *Their Highest Potential: An African American School Community in the Segregated South* (Chapel Hill, NC: University of North Carolina Press, 1996).

22. This is in line with Butts' argument that the history of social and civic education reveals distinct patterns of civics and citizenship curriculum initiatives that were instituted during times of social, political, and economic crisis. Butts, "Historical Perspective on Citizenship Education in the United States," 47.

23. Reese, *Power and the Promise of School Reform,* 40.

24. Mary Harmon Weeks, "What Constitutes a Good Mother?" *Child-Welfare Magazine* 4, no. 4 (1910): 235.

25. Alice McLellan Birney, *Childhood* (New York: Frederick A. Stokes Co, 1905), 106. In many ways, Birney continued the tradition of the early national period of republican motherhood. Republican motherhood was a solution to the challenge of popular sovereignty by placing the onus of civic education on mothers to educate the nation's sons to become virtuous citizens. Linda K. Kerber, *Women of the Republic: Intellect and Ideology in Revolutionary America,* 2nd ed. (New York: W. W. Norton & Company, 1986 [1980]). See especially Chapter 9 "The Republican Mother: Female Political Imagination in the Early Republic," pp. 265–288.

26. Butts, 55.

27. Mary Lowe Dickinson, "Response to Address of Welcome," *Proceedings of the Second Annual Congress of Mothers,* reprinted in *National Congress of Mothers: The First Conventions,* eds. David J. Rothman and Sheila M. Rothman (New York: Garland Publishing, 1987, [orig. pub. 1898]), 23–24.

28. "Mothers' Last Words," *The Washington Post,* 20 February 1897; located in PTA scrapbook, PTA Archives Collection, Chicago, Illinois. See also Nancy F. Cott, *The Grounding of Modern Feminism* (New Haven: Yale University Press, 1987), 94. Also, see the discussion on maternalism in *Journal of Women's History* (Fall 1993).

29. Mrs. Theodore Birney, "Address of Welcome," in Rothman and Rothman, 19.

30. *Washington Post*, 8 May 1898; located in PTA scrapbook, PTA Archives Collection, Chicago, Illinois.

31. Mrs. Theodore W. Birney, "Address of Welcome," *Work and Words of the National Congress of Mothers* (Washington, DC: National Congress of Mothers, 1897), 8.

32. B. Edward McClellan, *Moral Education in America: Schools and the Shaping of Character from Colonial Times to the Present* (New York: Teachers College Press, 1999), 46.

33. National Congress of Mothers, "Resolutions Adopted by the Second International Congress on Child Welfare," *Child-Welfare Magazine* 5, no. 10 (1911), 189.

34. Henry Sabin, "The Duties of Parents in Training Children for Citizenship," *Quarterly Report [of the National Congress of Mothers]* 1, no. 2 (1900): 93, 96, 97.

35. Francis W. Parker, "The Ideal Education," *Quarterly Report* (March 1901): 142.

36. *National Congress of Mothers Third Annual Convention, 1899*, Rothman and Rothman, 273.

37. Helen Grenfell, "The Influence of Women's Organizations on Public Education," *National Education Association Proceedings, 1907*, 130.

38. "Report of the Department of National Organizations of Women," *NEA Proceedings, 1908*, 1217.

39. "Resolutions Adopted by Second International Congress on Child Welfare, National Congress of Mothers," *Child-Welfare Magazine* 5, no. 10 (1911): 189.

40. Weeks, "What Constitutes a Good Mother?" 233. Weeks was referring to community relations and activities in her use of the term "domestic relations."

41. A discussion of community civics and its similarities to the work of women's associations of the Progressive era lies beyond the parameters of this chapter. I discuss this more fully in Christine Woyshner, "Women's Associations and the Origins of the Social Studies: Volunteers, Professionals, and the Community Civics Curriculum, 1890–1920," *International Journal of Social Education* 18, No. 2 (2003–2004): 16–32.

42. Reese, *Power and the Promise*, 242.

43. National Congress of Mothers and Parent-Teacher Associations, "State News" *Child-Welfare Magazine* 12, no. 10 (1918): 200.

44. "State News" *Child-Welfare Magazine* 12, no. 10 (1918): 201.

45. Mrs. Frederic Schoff, "President's Desk," *Child-Welfare Magazine* 7, no. 6 (1918): 89.

46. Mrs. O. Shepard Barnum, "The Past, Present, and Future of the Patrons' Department," *NEA Proceedings, 1917*, 641–642.

47. See *Child Welfare*, vol. 13.

48. Molly Ladd-Taylor, "'When the Birds Have Flown the Nest, the Mother-Work May Still Go On': Sentimental Maternalism and the National Congress of Mothers," in *Mothers and Motherhood: Readings in American History*, eds. Rima D. Apple and Janet Golden (Columbus: Ohio State University Press, 1997), 456–457.

49. NCM-PTA, "State News," *Child-Welfare Magazine* 12, no. 10 (1918): 210.

50. "State News—Tennessee," *Child-Welfare Magazine* 12, no. 10 (1918): 210.

51. *Child-Welfare Magazine* 12, no. 8 (1918): 137.

52. Mrs. Frederic Schoff, "President's Desk," *Child-Welfare Magazine* 7, no. 7 (1918): 113.

53. The PTA was among those women's organizations listed on the infamous "Spider Web Chart" of 1924, which was created to draw attention to domestic subversion in the nation. Nancy Cott, *The Grounding of Modern Feminism* (New Haven: Yale University Press, 1987), 242, 248, 249.

54. Jamestown, New York PTA, Nov. 13, 1934 meeting, "PTA Scrapbook," located at Fenton Historical Society, Jamestown, NY.
55. Jamestown, New York PTA, Oct. and Nov. 1936 meetings.
56. Jamestown, New York PTA, April and Nov. 1942 meetings.
57. Woyshner, "Race, Gender, and the Early PTA," 536.
58. Annette Smith, "The Need for Tolerance," *National Parent-Teacher* (November 1939): 6.
59. See Ruth Benedict, "Let's Get Rid of Prejudice," *National Parent-Teacher* (Feb. 1946): 7–9 and Frank W. Hubbard, "The Unique Function of the P.T.A. in American Democracy," *National Parent-Teacher* (June–July 1940): 10–13. This non-direct approach reflected larger trends in the intercultural education movement. See Montalto, *A History of the Intercultural Education Movement.*
60. Hubbard, "The Unique Function of the P.T.A. in American Democracy," 13.
61. Harry Overstreet and Bonaro Overstreet, *Where Children Come First: A Study of the PTA Idea* (Chicago: National Congress of Parents and Teachers, 1949), 158.
62. Overstreet & Overstreet, 165.
63. As cited in Butts, 63.
64. As cited in Overstreet & Overstreet, 165, 168.
65. As cited in Overstreet & Overstreet, 214.
66. Dale as cited in Cutler, 166.
67. O. L. Davis, Jr., "Rachel Davis DuBois: Intercultural Education Pioneer," in *"Bending the Future to Their Will"* eds. Margaret Smith Crocco and O. L. Davis, Jr., 173, 178. See also Montalto, *A History of the Intercultural Educational Movement.*
68. Rachel Davis DuBois, *All This and Something More: Pioneering in Intercultural Education* (Bryn Mawr: Dorrance & Company, Inc., 1984), 106–107.
69. Little is known about how racial and ethnic minorities felt about the goals of intercultural education or how they adapted its programs. One scholar to examine the involvement of black professional women in intercultural and intergroup relations efforts argues that black women were exploited by white managers who enlisted them in cultural sensitivity groups because of their orientation toward social justice and racial uplift and willingness to work on behalf of these issues for little or no wages. Stephanie J. Shaw claims that those white managers who embraced intercultural education did so out of fear of the emerging radical left. My analysis of the black PTA's use of intercultural education leads me to believe otherwise, as African American members sought to use the intergroup relations movement to their advantage by employing such groups in gaining equal resources in schools, and especially after desegregation became inevitable. Stephanie J. Shaw, *What a Woman Ought to Be and Do: Black Women Professional Workers During the Jim Crow Era* (Chicago: University of Chicago Press, 1997), 188, 189.
70. W. McKinley Menchan, "Adult Education Programs of Negro Parent-Teacher Associations," *Journal of Negro Education* 14, n.3 (1945): 415.
71. DuBois is mentioned in the National Congress of Colored Parents and Teachers publication *Our National Family.* See, for example *Our National Family* (May–June 1951): 6 and *Our National Family* (August 1951): 12.
72. Overstreet & Overstreet, 166.
73. DuBois, 121.
74. Susan Crawford and Peggy Levitt, "Social Change and Civic Engagement: The Case of

the PTA," in *Civic Engagement in American Democracy,* eds. Theda Skocpol and Morris P. Fiorina (Washington, DC: Brookings Institution Press, 1999).

75. Minutes, Board of Managers of the Kentucky Congress of Parents and Teachers, Sept. 18, 1956. Special Collections and Archives, Eastern Kentucky University.

76. DuBois, 120.

7

Andrew Mullen

"SOME SORT OF REVOLUTION":
REFORMING THE SOCIAL STUDIES
CURRICULUM, 1957–1972

"On the whole," declared educational theorist Ralph Tyler in 1963, "the social studies are the least effective educationally of any of the basic areas taught in the
American public schools." The field was in a "sorry condition." The social studies
curriculum was poorly planned, social studies teachers poorly prepared. Educators
and the public-at-large were confused about the field's essential purposes. Too few
competent social scientists had been involved heretofore in curriculum planning.
It was high time something was done.[1]

On this last point, at least, Tyler's fellow speakers at Stanford University's annual Cubberley Conference enthusiastically agreed. Precollegiate curricula in
mathematics and the natural sciences were currently undergoing a fundamental reorientation. The federal government and private foundations, whose resources had
made such reorientation possible, were now extending their largesse to the social
sciences. This very conference, in fact, was being subsidized by the United States
Office of Education's Project Social Studies, an early demonstration of the
"money and manpower [that had] . . . recently been allocated to the social studies
in a major way." It was evidently incumbent upon social studies educators to join in
what some contemporaries were anticipating to be a comprehensive curriculum
"revolution."[2]

The speakers at the Cubberley Conference were not altogether specific as to
what form the impending revolution should assume. They did articulate, however,
a number of underlying beliefs that might serve to guide the revision process.
Among other assumptions, the contemporary world was so radically different

from the past that a de facto national curriculum framework dating from 1916 was plainly obsolescent. The age of space and an era of continuing scientific revolution demanded a new framework, ideally one that provided a logical, sequential plan for each year of schooling, K-12. Secondly, the social studies curriculum had too long been dominated by history, at the expense of the non-historical social sciences. Sociology, psychology, and anthropology especially, were identified as disciplines significantly underrepresented in the existing social studies curriculum. Thirdly, the inductive instructional strategies currently being promoted in the natural sciences were believed to provide appropriate models for instruction in the social studies. In a world of exploding knowledge, it was increasingly impossible and increasingly unnecessary for students to focus on discrete facts. What was essential, the speakers made clear, was enhancing students' ability to develop useful generalizations from available data. Finally, the schools were in need of help from "highly competent social scientists." If "school people" and scholars could be brought into effective partnership, it appeared to a number of speakers that the social studies were on the "threshold of great opportunities for progress."[3]

Neither the critiques of social studies nor the hopes articulated by would-be reformers at the Stanford conference in 1963 were entirely novel, of course, nor worthy of attention strictly on their own account. As long as there has been a portion of the school curriculum identifiable as social studies, there have been those like Tyler, for instance, who thought the field in a "sorry condition." The sentiments expressed at the Stanford conference may be seen, however, as representative of a larger reform movement that shook the field between 1957 and 1972, and helped to shape in important ways what we think of as social studies today.

Two Critical Moments

In the pages that follow I wish to consider this larger period of reform in the social studies from the perspective of two loosely defined "moments." The first of these, a perceived "threshold of progress," I shall characterize as a moment of anticipation. This moment represents the culmination of events dating back to at least 1957, but as I have framed it, consists primarily of the climactic years 1961 to 1963. The second moment to be examined, at the turn of the next decade, I shall characterize as a moment of assessment, or at least attempted assessment. I characterize this as a moment of assessment in a double sense, as both an occasion when professionals working at the time were pausing to assess recent developments, and as an occasion for us in hindsight to consider the course of the revolution anticipated a short time before.

While I shall introduce various strands of curriculum reform and attempt to place these in larger social and educational contexts, it is not my purpose, even were it possible under present constraints, to provide a comprehensive review of such a turbulent and multi-faceted period. I wish to offer, rather, a broadly interpretive essay, examining first of all the agendas of different groups of would-be reformers at the beginning of the decade. To what extent did reformers speak in one voice, and in what particular ways did their goals differ? How do we account for the apparent near-unanimity on the pressing need for change in this period, well before the widespread social unrest that characterized the decade's later years? In the second half of the chapter I shall consider the extent to which these different agendas were validated, if not realized, by decade's end, particularly as these hopes were—or were not—expressed in the official National Council for the Social Studies (NCSS) Curriculum Guidelines published in 1971. In the latter context, moreover, I wish to consider the significance, for contemporaries and curriculum historians alike, of a relatively neglected set of curriculum documents. Finally, I wish to consider precisely "what sort of revolution," if any, occurred during this period.

The standard account of the period of reform under consideration, developed most fully by participant-historian Hazel Hertzberg (1981) and reasserted more or less in the most authoritative summaries of curriculum research since then, speaks of two distinct movements.[4] The first of these, what quickly became known as the "new social studies," was inspired by Cold War concerns, a desire to enhance academic rigor, and the educational psychology of Jerome Bruner. Supported by both federal and private foundation money, it consisted primarily of efforts to develop new curriculum materials written by or under the direction of university scholars. A core emphasis in most projects was to introduce students to the "structure," key concepts, methodology, and/or habits of mind of the particular discipline in question. Estimates of the number of projects vary, and only twenty-six widely recognized projects would be reviewed in a major published assessment at decade's end.[5] According to Hertzberg's estimate, however, there were by 1967—the movement's putative peak—more than fifty of these national, discipline-centered curriculum development projects underway.

By 1968—the year of the King and Kennedy assassinations, an escalating war in Vietnam, and associated social unrest—the New Social Studies movement was by Hertzberg's account replaced or eclipsed by a second movement. This reform effort she characterized as the "social problem/self-realization" social studies, or a shift toward "relevance, activism, and identity." Unlike the first movement, originated by the federal government, foundations, and professional associations, and which to a great extent was imposed on the schools top-down, Hertzberg saw this second movement as arising in large part from young people themselves. Both adolescents still in school and young teachers bringing into the schools their recent life-experience on university campuses sought ways to make the curriculum more personally and socially meaningful.

There is, in broad strokes, some obvious validity to Hertzberg's "two-movements" model—the rational, top-down reform movement of the head, railroaded by an affective, grass-roots movement of the heart. A model, moreover, of a movement conceived in perceived threats from outside the nation (in particular, the threat represented by *Sputnik*), overrun by a movement attuned to domestic problems. Such an interpretation obscures, however, the degree to which the two movement's concerns overlapped, and were experienced by at least some contemporaries as one continuous—if multistranded—stream of reform.[6] Moreover, as we shall see, this standard interpretation obscures the extent to which even the initial impulse for reform that characterized the decade's early years was itself divided. To the extent that the anticipated revolution would not live up to certain of its expectations, we may account for this in part by tracing the anticipated revolution's tangled roots.

"Urgency, Urgency, Urgency"

The three hundred teachers and scholars registering for the Cubberley Conference at Stanford that summer of 1963 were not the only ones discussing potential reforms in the teaching and learning of social studies. At the November 1961 NCSS convention in Chicago nearly two years before, a reporter had acknowledged "a sense of urgency," and a "gnawing realization that social studies instruction cannot stand still." He called readers' primary attention, however, to an atmosphere of "frustration with the slow progress of social studies education" as compared with gains in other subjects.[7] A spate of articles, volumes, and special forums on the social studies throughout 1962 and 1963, however, suggested that the social studies were quickly gaining ground. In 1962, the federal Office of Education announced its Project Social Studies, which immediately began to fund curriculum study centers, underwrite individual research projects, and offer support to a variety of "developmental activities," including scholarly conferences. A joint project of the NCSS and the American Council of Learned Societies, begun in 1958 and designed to bring scholars together for a re-examination of the social studies curriculum, finally bore fruit in the form of two volumes from major publishers.[8] A number of educational periodicals, including *Phi Delta Kappan* (October 1962), *Teachers College Record* (March 1963), and the NCSS's own *Social Education* (April 1963), devoted theme issues to the perceived "ferment" in the field, and several additional periodicals would quickly follow suit. With good reason, then, a contemporary might report, "everything is in turmoil. What we have is a multitude of pressures and proposals that are leading in many directions. The social studies are in a crisis, and some sort of revolution is coming."[9] The question at the moment was exactly what sort of revolution it would turn out to be.

Throughout the coming decade educational literature would continue to refer regularly to "turmoil," "a great state of flux," and even "a considerable number of rebellions" in the social studies. The overall sense of expectancy, however, would never match that of the decade's early years. The year of 1963, then, when "criticisms of the social studies [had become] as common as beer cans by a well-traveled highway," may be seen in hindsight as the acme of expectation for reform, recognized as such even by one contemporary.[10]

Whatever else was open to debate in 1963, near consensus existed within the professional social studies community on the need for immediate action. As one observer who evidently did *not* share fully this opinion put it in November, "many discussions of the social studies [have] become cluttered with irrelevant references to *Sputnik,* space travel, threats to peace and to mankind, and urgency, urgency, urgency."[11] Before considering the different camps' differing agendas, it may be instructive to contemplate this near-universal sense of the urgent.

To begin with the issues identified by the writer above, the issues represented by *Sputnik,* including the "threats to peace and mankind," did not seem at all irrelevant to many contemporaries. Since the launching of *Sputnik* (1957), several additional reminders of tension between the world's superpowers had surfaced; much of the discussion about curriculum reforms was being carried on in the shadow of developments in Berlin, Cuba, and the ever-present specter of nuclear annihilation. The frequently apocalyptic tone and language in the reform literature during this period—routine references, for example, to sentiments such as the "grave issue of the survival of our civilization and possibly of mankind itself"—may have been partly an indulgence in shibboleth. And partly even self-serving rhetoric as well—often employed, as they were, in the context of arguments to justify funding the social studies as generously as other areas of the curriculum.[12] At the same time, the rhetoric of "crisis" with respect to reforming the curriculum may also genuinely reflect a deep sense of uncertainty on other fronts. As one perceptive contemporary suggested, "the Cold War occupies more and more of the emotional life of many people . . . Frightened people in times of crisis take a special interest in the education of the young. People who are unable to solve their most vexing problems look to insure that the new generation will be better prepared to settle matters."[13]

Aside from Cold War tensions, the perceived need for immediate action may be explained by a growing awareness even by 1963 of the kinds of issues that would attract so much attention by decade's end. Articles and books on curriculum reform from these years call particular attention to the population explosion and associated concern about the adequacy of natural resources, air and water pollution, the urbanization of society, race relations, the needs of newly independent nations in Africa and Asia, and a perceived "crisis in values," including a loss of certainty about moral absolutes.[14]

To the extent, then, that there would be a major change of direction in the field of social studies during the coming years—and opinion on this point is by no means unanimous—it may be traced in part to the following two factors. One, that there was *no* one in these years arguing for the status quo. Virtually all parties involved in the professional conversation contributed to a state of potential destabilization, in lobbying for change of one kind or another. Secondly, a change of direction was facilitated, quite simply, by the willingness to *embrace* change, prompted by the perceived depth and number of crises in the world to which some sort of curricular response was apparently required.

Different Agendas Obscured by Common Rhetoric

A shared belief that radical reform of the curriculum was both needed and imminent, and a shared assumption about the urgency of the current situation did not, however, mean that all those who called for, or anticipated, a revolution in the curriculum were seeking the same thing. The rhetoric of radical reform was in fact employed at this time by three or more fairly distinct, if occasionally overlapping, camps.[15]

Arguably the least revolutionary in their vision for change, historians were nonetheless among the first to introduce such language. As early as the spring of 1961, Charles R. Keller, former director of the College Board's Advanced Placement program, had used the term "revolution" at least four times in a subsequently much-quoted article. Social studies teachers needed to come out from the "educational doldrums." The slow progress in social studies reform relative to other fields Keller attributed to the separate directions college historians and K-12 social studies teachers had apparently gone after 1916, when the term social studies was first popularized. Keller's "invitation to some kind of revolution," then, was an invitation to reconnect the two worlds of college history and precollegiate social studies. As the first step in creating the revolution, Keller advocated "elimination of the term social studies," substituting the "more exact and therefore . . . more meaningful" history and the social sciences. Secondly, Keller proposed establishing a less ambiguous, more intellectually focused, set of purposes. "I suggest that we rid ourselves of the idea that these subjects have the job of making good citizens." Finally, he stressed the need for a more coherent scope and sequence—a clear vertical plan "all up and down the academic ladder"—from elementary school through graduate school.[16]

To what degree Keller was speaking for the historical guild as a whole is not clear. Historians who contributed to published symposia on the social studies in these years, however, did generally echo Keller's concerns and agenda. Like Keller, University of California–Santa Barbara historian James High called for a "redefinition of social studies" and less "obfuscation of meaning" in discussions of its purposes. Social studies was "not a definable, identifiable body of discrete knowledge" and "therefore, not a solid core of teacher preparation or instructional material." Schools should be less concerned with the integration and application of knowledge, and more concerned with furnishing delimited bodies of knowledge, presenting historian's "findings to students as history."[17] Former American Historical Association (AHA) liaison with the social studies community Thomas Mendenhall attributed much of the weakness of the curriculum (frequently an "ill-digested mixture of poor history and worse social science") to the fact that social studies teachers had been "deprived of professional discipline-oriented leadership from the universities."[18] To the extent that current reform efforts in the natural sciences emphasized a greater role for disciplinary scholars and a greater alignment of K-12 curriculum with university coursework, then, these historians embraced the call for reform of precollegiate education in general. To do so was in fact merely continuing the work of the previous decade, when professional historians had supported the Council for Basic Education in working for higher academic standards in the schools and established the AHA Service Center for History Teachers. For all the talk about a new role for the non-historical social sciences, most historians seemed to take for granted that history would remain the core of the social studies curriculum. More effective organization of the curriculum, more cooperation between scholars and teachers, more precise and delimited aims, and more attention to academic content—particularly in teacher-preparation programs— would ensure the triumph of "valid history as opposed to the kind of 'social studies' rubbish that [had] dominated too many schools for the last two decades."[19]

Social scientists were starting the decade in a different position than the historians with respect to the existing precollegiate curriculum. Whether social studies courses had lived up to historians' standards, history had nonetheless served as the traditional core of the social studies. Of the leaders in the field holding doctorates in an academic discipline, most were historians, and few non-historical social scientists wrote for either the specialized or general-interest periodicals for K-12 educators.[20] With the exception of political science/government and possibly economics, few non-historical disciplines were typically taught as separate subjects. At the beginning of the 1960s it was widely assumed that the non-historical social sciences would assume a greater role in the social studies of the future, but exactly which social sciences would be represented, which given priority, and how any or all might be organized in the K-12 curriculum was not clear. Seven or eight different fields were often mentioned as having a potential claim in the curriculum: in addition to history and the "older" social sciences (economics, political science, and geography) were the still relatively novel sciences of anthropology, sociology, and behavioral science or psychology. A proliferation of distinct Area Studies— sometimes subsumed under history or geography, but in other contexts each listed separately—made the overall list of subjects with a reported claim to the precollegiate curriculum even more daunting.

With respect to the anticipated revolution in the field, and with respect to the periodical literature in education, far more was actually said on behalf of the social sciences than articulated by social scientists themselves, either as individuals or as professional associations. Many of the social scientists represented in the most publicized forums on curriculum reform were not, in fact, particularly forward in pressing their disciplinary claims. They even occasionally expressed doubt that students below the college level were capable of valid study in their fields. Jerome Bruner, a behavioral scientist, was of course widely quoted, but Bruner's initial call was merely for the application of psychology to education in general, not a call to include more psychology in the curriculum as such. Only later in the decade would he press the case for anthropology through his work on the *Man: A Course of Study* project. Bruner, however, was throughout this period a spokesman for the non-historical social sciences as a whole, "for a shift away from history toward the social or behavioral sciences." His belief that it was "the behavioral sciences and their generality with respect to variations in the human condition that must be central to our presentation of man, not the particularities of his history" was consistent with the arguments of the social science associations as a whole.[21]

If they rarely addressed educators directly, however, both individual scholars and professional associations were not reticent in stating the case for reform of the social studies, particularly within their own disciplinary forums. Annual reports of the Committee on Social Studies Curriculum of the American Sociological Association (ASA), for example, reveal the depth of scholars' disdain for the existing social studies—a "soft spot," they claimed, in K-12 education. A November 1963 statement from the ASA to the National Science Foundation speaks of the "urgent need to upgrade the so-called social studies. The present offerings are acknowledged, by common consent, to be poorly organized, lacking in vigor . . . confused in objectives," and hopelessly out of date.[22] Political scientist Franklin Patterson of Tufts University both summarized current developments and extended the call for further "modernization" of the social studies curriculum in a 1962 article for the *American Behavioral Scientist*. Like the historians, he and the scholars he quoted from other disciplines emphasized the need for experts to update a curriculum that was increasingly "obsolescent." The schools were not capable of reform on their own. Academic rigor was a definite concern, but unlike most historians, the fellow social scientists Patterson quoted were less anxious to preserve disciplinary integrity than concerned to be represented in the social studies at all. One of the major obstacles to reform, it was reported, was the "dominant role that one discipline, history, plays in the existing curriculum." The summer before, Patterson noted, a sociologist had declared in "the strongest possible terms that we shall make no progress in transforming the social studies into social sciences until we slaughter the sacred cow of history." As Patterson added, however, the cow in question was "tough as well as venerable and may take more than a sociologist's words to slay."[23]

A third cluster of voices calling for major change in the early years of the 1960s was a loose coalition of educators whose disciplinary roots were neither in history nor the non-historical social sciences, but rather educational philosophy and the social foundations of education. Particularly dominant in the public universities of the lower mid-west, espousing ideals associated with the now-defunct Progressive Education Association (PEA), they would later be identified as part of the "reflective inquiry" tradition in social studies.[24] A majority of the voices included in a *Social Education* symposium on curriculum reform in 1963 represented this tradition: Indiana educationist Shirley Engle, his former student Byron Massialas, and Illinois educationist and former PEA journal editor Lawrence Metcalf. All of these voices welcomed major reform, and particularly applauded current efforts underway to introduce more non-historical social science. Like Samuel McCutchen, who, in his 1962 NCSS presidential address, had spoken of re-fashioning the unintegrated "goulash" of current social studies into its own distinctive social studies "discipline," the contributors to this symposium appropriated much of the fashionable Brunerian language.[25] They emphasized, like Bruner, the primacy of concepts or generalizations over discrete facts; and like the social scientists, spoke disparagingly of history, which was allegedly "totally lacking in structure."[26] On the surface, then, their call to reform seemed congruent with that of the social scientists.

In fact, however, Engle and others tried to develop an explicit contrast between social studies and the social sciences. The latter were putatively focused on the *generation* of knowledge. Social studies was to be about the utilization or application of knowledge in solving contemporary social problems. In contrast to the supposed rational and value-free social sciences, social studies would always have a valuing component (or as Metcalf put it, would include the development of a rational process for inquiry into values). Engle stated the essence of his position a few years earlier, as follows: "My thesis is simply this, decision making should afford the structure around which social studies instruction should be organized."[27] These ideas did not translate easily into a concrete agenda for reform. Metcalf did offer, however, at least a summary of the areas that needed to be addressed: among others, articulating clear purposes for instruction, addressing motivation issues through more relevant content, helping students grapple with personally meaningful problems, and adding more social science to the curriculum.

While these were the three major sets of voices throughout the early years of the decade, we may see in retrospect signs of an incipient fourth movement that would soon rapidly gain steam. In November of 1963 John Hope Franklin, an African American and chair at that time of history at Brooklyn College, addressed a general session of the NCSS. He began by reflecting on President Kennedy's assassination just eight days before, discussed Kennedy's hopes for American race relations, and called attention to the hundredth anniversary of the Emancipation Proclamation. In light of all three, he challenged social studies educators to work for the dignity of *all* men, and to be honest in examining the nation's failure in the past to do so.[28] That only a few months later the NCSS House of Delegates would go on record "in support of textbooks . . . which deal frankly, accurately, and honestly with the historical development of minorities in our country and the concomitant problems which arose and still exist in relation to these minorities" suggests that the words of Franklin and others like him were beginning to take effect.[29] Scattered articles in *Social Education* throughout the early years of the decade had raised similar concerns, for instance a call for greater attention to a range of "neglected minorities . . . the immigrants, the Negroes, and even the women."[30] Another writer reminded teachers in similar fashion that "the girls in history classes need help in seeing people like themselves in the history they study, and for obvious reasons the boys should know that history is only about half 'a man's subject.'"[31] While not yet an organized movement for reform, these voices did foreshadow what lay ahead. If they did not speak in language as radical as that of other camps, they nonetheless articulated hopes that may have seemed at the time the most revolutionary of all.

Taking Stock

Early in 1967 future NCSS president Jack Allen declared that "it was reasonably apparent that the educational historian of, say, the 1990s, reflecting on the present decade, will report it as one of the most productive periods of change in the chronicles of American education."[32] For many in the social studies community, however, the 1990s was too long to wait. Throughout the years of 1970 and 1971 articles appeared attempting to size up the years just past. Partly it was coming to the end of the decade, partly also perhaps a reflection of American society's relative calm between Kent State and the first news of Watergate. Within the social studies community, it was a time of celebrating the fiftieth anniversary of the NCSS and speculating on the directions the organization and field might go in the future. Finally, there was a sense that the excitement over the anticipated revolution was winding down. With respect to the highly funded curriculum proposals of the period, it would soon be reported, "most of the projects have completed their work and their staffs have disbanded."[33]

"It has been ten years since Charles Keller boldly announced the need to 'revolutionize' social studies," wrote one New Jersey administrator, "almost ten years since Bruner's *The Process of Education* . . . Perhaps it is time to ask, 'How is the revolution going?'" The writer concluded that "the rhetoric of revolution [had] been most impressive," yes, but on the whole the revolution had "not lived up to the expectations of its zealous prophets."[34] In the fiftieth anniversary issue of *Social Education,* one historian concluded that "the social studies revolution is faring better than most revolutions in history," although a later rebuttal claimed that the writer had offered no evidence to support his judgment.[35]

Without weighing in directly on the debate over the status of the revolution, the NCSS took advantage of an "opportune" moment of collective reflection to release its Curriculum Guidelines and a companion set of less comprehensive standards on teacher education. It was the first organizational attempt since the anticipated revolution began to address a range of insistent issues and to synthesize the decade's thinking. It offered the potential for the association to assume what the preceding year's president Shirley Engle characterized as its function to serve as "the responsible weathervane of social education." It offered an opportunity to choose between continuing "to afford our members a kind of smorgasbord of educational goodies and services [but no] cogent philosophic or pedagogical position;" or to define clearly what the organization stood for.[36]

The 1971 Curriculum Guidelines arrived on the scene with a clear organizational imprimatur and an explicit acknowledgement to readers of the NCSS's responsibility to articulate and clarify "precisely what constitutes soundly based professional practice." As such, the document serves perhaps as well as any measure as an indicator of how social studies educators were attempting to make sense of the field at this time. It is an indicator as well of the kind of vision for social education NCSS leaders were conveying to those outside the field. As president John Jarolimek was careful to point out, "the present document represents the official position of the National Council of the Social Studies on the social studies curriculum," and was to be used by all pertinent parties in making curriculum decisions.[37]

With four members, the task force that drafted the Curriculum Guidelines was smaller than any of the famous numerically named committees of earlier in the century. Appointed in 1969, its members included two future presidents of the NCSS, and with one woman, provided some degree of gender balance. At the same time all four were relatively young and had yet to establish themselves in the field: three of the four received their doctorates in 1970. Anna Ochoa and Gary Manson had earned degrees in education from the University of Washington and had worked together previously, helping to write a set of curriculum standards for that state. The other two members, Gerald Marker and Jan Tucker, had both received degrees, again in education, from the University of Indiana. For all the talk a decade before about involving scholars in constructing the curriculum, none of these four had a terminal degree in a traditional academic discipline.

At thirty-one pages, the Curriculum Guidelines represented an effort of a completely different scale than, say, the recommendations of the famous AHA Commission on the Social Studies of the 1930s, issued in seventeen sometimes-hefty volumes. Unlike most comparable efforts, the Guidelines came with almost no accompanying explanation as to the professional, philosophical, or methodological basis for the recommendations. This was clearly a more casual approach, then, to the process of offering curriculum guidance than the social studies world had been accustomed to—curriculum-making lite.

The document itself was divided into three parts. An overall rationale reminded readers that social studies consisted of "knowledge, thinking, valuing, and social participation." This was followed by nine general statements, broken down into fifty-seven elements, single statements ranging from "The social studies program should be directly related to the concerns of students" to "Evaluation should be useful, systematic, comprehensive, and valid for the objectives of the program." A checklist at the end restated in question form, for purposes of evaluating programs, the fifty-seven elements previously identified.[38]

In characterizing an earlier set of curriculum recommendations, Hazel Hertzberg noted wryly that its conclusions were so "full of qualifications that a fair summary is difficult to make . . . the summary volume often took back with one hand what it offered with the other.[39] At times, such a characterization applies to the 1971 Guidelines. "Young people should not be expected to fit themselves into uniform or rigid programs." At the same time some sort of unspecified flexible structure was "possible and desirable. . . . Disorder and lack of direction stand in the way of continuous reorganization of experience." The document noted that while many schools were developing a traditional, systematic scope and sequence, other schools had abandoned the notion of any kind of framework in order to offer teachers and students more freedom. "This document," the task force announced, "seeks to serve and encourage both of these trends."[40]

On two issues, however, the guidelines were unambiguous. One, the curriculum should emphasize contemporary social issues and problems, and involve students in resolving such. Among the specific issues identified were war, racism, pollution, poverty, deteriorating cities, alienation, and "an unfulfilled quality in living." Secondly, and equally unambiguously, the guidelines emphasized the role of the student as curriculum resource and agent. "In a rapidly changing society it is often young people who have greatest access to [the society's] emergent knowledge." Accordingly, the students themselves needed to be consulted as to what was most meaningful to study. The document did not explore the possibility that these two principles might ever be in tension, nor consider which should take priority if students' felt concerns and contemporary social issues did not coincide.[41]

With respect to the kinds of expectations raised at the beginning of the 1960s, the Guidelines were as notable for what they did not address as for what they did say. Items on the historians' earlier agendas were in particularly short supply. Needless to say, the guidelines had not accepted the invitation to change the field's name, nor invited by precept or example the involvement of historians in curriculum decision-making. Although the document spoke of the importance of "knowledge" for teachers, its framers declined to delineate what that knowledge might be, other than to suggest that the program as a whole should draw upon each of an itemized list of social sciences. The "function of knowledge, whatever its source, is to provide the reservoir of data, ideas, concepts, generalizations, and theories . . . which can be used by the student to function rationally and humanely." The one substantive discussion of history, in fact, consisted of an indictment of the field, to the extent that in its "school" form, it was often "repetitive, bland, merely narrative, inattentive to the non-Western world" and distorted by ignoring the experiences of cultural minorities. Least of all did the guidelines fulfill the hopes of historians for a more coherent scope or sequence, the "clear vertical plan up and down the academic ladder" that Charles Keller had dreamed of only a few years before.[42]

Items on the social scientists' agenda fared somewhat better than those on the historians' list. No, the Guidelines did not insist that scholars from the social sciences be consulted in developing the curriculum, any more than historians. But to the extent that a major goal of the social science associations was simply to be acknowledged as deserving space in the curriculum, the Guidelines seemed to vindicate their wishes. And to the extent that devoting less attention to history might be necessary to accomplish this, the document's censure of history was consistent with earlier references to "slaughtering the sacred cow." Even so, the framers did not give a nod to all of the non-historical social sciences equally, at least as commonly taught. While stating that anthropology, economics, social psychology, and psychology were underrepresented—and exempting these four from criticism—"ideas from political science and geography are often badly out-of-date." Moreover, the document took pains on numerous occasions to distinguish the utilization of social science from the teaching of social science concepts or methodologies for their own sake. "The primary purpose of a social studies program is neither to advance the frontiers of knowledge nor to produce social scientists." What was essential was for students to learn to "apply their knowledge, abilities and commitments toward the improvement of the human condition."[43]

The Guidelines affirmed at least in broad strokes the hopes of those earlier in the decade concerned that the social studies curriculum include greater attention to cultural minorities. While the Guidelines never mention women or gender concerns, numerous references can be found to combating racism; viewing the world through other than white, middle-class eyes; and giving attention to "Blacks, Chicanos, native American Indians, Puerto Ricans, and Oriental Americans."[44]

The real winners in the Guidelines, however, were those who in 1963 had outlined the least detailed agenda. Not surprisingly, given the constituency and pedigree of the task force, the Guidelines were a strong affirmation of the "Indiana" tradition of Shirley Engle—those soon to be identified as belonging to the school of reflective inquiry. The Guidelines did not validate earlier hopes to formulate a separate discipline, but philosophically, the document represented a major victory for the camp, at least in the contest to articulate a vision for the field. If the document had not totally fulfilled the sponsoring organization's stated responsibility to articulate and clarify "precisely what constitutes soundly based professional practice," it had defined more or less clearly, as Shirley Engle had hoped, what the organization stood for.[45]

The Radicalism of the Revolution

At this point we need to return to the question of what sort of revolution, if any, occurred during this period. In light of our conclusions in the section above, one might be inclined to argue that a particular and—in 1963, relatively less influential—philosophical wing of the social studies field had scored a coup. It was either a major or minor coup, depending on how symptomatic, and/or influential, one takes official statements of curriculum standards to be. In the contest to articulate a key organization's vision for the curriculum, a camp of like-minded Midwesterners had apparently begun to exercise a kind of professional hegemony. The author happens to hold that interpretation, and believes moreover that the coup was not altogether minor. But these are not my central arguments, nor do they constitute my final answer to the question posed above about what sort of revolution, if any, occurred.

The 1971 Guidelines, in fact, provide more than an indicator of the gains and losses among different camps in controlling professional discourse. They also provide an indicator of a shift in attitudes with respect to curriculum authority, and with respect to the very notion of curriculum itself. In 1968 a New York City educator writing in *Social Education* had argued for a "non-curriculum:" in effect, that teachers and students should be free to examine whatever problems were "likely to be relevant to youth and adults." The author's examples ranged from "traffic and transit" and "adult crime and juvenile delinquency," to "urban and rural slums" and "protest—violent and non-violent." But these specific topics were not the point. Any established curriculum, by its nature, interfered with effective teaching and learning. Curriculum-making was "an embalming process in which the life blood is drained from the heart of the social studies." "By preparing a curriculum bulletin we are saying in effect that we know what should be taught at a given grade and to a given age group. . . . Do we really know what social studies students should learn today that will be of value to them tomorrow? . . . In a world in which the rules of the game are changing daily, even to try to do so is sheer presumption."[46] Maybe, as longtime social studies leader Edgar Wesley expressed in 1972, "it really does not matter much what you teach or what the student studies so long as he finds a highway from ignorance to understanding."[47]

Throughout the preceding decade, administrators, teachers, historians, social scientists, educationists of different stripes spoke—not unanimously, but with a considerable degree of consensus—about the desirability of establishing some minimal degree of consensus on a framework within which to operate. Of the need to "end the confusion in the current social studies program," of the need for clarity of purpose and for some baseline for curriculum conversation. Of the desirability of articulating a "firm set of recommendations for the nation's schools," the need for "a comprehensive, cumulative, and coherent program for the entire range of grades," of the desirability of an organizational framework that would end unfruitful repetition and provide a "logical sequence through the various grade levels." Lewis Paul Todd, textbook author and longtime editor of *Social Education,* managed to capture the sentiment in just three words: "What and where?"[48] Such statements frequently included an acknowledgement of the danger of imposing an overly rigid uniform design, but came down on the side of establishing some minimal degree of consensus, or at least establishing some attractive sets of options.

In addition to the desire for some overall framework, contributors to the curriculum conversation expressed a number of specific recurring questions, including how best to organize and/or integrate history and the social sciences, what alternatives to the expanding environments sequence for the elementary school might be available, and how the schools might pay more systematic attention to Latin America and the non-Western world.

Given the virtual silence of the 1971 Guidelines on all these questions, the document's framers delivered a strong message about the value of the entire enterprise of curriculum planning. In declining to offer or even refer to particular scope and sequence patterns, they implicitly disavowed the need for such. As one of the document's co-authors expressed in another context the following year, it was a time in the social studies for "letting a hundred flowers bloom." If this created tension and pain, well, it was all part of a field "seeking its identity." And ultimately the tension and pain held potential for creative growth in the future.[49] Rhetorically, at least, and relative to any previously published set of official curriculum guidelines, this represented a much more radical revolution than members of any camp had imagined back in 1963.

Sufficiently radical, in fact, that it would not be long before many in American society and American education would once again say it was time for a change. Not long, that is, before many began to complain that the same "hundred flowers blooming" had gone to seed. Throughout the 1970s, it was reported, for example, that "many social studies teachers have confused innovation and creativity with a do-your-own-thing academic anarchy."[50] In this allegedly "permissive" environment, the "grab-bag approach" to curriculum-making was said to have triumphed.[51] Social studies educators were having "great difficulty in deciding whether to teach 'this and not that.'"[52] "The conversations I have heard at professional gatherings," claimed one teacher-educator, "manifest a generalized kind of confusion, a sense that neither pupils nor public would care very much if social studies disappeared from the curriculum altogether."[53] As early as 1975, in fact, discussions were starting to crystallize that led to both the Bradley Commission on History in the Schools (active 1987–1988) and the NCSS's own Commission on Social Studies in Schools (report published 1988). The perceived freedom and license of which the 1971 Guidelines were symptomatic, if not fully responsible, may be interpreted, then, as planting the next cycle of reform.

Notes

1. Ralph W. Tyler, "An Assessment: The Edge of the Future," in *The Social Studies: Curriculum Proposals for the Future*, ed. G. Wesley Sowards (Chicago: Scott, Foresman, 1963), 120–32. This and the following two paragraphs are based closely on language from the author's "Clio's Uncertain Guardians: History Education at Teachers College, Columbia University, 1906–1988," (Ph.D. diss., Columbia University, 1996), 219–221.
2. Sowards, *The Social Studies*, 5, 9, 91.
3. Ibid., 91.
4. Hertzberg, *Social Studies Reform, 1880–1980* (Boulder: Social Science Education Consortium, 1981); Gerald Marker and Howard Mehlinger, "Social Studies," in *Handbook of Research on Curriculum*, ed. Philip W. Jackson (Macmillan, 1991), 830–851; Michael B. Lybarger, "The Historiography of Social Studies," in *Handbook of Research on Social Studies Teaching and Learning*, ed. James P. Shaver (Macmillan, 1992), 3–15.
5. Karen Wiley and Irving Morrissett, eds., "Evaluation of Curricular Projects, Programs, and Materials," *Social Education* 36 (November 1972): 712–771.
6. William W. Goetz, Curriculum-Making in a Suburban New Jersey High School from 1957 to 1972," (Ed.D. diss., Teachers College, Columbia University, 1981), esp. 262–263.
7. "Reviewing the 41st Convention," *Social Education* 26 (February 1962): 85.
8. ACLS and NCSS, *The Social Studies and the Social Sciences* (New York: Harcourt, Brace, & World, 1962); Martin Mayer, *Where, When, and Why: Social Studies in American Schools* (New York: Harper & Row, 1963).
9. "Review of the 42nd NCSS Convention," *Social Education* 27 (February 1963), unnumbered insert pages.
10. Donald W. Robinson, "Ferment in the Social Studies," *Social Education* 27 (November 1963): 360; J. Wade Caruthers, "Social Education Looks at the History Curriculum: An Eleven-Year View," *Social Education* 31 (February 1967), 95.
11. Robinson, "Ferment in the Social Studies," 361.
12. See, for instance, Merrill Hartshorn, "Statement on HR 6774," *Social Education* 25 (Oc-

tober 1961): 295–297; Lewis Paul Todd, "The Hour Glass," *Social Education,* 25 (October 1961): 275, 320.

13. Eugene McCreary, "The Crisis Threatening American Education," *Social Education* 26 (April 1962): 177–179.

14. See, for instance, Merrill Hartshorn, "A Current Critical Issue in Secondary Education—Social Studies in the Comprehensive Secondary School," *Bulletin of the National Association of Secondary School Principals* 45 (April 1961): 312–322.

15. Although my "three-camp" argument was developed independently, this interpretation is similar to that of Leonard Kenworthy in "Changing the Social Studies Curriculum: Some Guidelines and a Proposal," *Social Education* 32 (May 1968): 481–486.

16. Keller, "Call to Revolution in the Social Studies," *College Board Review* 44 (Spring 1961): 13–16. See also, Keller, "Needed: Revolution in the Social Studies," *Saturday Review,* 16 (September 1961), 60–62.

17. High, "Scholarship and Nonsense in the Social Studies," *Teachers College Record* 64 (March 1963): 445–455.

18. Mendenhall, "Social Studies, History, and the Secondary School," *Social Education* 27 (April 1963): 202–204.

19. "The Year's Business [1964]," *American Historical Review* 70 (April 1965): 963.

20. For a quantitative study of articles published in *Social Education,* see June R. Chapin and Richard E. Gross, "A Barometer of the Social Studies: Three Decades of *Social Education,*" *Social Education* 34 (November 1970): 788–789.

21. Bruner, "Education as Social Invention," *Saturday Review,* 19 (February 1966), 103.

22. "Report of the Committee on Social Studies Curriculum in American Secondary Schools," *American Sociological Review* 29 (December 1964): 907.

23. Patterson, "Social Science and the New Curriculum," *American Behavioral Scientist* 6 (October 1962): 28–31.

24. Robert Barr, James L. Barth, and S. Samuel Shermis, *The Nature of the Social Studies* (Palm Springs, CA: ETC Publications, 1978); C. Benjamin Cox, "Shirley's Simple Theme," Social Studies Development Center, Indiana University: Occasional paper #1, 1978.

25. McCutchen, "A Discipline for the Social Studies," *Social Education* 27 (February 1963): 61–65.

26. Lawrence E. Metcalf, "Some Guidelines for Changing Social Studies Education," *Social Education* 27 (April 1963): 200.

27. Engle, "Decision Making: The Heart of Social Studies Instruction," *Social Education* 24 (November 1960): 303.

28. Franklin, "The Dignity of Man: Perspectives for Tomorrow," *Social Education* 28 (May 1964): 257–260, 265.

29. "Report of the Meeting of the Seventh House of Delegates," *Social Education* 28 (March 1964), 158.

30. Thomas A. Bailey, "Revitalizing American History," *Social Education* 24 (December 1960), 373.

31. Erwin J. Urch, "The Other Half of History," *Social Education* 25 (April 1961), 192.

32. Allen, "Assessing Recent Developments in the Social Studies," *Social Education* 31 (February 1967), 99.

33. "Editorial Reflections," *Social Education* 36 (November 1972), 711.

34. William W. Goetz, "The 'New' Social Studies: Boon or Bust?" *Clearing House* 45 (March 1970): 404–406.

35. Mark M. Krug, "The Future of the Social Studies," *Social Education* 34 (November 1970): 768–776.
36. Shirley Engle, "The Future of Social Studies Education," *Social Education* 34 (November 1970), 780. In his argument concerning the proper role of the NCSS, Engle appears to have intended the term "bellwether." Speaking descriptively rather than prescriptively, however, "weathervane" may be a more accurate term.
37. NCSS, *Social Studies Curriculum Guidelines* (Washington: NCSS, 1971), 3–4.
38. Ibid., 7, 16, 25.
39. Hertzberg, *Social Studies Reform,* 50.
40. *Social Studies Curriculum Guidelines,* 16, 24, 5.
41. Ibid., 13, 10.
42. Ibid., 10, 19.
43. Ibid., 19, 17, 8.
44. Ibid., 19–20.
45. Ibid., 3.
46. Gerald Leinwand, "The Year of the Non-Curriculum," *Social Education* 32 (October 1968): 542–545.
47. Wesley, "Commentary on *Social Studies Curriculum Guidelines,*" *Social Education* 36 (March 1972), 264.
48. Todd, "Afterword: Revising the Social Studies," in *The Social Studies and the Social Sciences,* ed. ACLS and NCSS, 297.
49. Jan L. Tucker, "Teacher Educators and the 'New' Social Studies," *Social Education* 36 (May 1972), 560.
50. "Reader's Round-Table," *Social Studies* 69 (March/April 1978): 82–83.
51. Richard Whittemore, "The Decline of School History," unpublished paper presented at Teachers College Conference on History in the Schools, 23 April 1977, Social Studies Department files, Special Collections, Teachers College, Columbia University, 13.
52. Hazel W. Hertzberg to Irving Morrissett, 10 February 1978, Box 3B, Hertzberg Papers, Special Collections, Teachers College, Columbia University.
53. Whittemore, "Decline of School History."

8

Tyrone C. Howard

SOCIAL STUDIES DURING THE CIVIL RIGHTS MOVEMENT, 1955–1975

In 1950, acclaimed historian John Hope Franklin writing in *Social Education* proclaimed the need for "New perspectives in American Negro history."[1] In his call, Franklin cogently argued for social studies educators to give new meanings, accurate interpretations, and more comprehensive accounts of Black life in the United States. Moreover, Franklin believed that for Blacks to be viewed in a more positive manner, history textbooks in particular would have to offer new accounts of African Americans and their contributions to the development of the United States. Franklin explains, "Distortion and misrepresentation of any group's history are serious enough when confined to general literature for scholars and laymen. But irreparable damage is done when these practices are carried over into the writing of textbooks for our schools and in the teaching of our children."[2] With this charge, Franklin became one of the earliest scholars to challenge social studies educators to rethink the portrayal of African Americans in history textbooks. Franklin's call for "new perspectives" was not the first of its kind. His call was important, however, because it marked one of the first times that an African American scholar had contributed to a mainstream educational outlet advocating the need for content reform in the portrayal of African Americans.

Franklin challenged social studies educators to recognize the pillars upon which the discipline boldly proclaimed its beliefs. He stated that "the field of social sciences, perched on its pedestal of tentative respectability, can ill afford, when it comes to studying the Negro, to turn its back on the very principles that have given it some claim to its position."[3] He continued in his poignant, yet penetrating words by proclaiming:

> Just as surely as the presence of the Negro in American life provides the acid test for democratic institutions, so does the factor of the Negro in our history constitute the acid test to our adherence to truth and dispassion. We shall achieve real democracy only as our intellectual integrity becomes strong enough to support the searching and far-reaching implications of so noble a goal.

It is with this premise that this chapter unfolds. Contemporary social studies scholars have engaged in an increasing amount of research and scholarship regarding African American history, the quest for equality, cultural diversity, and the civil rights movement. Yet, how did the social studies as a discipline engage in telling the story as it unfolded during the 1950s, 1960s, and 1970s? The purpose of this chapter will be to engage in a historical journey in the social studies to examine how the discipline addressed issues of cultural diversity and the struggle for equality during three turbulent decades. To that end, the chapter will have three aims that investigate the social studies during the civil rights movement. The first aim will be to examine the social studies in the mid-to-late 1950s and early 1960s as theorists grappled with the idea of how to create more inclusive social studies. The second aim will be to uncover the emergence of research and scholarship directly concerned with the civil rights movement and equality for African Americans. During the mid-to-late 1960s key individuals played important roles in persuading social studies scholars to begin incorporating new paradigms that would debunk traditional notions of African Americans and the quest for equality. The final aim will be to examine how history textbooks addressed the issue of civil rights. Given the salience that textbooks have in the social studies, examining the manner in which they incorporated issues about struggle, diversity, and the quest for democracy is essential to gauge the pulse of the discipline at the time.

I want to be explicit that I am by no means attempting to provide an exhaustive account of the forces, scholars, and issues that shaped the emergence of the social studies during the civil rights movement. Time and space limits the inclusion of countless contributors to a vital period in United States history. My purpose is to shed light on some of the critical developments, key scholars, and important paradigm shifts that occurred in the social studies during this critical time in the discipline's evolution. More specifically, I am concerned with how social studies research and scholarship addressed issues of diversity, oppression, and equality during the civil rights movement and the emerging role of African Americans and other non-Whites in mainstream society. I am interested in answering questions such as: What role did social studies organizations play in helping educators address the changing dynamics of the nation during the tumultuous times of the 1950s and 1960s? Who were some of the social studies scholars who challenged hegemonic notions of social studies education? How did social studies textbooks at the time tell the stories of African Americans, and other oppressed groups during the civil rights movement? These questions are critical because they begin to provide insight into how the discipline interpreted events that occurred around it. The solutions to these questions also hold implications for today's social studies educators because the nation continues to experience unprecedented diversity. And while progress has been made in contemporary social studies research, theory, and practice, room for improvement remains. Examining some of the historical precedents about creating more inclusive social studies may offer strategies for contemporary scholars in an increasingly multicultural and multiracial society.

New Forces in the Social Studies

In the 1955 NCSS yearbook, Roy Larsen and Henry Toy, Jr. discussed forces affecting curriculum improvement in the social studies.[4] In their examination of the social studies they were explicit about the countless forces that would continue to shape the field. Their contention that the unique nature of America's schools invited internal and external pressures about what students should learn was a topic of concern for many social studies educators. One of the areas that Larsen and Toy identified as an important topic for social studies educators to take on was the increasing demand of different racial groups who were expressing what they thought that schools should and should not teach. Larsen and Toy were not prescriptive about how the social studies should address the needs of different racial groups, but they were clear that the issue was one of increasing significance within schools and society, and that the social studies should be a part of the discussion.

By and large, prior to 1960 the social studies had not engaged in much discussion of the needs of African Americans or other groups of color, and how their stories should be told in the social studies. Among the rare notable mentions of Blacks prior to the 1960s were the Rugg books of the 1930s. FitzGerald maintains that Rugg, as one of the more progressive social historians of his time, was among the first social studies educators to mention African Americans in his scholarship.[5] Even Rugg's accounts of Blacks, however, were phrased in mildly negative overtones. Rugg frequently referred to Blacks as a "social problem," called for greater tolerance to be shown to the group, and cited notable exceptions such as Booker T. Washington and George Washington Carver as examples of Blacks who had made positive contributions to society. Rugg's works were among the first to call for greater inclusion, racial tolerance, and national unity for the optimal existence of a democratic nation. His advocacy for democratic values and social reconstruction were radical for the time, but would be later used as an essential foundation for subsequent scholars.

While the social studies existed for close to a half-century in silence and denial about the history of African Americans, a growing cadre of African American scholars called for schools to acknowledge accurate and positive portrayals of African Americans. Notable scholars such as George Washington Williams, W. E. B. DuBois, Carter G. Woodson, Charles H. Wesley, Horace Mann Bond, and John Hope Franklin spent years conducting research and scholarship on Black history and life in the United States.[6] Moreover, these scholars fought tirelessly to challenge the distorted notion of African Americans as being inferior to Whites, docile, lazy, and uneducable.

W. E. B. DuBois was among an early set of scholars who challenged Blacks to evaluate the quality of education they received in segregated and mixed schools in his classic work, "Does the Negro Need Separate Schools?" DuBois strongly asserted, "Negroes must know the history of the Negro race in America."[7] In a direct reference to school knowledge and the construction of Blacks at the time, he questioned the likelihood of Blacks to receive sympathy, knowledge, and truth in institutions that excluded their contributions in history. Mainstream social studies educators engaged in theory and practice about how to prepare citizens to live in a democratic society during the first half of the twentieth century largely ignored the efforts of DuBois. Thus, the scholarly works of Black historians, sociologists, and educators were never taken into consideration about what social studies education should look like for a changing nation such as the United States. Nevertheless, the work of these preeminent Black scholars of the first half of the twentieth century would provide a vital foundation for subsequent African American scholars intent on incorporating the life and history of African Americans into social studies curriculum in the late 1960s and early 1970s.

Addressing Neglected Subjects

The year 1961 was an important time in the evolution of diverse perspectives within the social studies. Scholars such as William Cartwright and Richard Watson talked about the need for "new interpretations" of historical truths and called for social studies teachers to promote critical thinking in historical study.[8] These developments were critical because they began to lay the groundwork for future scholars to challenge traditional canons about various groups and historical developments. Claude VerSteeg wrote about the "neglected subjects" in the social studies, most notably the history of slavery and how social studies educators needed to be involved in "greater precision and understanding" of historical events.[9] These works played instrumental roles in calling into question the manner in which the social studies addressed issues involving non-Whites. Though there was minor discussion and theorizing about marginalized groups and their histories, little evidence existed of advancement in social studies textbooks, research, or scholarship about important events occurring throughout the late 1950s and early 1960s.

For example, no mention was made of the tragic death of Emmitt Till, the Montgomery bus boycotts, or student sit-ins, all of which have subsequently been considered critical developments in the early years of the civil rights movement. For the most part, social studies textbooks at this time ignored the contributions and struggles for equality of Blacks in the U.S. Exceptions to this pattern were stereotypical depictions of Blacks as "happy slaves,"[10] included in textbooks without analysis of the institution of slavery, its long term effects, or Black perseverance through these trials. Many textbooks simply made neutral statements about this topic, such as "there were arguments for and against slavery." The status of African Americans in social studies textbooks in the 1960s were best described by the title of Ralph Ellison's important work a decade earlier, "The Invisible Man."

Since much of the general education literature of the late 1950s and early 1960s was concerned with *Sputnik,* scientific development of the nation's youth became a priority within education. Thus, many of the issues germane to the social studies did not occupy the nation's attention. Ronald O. Smith, president of NCSS in 1969, stated, "foundations and public funds in vast sums were being made available to implement scientific education. Social studies education was still in the doldrums."[11] Still, important events of the 1960s catapulted issues critical to social studies education to the forefront of the nation's consciousness. During the 1960s, the nation witnessed increasing civil unrest, growing frustration on the part of African Americans, and the tragic assassinations of President Kennedy, Robert Kennedy, and Dr. Martin Luther King. Consequently, for the first time since the Civil War 100 years earlier, the U.S. was confronted with how it could coexist peacefully as one nation. The importance of social relations and the quest for equality now captured the nation's mind, yet the social studies were still not responsive to the demands of an increasingly diverse and socially fractured nation.

During this period, social studies practitioners heard calls for "new social studies programs," "relevant social studies curriculum," and "revised social studies textbooks." The social studies, perhaps more than any other discipline, felt the full impact of the forces of change brought on by the civil rights movement. Dorothy McClure Fraser talked about a "revolution" in the social studies as the field came to grips with its newfound prominence. Fraser poignantly discussed the changing scene in the social studies, and its need to pay close attention to human rights and equality. Fraser posed the question: "Will an open society, in which prejudice and discrimination are replaced by mutual respect and truly equal opportunities, be evolved in the United States? Will racial, ethnic, and religious hostilities among the people of the world be ameliorated or even eliminated? Or will they continue to plague efforts at constructive, cooperative action among the nations of the earth?"[12]

Emerging Scholars in the Social Studies

The late 1960s and early 1970s marked an important shift in social studies literature regarding the inclusion of African Americans and the civil rights movement. James Banks, who would become a major figure in the infusion of greater ethnic content into the social studies, opened the 43rd NCSS yearbook, published in 1973, with these strong words about its theme:

For any reader, this book will be a profound experience. It will evoke a wide range of emotions, including pain, anger, compassion, disillusionment, despair, admiration, and hope. It is a hard-hitting book written by a group of fighters who have an unrelenting commitment to social justice. Their words are sometimes bitter and incisive, but their restraint is a tribute to their wisdom and scholarship.[13]

Banks' work would be seminal in providing the framework for the emerging discourse on ethnic diversity in the social studies. The 43rd yearbook was influential because it marked the first time that a yearbook from the NCSS was devoted exclusively to the problem of racism and its effects on minority students. This contribution would serve as the catalyst for later inclusion of issues pertaining to equality, social justice, and multicultural education that would eventually become integral parts of the social studies.

Although only scant attention was paid to these issues in the social studies literature in at this time, signs existed that the discipline was slowly moving toward discussing topics that had been grossly overlooked in previous years. Approximately one year after the death of Dr. Martin Luther King, *The Social Studies* devoted an entire issue to "Black Americans and the Social Studies."[14] A number of prominent scholars, Black and White, discussed critical issues that had rarely been seen on the pages of a social studies journal. The topics ranged from strategies to improve the teaching of Black history to examining history textbooks about the experiences of minority groups. It was no coincidence that many of the topics being discussed by social studies theorists were occurring as the civil rights movement continued to happen. With the rise of Black Nationalism, the Black Power Movement, and the overall frustration with the state of race relations in the United States, Black scholars sought greater inclusion and representation in school curricula. Pleas were made that Black students were not the only ones negatively affected by their invisibility in school textbooks and curriculum. Several scholars claimed that White students were also negatively affected by the negative stereotypes of Blacks, and as a result, would continue to internalize prejudice towards Blacks if they were not educated about the life, history, and contributions of Blacks.

The late 1960s witnessed the emergence of a new group of scholars contributing to the promotion of Black history in the schools. In *Social Education,* Nathan Hare provided a sociological framework on teaching Black history and culture in the social studies.[15] Hare suggested that teaching Black history had a therapeutic value for Black students, and could foster community consciousness and awareness. He called for an approach to social studies that would offer curriculum transformation as opposed to cultural transmission. He encouraged social studies educators to focus more on transmitting critical knowledge to students and to move away from offering political dogma or abstract ideology in social studies education.

Louis Harlan, one of the few non-minority scholars contributing to Black history at the time, discussed how social studies education could be inclusive of the Black experience.[16] Yet, Harlan offered a divergent method for incorporating Black history. He cautioned educators against creating a propagandistic form of Black history that overemphasized Black nationalism and separatism. In his address at the 48th annual meeting of NCSS, Harlan urged educators to develop a comprehensive account of Black history and culture. He asserted, "I urge you to acquaint your students with the beauty as well as the pathology of Black life in America." Harlan's call represented a different emphasis than many other scholars were supporting. He recommended that issues pertaining to slavery and all its unpleasantness become a part of social studies discourse. The biographer of Booker T. Washington, Harlan encouraged students to read biographies about famous Blacks. Through these endeavors, students would learn about notable figures in Black history and their struggles and setbacks, tragedies and triumphs.

Prominent advocates of the "New Social Studies" programs of the early 1970s joined in the chorus for rethinking how issues of cultural diversity could be introduced. Edwin Fenton, one of the leaders of this movement, disagreed with Louis Harlan's idea of studying biographies as an effective means of introducing Black history into social studies education.[17] Fenton suggested that the new social studies should help students identify problems, develop problem-solving skills through collection and analysis of data, and reach conclusions based on findings. Fenton believed that this inquiry approach to issues concerning diverse groups would be more meaningful and in line with social studies objectives than mere recitation of names, facts and figures. Although disagreement existed about how best to achieve these ends, these individuals did not dispute the fact that issues pertaining to equality, struggle, and the elimination of discrimination should at least became part of the discussion taking place in social studies. This concession represented considerable progress, given the little attention these topics had received in previous years.

In addition to scholars such as Banks, Harlan, Hare, and Fenton, the social studies were witnessing the emergence of a new generation of scholars who would be assuming an important role in examining relevant topics that had largely been ignored in the social studies.[18] Scholars such as Geneva Gay discussed racism in teaching ethnic studies; she would play an instrumental role over the next two decades in the area of multicultural curriculum in the social studies. Carlos Cortes addressed issues pertaining to the Chicano experience in the United States. This contribution to the social studies would help to provide a more multiethnic account of the United States. Larry Cuban, Barbara Sizemore, David Ballesteros, and a growing list of new scholars would assume leadership roles in the development of new research and scholarship germane to more inclusive forms of social studies education. In the face of these contributions, Banks maintained that Whites could certainly engage in research and discussion about ethnic minorities but emphasized the importance of seeking scholars from ethnic minority groups to engage in this work as well. He stated that "we have reached a point in our history in which we must hear from the victims of racism since for too long most books have been written by writers who were members of powerful and ruling groups."[19]

The Changing Nature of the Social Studies

The arrival of new scholars of color and the growing attention to social issues and racial prejudice during the civil rights movement witnessed an increase in social studies scholarship on issues affecting African Americans and the quest for equality. Not all scholars were in accord, however, about the need to address issues historically omitted from social studies discourse. In a *Social Education* issue published in late 1970, John Guenther and Wayne Dumas titled their article "Black History for What?"[20] They questioned the usefulness of ethnic content in U.S. history classes if it were not centered on clear goals, obtainable objectives, and an appropriate curricular fit. Guenther and Dumas raised the point that White teachers, with very little background knowledge about the experiences of African American students, would fail to see the value of teaching Black history. In a study they conducted with 250 public high school teachers in the state of Missouri, Guenther and Dumas found that teachers rated core civil rights movement issues such as Black Power, Black Unity, Black contributions, and Black problems, as "low priority" issues in teaching U.S. history. Even as neglected subjects were gaining increased visibility in the early 1970s, scholars still faced an uphill battle for inclusion of diverse groups in social studies curriculum and literature.

In examining publications within the social studies during the 1950s, 1960s, and 1970s, it becomes painfully obvious how issues pertaining to race and equality were simply omitted, except for the works of a handful of emerging scholars. In a review of the literature that touched on this subject, Chapin and Gross wrote that prior to the late 1960s articles focusing on cultural diversity in *Social Education* were virtually non-existent.[21] They supported their criticism of NCSS concerning its lack of attention to racism, the urban crisis, and issues affecting minority groups by documenting the few words published in *Social Education* addressing these issues. Years later in a separate retrospective analysis, Jesus Garcia and Edward Buendia reconfirm this evaluation of works published in *Social Education* during the 1960s and 1970s.[22] They contend that an examination of articles published in *Social Education* during the period 1961 to 1976 yields only a small number addressing minority concerns and issues relating to diversity. Furthermore, discussion of the general contributions made by Blacks and other minority groups to American culture was extremely limited.

Social Studies Textbooks: A Period of Omission and Invisibility

One of the primary targets of criticism by scholars advocating change in the social studies was the inadequacy of school textbooks, namely history textbooks. School textbooks have always played a crucial role in the development of educational ideology. Venezky describes textbooks as "a *cultural artifact* and as a *surrogate curriculum*."[23] His contention is that school textbooks have often assumed the role of maintaining societal judgments and national values, some of which have not been fully inclusive of all Americans. He says, "Throughout American history, text-books have reflected mainstream, conservative interests. In part, this is to state that the means for producing and consuming textbooks have been in the hands of these sectors of society."[24]

Harris Dante, president of NCSS in 1973, used Jim Banks' call for greater cultural pluralism in the 1973 NCSS yearbook as an opportunity to challenge social studies textbook authors to revisit traditional content. Dante maintained, "textbooks and school curricula too often have sustained the status quo, helped entrench stereotypes, and narrated the myth and the folklore."[25] Other scholars echoed Dante's and Banks' calls for greater representation of issues affecting African Americans, and the civil rights movement in school curricula. Robert Tresize, in an issue of the *Social Studies,* charged that the "civil rights revolution" had been largely ignored by the "white world of school textbooks,"[26] and claimed that social studies educators had an obligation to include the relevance of the civil rights movement in their research and practice. Tresize's work was important because he cited studies examining history textbooks and their inclusion of ethnic-specific content. For example, he cited findings from the Michigan Department of Education indicating that history texts used in state schools were grossly inadequate and inaccurate in portraying the African American experience. The study also discusses the limited coverage given the civil rights movement, and claims that most textbooks' conclusions about the movement were "misleading" and "incorrect." The study concluded, "the discussion lacks an important dimension because the student is never given a full explanation of what Negroes are fighting against."[27]

Other scholars of the day also examined school textbooks. Banks' doctoral dissertation in 1969 was a content analysis of the Black American in school textbooks. He looked at elementary school history textbooks to discover what themes were associated with Blacks and race relations.[28] Banks' study found that textbook authors "rarely take a moral stand when discussing such issues as racial discrimination and racial prejudice."[29] He also suggested that, given the widespread racial violence and conflict afflicting the nation at the time, textbook authors needed to improve the degree to which they addressed issues of racial prejudice.

Robert Bierstedt noted the rampant racial bias in textbooks as early as 1955.[30] He charged that much of the language in school textbooks used in describing ethnic minorities was degrading and stereotypical, and omitted positive information about these groups. Furthermore, Bierstedt argued that textbook authors refused to take moral stands about issues pertaining to segregation and racial discrimination. Claims such as Bierstedt's were consistent with FitzGerald's contentions that history textbooks were often too extreme in their nationalism and failed to discuss many of the challenges and tensions the nation faced. In her analysis of the "New Social Studies," FitzGerald contended that the old social studies programs were not easily swept away, and that many social studies educators resisted changes in social studies textbooks and curriculum. She commented, "[t]he public school system is, after all, one of the most conservative of American institutions, it has a protoplasmic quality that combines a superficial sensitivity with a profound resistance to change."[31]

Challenges to mainstream textbooks during the late 1960s and early 1970s were not new. The inaccurate depiction of Blacks in particular was a source of concern to minority organizations in the 1930s and 1940s. Groups such as the NAACP and the Association for the Study of Negro Life and History (ASNLH) raised concerns about the racist orientations in many of the commonly used history textbooks.[32] James Anderson notes that as early as 1933 Lawrence Reddick's work on racial attitudes about history textbooks in the South was among the first to call into question the misrepresentation of Blacks. Anderson also documents the work of scholars such as Edna M. Colson and Marie E. Carpenter who followed suit in challenging distortions and falsehoods about the Black experience.[33] The ASNLH, founded by Carter G. Woodson in 1916, devoted much of its attention to disrupting commonly accepted accounts of Blacks during the 1930s and 1940s. Woodson's work during this time was most instrumental as his organization continually fought mainstream depictions of Blacks. Woodson ultimately initiated his own journal, *The Journal of Negro History*, to provide a venue for scholars who wanted to provide more positive and realistic portrayals of Black life and culture.[34]

During the mid-1960s, there were several non-minority scholars who also engaged in the criticism of social studies textbooks. Louis Harlan's work *The Negro in American History*[35] and Irving Sloan's *The Negro in Modern American History Textbooks*[36] were highly critical of the shortcomings in U.S. History textbooks. Both challenged social studies textbook authors to come of age in providing a more balanced and positive portrayal of African Americans. In 1970, Michael Kane echoed similar sentiment in his work, *Minorities in Textbooks: A Study of Their Treatment in Social Studies Textbooks*.[37] Kane conducted an investigation of forty-five leading history textbooks and concluded that they were largely steeped in a "white, Protestant, Anglo-Saxon view of America." Moreover, he concluded that the histories and contributions of minorities were largely ignored.

One of the more significant problems with textbooks during the civil rights movement is the fact that they remained stagnant amid social and political upheaval on several fronts. The 1960s witnessed Blacks' and other minority groups' fight for full inclusion into the U.S. democracy. Women continued to struggle for greater equality, and the war in Vietnam was a cause of concern for many citizens. An evaluation of U.S. history textbooks in the early 1970s could easily lead one to believe that citizens of the United States had coexisted peacefully since the end of the Civil War. There is no mention of the residual effects the Civil War had on the poor, women, or minority groups. Most textbooks completely excluded the struggle of Blacks during the period of Reconstruction, which essentially served as the genesis of the civil rights movement. Of greater concern was the fact that while many textbooks highlighted struggles for democracy in countries across the globe, or documented the unfair treatment of citizens in non-democratic nations, little attention was paid to such issues in the United States.

One of the more disturbing realities about the absence of topics related to justice and equality in social studies discourse is the notion that social studies education and social studies scholars should have assumed *the* leading role in this area.

Ideally, social studies educators could have led the charge in helping educators and the nation to examine, comprehend, and combat racial oppression and discrimination within schools and society. The movement of equality and discrimination should have moved from the fringes to the heart of a critical dialogue within the social studies. What discipline would be more suited to facilitate the discussion of race and racism within schools and society than the social studies? As a discipline charged with preparing democratic citizens and promoting civic interest in the pursuit of equality for all citizens, the social studies would seem to be well suited to address the salience of social relations, inequality, race and culture, and the elimination of oppression.

That the social studies were not actively engaging in a full-fledged discussion about critical topics such as discrimination, equality, and racism served as the rallying cry for the new generation of scholars. Banks noted that one of the purposes of the social studies is to emphasize the need for the entire polity to engage in the development of public policy that would address the nation's social problems.[38] Within the context of schools, Banks stressed the incorporation of concept development on critical issues such as racism, conflict, culture, capitalism, and power as a part of social studies education. Banks maintained that programs in social studies could be interdisciplinary and incorporate core knowledge about the experience of ethnic minorities. Thus, the social sciences did not have to be excluded in order to introduce core concepts to students. The introduction of these approaches to social studies were critical because they helped to deflect criticism from more conservative social studies scholars who argued that the incorporation of issues pertaining to diversity would come at the expense of traditional social studies based approaches.

Social Studies Organizations

Another indicator of how the social studies evolved during the civil rights movement is the status of the primary organization of the field, the National Council for the Social Studies. Prior to the late 1960s there is little documentation of NCSS taking assertive stands as an organization on issues pertaining to diversity and equity. The first several decades after its inception in 1921 found NCSS struggling to establish an academic identity. Much of the debate in the early decades centered on what should be the scope and nature of the social studies. The organization also sought ways to develop new ideas, inform practitioners and develop curriculum about social education, primarily within a history context.[39]

Not until the late 1960s and early 1970s did key scholars play important roles in incorporating issues pertaining to cultural diversity into the organizational framework of NCSS. For example, in the fall of 1970, the NCSS executive board agreed to establish a traveling clinic that would help "teachers deal with the 'Black-White' problem" in schools. The organization took other steps that would prove to be vital in providing a more honest examination of the field's treatment of ethnic minorities. A committee on Racism and Social Justice was established in the early 1970s. This committee's charge was in response to five recommendations that were made to the NCSS executive board by a group of Black educators.[40] To respond to the growing concerns of racism, social justice, ethnic studies, and inner city education, NCSS developed advisory committees to evaluate how they could best meet the needs of teachers in these areas. The advisory committees developed clinics that would be offered at the annual meetings that could help social studies educators teach ethnic studies, interrogate racism, and become more socially just in their work.

It is important to note the leadership at the time of the paradigm shifts that occurred in the social studies. Without question, the organizational leadership played a salient role in the development of new charges, the creation of active committees, and the implementation of proactive interventions to discuss sensitive topics. John Jarolimek and Jean Fair were presidents of NCSS in 1971 and 1972 respectively, when substantive action about addressing issues such as racism in the social studies began to emerge. The NCSS Racism and Social Justice Committee was formed under the leadership of Jarolimek, Fair, and Harris Dante. In the 1973 yearbook, Banks pays special tribute to Jarolimek and Fair, whom he described as "two distinguished NCSS presidents who struggled to eliminate racism and social injustice."[41] Jarolimek and Fair were intent on having the social studies assume an active role on critical issues that were affecting the nation. Each was determined not only to study racism and inequality, but also was adamant about working with teachers to improve their knowledge, content use, and instruction on these topics.[42]

The Racism and Social Justice Committee played a much-needed role within NCSS of keeping issues pertaining to race and social justice as an integral part of the NCSS agenda. Over the next decade, NCSS sponsored a multitude of programs, workshops, and presentations at the national and state levels to inform social studies educators about previously neglected topics. The topics examined included "comparative study for the treatment of Blacks in the past and present in U.S. History textbooks," "How to reduce racial prejudice," "Racism and Teacher Behavior in the classroom," and "Educating the Inner-City Poor." By the mid-to-late 1970s the social studies offered greater inclusion of the history, experiences, and contributions of non-Whites in programming and curriculum guidelines. The movement in programming was important, particularly within the context of curriculum development and social studies guidelines. As history textbooks were still slow to respond to the discipline's more inclusive focus, curriculum guidelines provided a viable alternative about the ideological state of the discipline and its primary goals and objectives. The 1971 Guidelines in particular included numerous references for topics such as racism, oppression, and the experience of ethnic minority groups, and reflected the slow shift that was occurring in the social studies as it addressed issues concerning racial and ethnic diversity.

While the 1971 Guidelines gave some mention to previously neglected topics, an increasing number of theorists in the discipline criticized omissions and exclusions in social studies textbooks, research, and scholarship. It was the work of these dedicated scholars that would lead to the evolution of multicultural education as a staple in the social studies framework. The shift in the discourse in the social studies during the 1960s and 1970s was slow, but much needed. The important work of numerous scholars helped to shape a discipline that is much more responsive to the needs of ethnic minorities, the quest for equality, and the value of cultural diversity than it was half a century ago. It goes without saying that the struggle for this new shift in research and scholarship in the social studies was not a smooth process. As the debates about the purpose and mission of the social studies continued throughout the 1970s, the new social studies would begin to take a more serious look at issues pertaining to diversity, oppression, and the experiences of marginalized groups. The decades of the 1970s, 1980s, and 1990s would witness the social studies beginning to tell a different story in comparison to the three prior decades. The need for progress in addressing issues of diversity in the social studies continues to exist. However, it is essential to note that attempts to move the social studies forward in the twenty-first century will be less difficult due to the invaluable work of courageous and influential scholars. These scholars should be recognized as leaders who refused to allow the discipline to move forward without examining critical issues that would leave a lasting influence on the country for years to come.

Notes

1. John Hope Franklin, "New Perspectives in American Negro History," *Social Education* 14 (May, 1950), 196–200.
2. Ibid., 197.
3. Ibid., 200.
4. Roy E. Larson and Henry Toy Jr., "Forces Affecting Curriculum Improvement," *Twenty-Sixth Yearbook of the National Council for the Social Studies* (Washington, DC, 1955), 5–15.
5. Frances FitzGerald, *America Revised* (Boston: Little, Brown, 1979).
6. James A. Banks, "Multicultural Education: Historical Development, Dimensions, and Practices," in *Handbook of Research on Multicultural Education,* eds. James A. Banks and Cherry A. McGee Banks (New York: Macmillan, 1995), 3–24.
7. W. E. B. DuBois, "Does the Negro Need Separate Schools?" *Journal of Negro Education* 4 (July): 328–355.
8. William Cartwright and Richard L. Watson, Jr. "Historical Scholarship and the Teaching of History," in *Thirty-First Yearbook of the National Council for the Social Studies* (Washington, DC, 1961), 1–11.
9. Claude Ver Steeg, "The North American Colonies in the Eighteenth Century, 1688–1763," *Thirty-First Yearbook of the National Council for the Social Studies,* 24–37.
10. Robert L. Trezise, "The Black American in American History Textbooks," in *Teaching Social Studies to Culturally Different Children,* eds. James A. Banks and William J. Joyce (Reading, Mass.: Addison-Wesley, 1971), 147.
11. Robert O. Smith, Foreword to the *Thirty-Ninth Yearbook of the National Council for the Social Studies* (Washington, DC, 1969), v.

12. Dorothy McClure Fraser, "The Changing Scene in Social Studies," in *Thirty-Ninth Yearbook of the National Council for the Social Studies*, 10.

13. James A. Banks, Introduction to the *Forty-Third Yearbook of the National Council for the Social Studies* (Washington, DC, 1973), xi.

14. *Social Education*, 33 (April, 1969).

15. Nathan Hare, "The Teaching of Black History and Culture in the Secondary Schools," *Social Education* 33 (April 1969), 385–389.

16. Louis Harlan, "Tell it Like it Was: Suggestions on Black History," *Social Education* 33 (April, 1969), 390–395.

17. Edwin Fenton, "Crispus Attucks is Not Enough: The Social Studies and Black Americans," *Social Education* 33 (April 1969), 396–399.

18. See James A. Banks and William J. Joyce, *Teaching Social Studies to Culturally Different Children* (Reading, Mass.: Addison-Wesley, 1971).

19. Banks, Introduction to the *Forty-Third Yearbook of the National Council for the Social Studies*, xiii.

20. John Guenther and Wayne Dumas, "Black History for What?" *Social Education* 34 (December 1970), 927–930.

21. June R. Chapin and Richard E. Gross, "A Barometer of the Social Studies: Three Decades of *Social Education*," *Social Education* 34 (November 1970), 788–795.

22. Jesus Garcia and Edward Buendia, "NCSS and Ethnic/Cultural Diversity," in *NCSS in Retrospect, Bulletin 92*, ed. O. L. Davis, Jr. (55–65).

23. Richard L. Venezky "Textbooks in School and Society," in *Handbook of Research on Curriculum*, ed. Philip W. Jackson, 436; italics in original.

24. Venezky, "Textbooks in school and society," 445.

25. Harris O. Dante, Foreword to the *Forty-Third Yearbook of the National Council for the Social Studies*, vii.

26. Trezise, "The Black American in American History Textbooks," 147.

27. Ibid., 149.

28. James A. Banks, "A Content Analysis of the Black American in Textbooks," *Social Education* 33 (December 1969): 954–957.

29. Ibid., 957.

30. Robert Bierstedt, "The Writers of Textbooks," in *Text Materials in Modern Education*, ed. Lee J. Cronbach (Champaign: University of Illinois, 1955), 96–126.

31. FitzGerald, *America Revised*, 190.

32. Banks, "Multicultural Education: Historical Development, Dimensions, and Practice," in *Handbook of Research on Multicultural Education*.

33. James D. Anderson, "Secondary School History Textbooks and the Treatment of Black History," in *The State of Afro-American History: Past, Present & Future*, ed. Darlene Clark Hine, 253–274.

34. Jacqueline Goggin, *Carter G. Woodson: A Life in Black History* (Baton Rouge: Louisiana State University Press, 1993).

35. Louis R. Harlan, *The Negro in American History* (American Historical Association: Washington, DC, 1965).

36. Irving Sloan, *The Negro in Modern American History Textbooks* (American Federation of Teachers: Washington, DC, 1967).

37. Michael Kane, *Minorities in Textbooks: A Study of Their Treatment in Social Studies Textbooks* (Quadrangle Books: Chicago, 1970).

38. James A. Banks, "Teaching Black Studies for Social Change" in the *Forty-Third Yearbook of the National Council for the Social Studies,* 148–179.
39. James L. Barth, "NCSS and the Nature of the Social Studies" in *NCSS in Retrospect, Bulletin 92,* ed. O. L. Davis, Jr. (9–19).
40. Minutes of NCSS Meetings from the NCSS Archives. Milbank Memorial Library, Teachers College, Columbia University, New York.
41. James A. Banks, Introduction to the *Forty-Third Yearbook of the National Council for the Social Studies,* v.
42. Minutes of NCSS Meetings from the NCSS Archives. Milbank Memorial Library, Teachers College, Columbia University, New York.

9

Margaret Smith Crocco

WOMEN AND THE SOCIAL STUDIES: THE LONG RISE AND RAPID FALL OF FEMINIST ACTIVITY IN THE NATIONAL COUNCIL FOR THE SOCIAL STUDIES

In 1976, Professor Jean Dresden Grambs of the University of Maryland used the following statement to introduce her edited volume, *Teaching about Women in the Social Studies: Concepts, Methods, and Materials,* issued by the National Council for the Social Studies (NCSS) as *Bulletin 48* in its series of official publications on the field:

> Human society has always been composed of male and female. Human history has been almost exclusively male. How or why this interesting development occurred is beyond the scope of our inquiry here. . . . What we do know is that the distortion that has resulted is neither true nor useful. . . . History becomes a poor guide to understanding the present or predicting the future if it is grossly out of touch with historical reality.[1]

To the degree that women's stories have been overlooked since Grambs made this statement, histories of the social studies have served as poor guides to understanding the field's past and present or suggesting the shape of its future.[2] Women have been a sizable group within the social studies since its inception, serving chiefly as practitioners and teaching supervisors, with the number of administrators and professors growing substantially over the course of the twentieth century. Although few women were directly involved in founding NCSS in 1921, many women joined the organization and took on committee work from the early years.

Women's visibility, especially in claiming authority as theoreticians and leaders of social studies, would await emergence of feminist consciousness within NCSS during the 1970s, a period during which substantial feminist activity characterized the organization. But as slowly as this activity built within NCSS, just as rapidly it declined. By the last decade of the twentieth century, few signs could be found of sustained feminist activity in the organization.

In this chapter, I consider the place of feminism within social studies as assessed through evidence of feminist activity within NCSS over the course of the twentieth century. I recognize that NCSS is not isomorphic with either social studies or social education, but use the organization as proxy for these larger entities because it provides a convenient and highly visible symbol of a rather amorphous educational enterprise. In analyzing the place of feminism within the social studies, I consider factors both inside and outside the organization: the early twentieth century challenges women faced in gaining advanced educations, joining college faculties, and serving as leaders of professional organizations; the mid-twentieth century rise of a new women's movement; and the new status and hybrid nature of the social studies in the first half of the last century, including activities in both schools and colleges of education. Together, these factors help explain the long rise and rapid fall of feminist activity within the social studies.

Towards a Theory of Feminist Consciousness in the Social Studies

NCSS published *Bulletin 48, Teaching about Women in the Social Studies,* during a period of ferment in women's status in the United States. The authors whose work appears in this volume were largely applying the lessons of the women's movement of the sixties and seventies to their own professional domain. Their chapters offer a critique of women's invisibility in social studies curriculum but stop short of providing a parallel feminist analysis of their own professional situation as social studies educators. Nevertheless, for our purposes here, Grambs' statement can be successfully applied to both topics and their respective histories.

Reviewing histories of the field reveals the degree to which women's place in social education has gone largely unremarked.[3] One reason for this fact may be the paucity of such works overall.[4] Not until the 2002 NCSS publication of *Building a Legacy: Women in Social Education 1784-1984, Bulletin 100,* has an effort been made to provide an overview of women's contributions to the social studies.[5] The renewed attention to women and the social studies found in this volume depended on resurgence of feminist consciousness in the social studies, a necessary precondition to raising questions about women's roles, visibility, and power within an institution or organization.

Historian Gerda Lerner defines feminist consciousness as follows:

> The concept "feminist consciousness" is derived from and parallels the concept "class consciousness" as a means of defining the awareness of a group of its own oppression and of its struggle against that oppression. Deriving as it does from a Marxist conceptual framework, it assumes an "oppression" model, which in the case of

women does not adequately describe the complex way they function in society and are structured into it. The use of this term tends to obscure the way women are simultaneously "oppressed" and may be themselves oppressors of other groups.[6]

Identifying feminist consciousness within NCSS demands that inferences be made from historical evidence about the motivating factors leading to activities that appear as feminist in nature.[7] Relying on Lerner's definition, this chapter will assume that feminist consciousness emerges with the first organized feminist activity found in NCSS. It is certainly possible that feminist consciousness existed on an individual basis prior to organized feminist activity but it is difficult to surmise this from the extant historical record. Likewise, the chapter will leave aside the question of whether feminist consciousness ceases with decline in feminist activity during the last decade of the twentieth century. By this logic, publication of *Bulletin 48* in 1976 and other feminist undertakings of that decade signal feminist consciousness within the social studies. The chapter will focus on the vibrant feminist activity in NCSS around this time, contrasting its visibility with earlier and later periods of virtual silence regarding women.

The reasons for this pattern of long rise and swift fall are complex; nevertheless, they relate closely to the social and cultural difficulties women, even well educated women working in a largely female domain, have experienced in gaining a sense of themselves as a distinctive human and professional cohort, challenging the gender norms to which they have been socialized, and offering a critique of their subordinated status. As Lerner's quotation notes, women have been both oppressors and oppressed in history; and they have not made much progress in recognizing their situation until the last century. In this regard, social studies women resembled the generally conservative women and men of the National Education Association (NEA) during the latter half of the twentieth century or schoolteachers in general.[8] Although women social educators may have differed from male social educators in the concerns, values, and approaches they brought to the profession, nevertheless, few women (or men) critiqued the status of women as recorded in official NCSS documents prior to the 1970s.

Lerner provides comprehensive and cogent analyses of women's subordination in two books, *The Creation of Patriarchy* and *The Creation of Feminist Consciousness*. In the latter book she notes the essential linkages between feminist insights and communal efforts at social change: "Women's history could not be created as an intellectual pursuit in the absence of a social movement of women."[9] Such a movement was unlikely to occur until most women gained access to education, which occurred in the United States only during the nineteenth century. Although some historians trace widespread use of the term "feminism" to the early twentieth century, it should be noted that organized women's rights movements occurred earlier.[10]

Scholars have identified three separate women's movements in this country: 1) the mid- to late-nineteenth century movement associated with the Elizabeth Cady Stanton and Susan B. Anthony; 2) the early twentieth century suffrage movement associated with passage of the Nineteenth Amendment; and 3) the modern feminist movement dating from the 1960s and 1970s.[11] In the first and second movements, social educators such as Mary Beard, Lucy Salmon, and Lucy Sprague Mitchell endorsed women's political and legal rights while also advocating that social and women's history and geography become part of social education.[12] Likewise, in the second and third movements, many women educators worked for equal economic and professional rights for women.[13] It was not until the third women's movement, however, that feminist educators launched a comprehensive knowledge transformation project to bring women's issues, biographies, and histories into mainstream social studies curriculum.

This knowledge transformation project rested on feminist consciousness of a more thoroughgoing order than that which characterized the earlier movements. Thus, publication of *Bulletin 48* signifies a watershed moment in the field of social studies. Designation of a publication focused on teaching about women as a "bulletin," or official NCSS product, signaled that women's issues had finally arrived as concerns with legitimate standing in the field. How can we explain, then, the considerable distance from 1921, the year in which NCSS was founded, to the 1976 debut of women's issues? Why did the large number of women in the field from its inception fail to espouse feminist ideas or engage in feminist activities?

Women's Efforts to Gain Professional Standing

During the first half of the twentieth century, women's situation in NCSS can only be understood within the context of the challenges women faced in gaining access to higher education. In brief, they found their opportunities for gaining college education limited and for seeking preparation beyond bachelor's degrees even more limited. Discrimination in college admissions was widespread, making their exclusion from positions of power in professional organizations an inevitable outcome of the inability to gain access to doctoral programs. Even where they managed to pursue advanced degrees, rarely were they able to use such training to help other women make educational progress:

> Shut out of institutions of higher learning for centuries and then treated with condescension or derision, educated women have had to develop their own social networks in order for their thoughts, ideas and work to find audience and resonance. And finally, the fact that women were denied knowledge of the existence of Women's History decisively and negatively affected their intellectual development as a group.[14]

The feminization of teaching occurred in the United States during the late nineteenth century. Gender ideology of the day posited affinities between women and children; likewise, gender disparity in wages made women attractive teacher candidates in states implementing compulsory education laws. Normal schools, also staffed mostly by women, handled the lion's share of teacher preparation until the call for bachelor's degrees moved teacher preparation into colleges and universities. Even so, colleges remained largely inhospitable places for women—for education and employment. As universities developed graduate education offerings during the late nineteenth century, such changes brought greater restriction, if not outright exclusion, of women from these programs in many coeducational institutions.[15] In sum, women faced many hurdles in becoming professors throughout the first half of the twentieth century, and arguably, beyond that.[16]

These problems became particularly apparent when women sought positions in which they operated as knowledge producers or authoritative voices in academic fields. Seldom did women gain regular appointments to a college faculty, except at all-female colleges. When they secured work, their jobs came with lower pay and slower promotion. Their positions typically lacked opportunities for securing research funding, assuming editorship of an important journal, or gaining serious recognition as a scholar. Women's limited access to first-rate academic positions inhibited their ability to create knowledge and develop professional expertise, "the hallmarks of professional achievement."[17]

Many women chafed under the restrictions imposed on them. Others accepted the norms of academic meritocracy into which they had been socialized, distancing themselves from other women and propagating norms that were inherently biased against them. Most made little public comment about gender norms, adapting themselves to the academic profession without challenging its modes of action, thought, and evaluation. Two scholars of women's educational history, Penina Glazer and Miriam Slater, comment: "They may have seen women's experience as distinctive. But they never translated this judgment into the more radical posture that might have required formulating a new set of intellectual questions that would have confronted the assumptions of the double standard."[18]

Glazer and Slater have identified four strategies for career management utilized by women seeking positions within the academic world during the period 1890–1940: "superperformance, subordination, innovation, and separatism."[19] Women adopted different strategies at different stages of their careers, but collectively these strategies provided women with the means of surviving professionally in male-dominated institutions. This framework illuminates the means used by social studies women in finding success and often satisfaction in their professional lives, without calling attention to and perhaps without fully recognizing their secondary status within the organization.

More concretely, this framework can be seen in the patterns of engagement found among social studies women described in *Building a Legacy: Women in Social Education 1784–1984*.[20] Superperformance can be found among the numerous female academics remaining unmarried during the late nineteenth and early twentieth centuries. Subordination was likewise dictated by the realities of patriarchal institutions but can only be surmised in the stories found in *Building a Legacy*. Separatism, or opting to work in all-female environments, can be identified among those female scholars seeking to relinquish daily competition with men. Finally, innovation is central to the story of women and the social studies. As a new academic subject, the social studies attracted many women. This factor may account for the relatively early ascendancy of women to positions of prominence in social studies.

Women's Place in NCSS

Glazer and Slater indicate that newer professional domains provided women with less hostile environments for career advancement.[21] This may help explain why social studies early on included a number of women on influential NCSS committees and why a woman was able to capture the NCSS presidency at a relatively early point: Bessie Pierce in 1926. Over the next thirty years, one woman ascended to the NCSS presidency every decade. By contrast, the first female president of the AHA, Nellie Neilson, was not elected until 1943; the second female president of the AHA was not elected until 1987.[22] Pierce took her Ph.D. degree in 1923 at the University of Iowa under the direction of Arthur M. Schlesinger. In educational stature, she fit the mold of earlier NCSS presidents, all of whom were prominent scholars. Not until 1939 did a schoolteacher, Ruth West, became NCSS president. In 1945, Mary Kelty became the third woman to hold the position. Between 1921 and 1980, twelve women served as NCSS presidents.[23] One woman was elected president in each decade between 1920 and 1950; from 1950 on, three women ascended to the position each decade.

Louis Vanaria's dissertation on the history of NCSS, written in 1958, sheds light on this change in patterns: "The culmination of efforts to democratize elections has resulted in the inclusion of such criteria for identifying leadership as representation according to geographical location, balance between the sexes, and levels of classroom instruction."[24] Thus, NCSS leaders made a deliberate decision in 1954 to rotate the presidency according to several factors, including gender. This decision registers the first formal acknowledgement of gender's role within the organization's archives. The timing of this decision may reflect concerns with the commitment of social studies to democratic norms after defeat of fascist regimes in World War II and with America's image abroad during the Cold War. Similar considerations played a role in the Supreme Court's 1954 decision in *Brown v. Board of Education*.[25] One additional note of interest: After reporting the change in policy, Vanaria questions the wisdom of the decision.

Looking back at the archives associated with the period 1920 to 1970, one is also struck by the infrequent attention paid to matters of race. Nevertheless, infrequent attention contrasts noticeably with silence about gender throughout these years. Why both matters merited so little attention needs further examination by historians of the social studies.[26] As early as the thirties, NCSS leaders commented on the problems posed by segregation in terms of the integrity of the organization's democratic commitments. Like other educational organizations during these years, however, NCSS accommodated rather than challenged Jim Crow arrangements whenever it held meetings in the South. By the forties, NCSS sponsored intercultural education efforts along with the Anti-Defamation League of B'nai B'rith and the National Conference of Christians and Jews. Likewise, the historical evidence indicates the self-awareness of NCSS members concerning the organization's avoidance of dealing with urgent contemporary social problems.[27]

In making sense of the silence on gender, these factors highlight several points made by Lerner, most especially, the contingency of feminist consciousness on organized women's movements, women's collusion in maintaining patriarchy, and the ability of a few "exceptional" women to gain perquisites denied other women. As Joyce Antler and others have shown, educated women and professionals during and after the 1920s worked in an environment characterized by a shortage of feminist organizations, leadership, and momentum. Between the two women's movements of the twentieth century a long period of retrenchment occurred, which can be explained in part by the onset of the Depression and World War II.[28] Feminist historians have labeled these decades "the doldrums," years that saw increased societal emphasis on marriage, motherhood, and family as the apex of female aspiration.[29] Still, educational historians such as Linda Eisenmann also suggest that women continued to make steady and significant progress in education throughout these years.[30]

Perhaps, then, it is not surprising that, in the first half of the twentieth century, "Exceptional women . . . felt they could create a new identity and succeed on a personal basis without constructing an organized political base for change which would ultimately benefit all women."[31] Only in rare cases, according to this line of analysis, did women acknowledge their status as women, for doing so might undermine the perception of their seriousness, commitment, or objectivity as scholars. Women, as well as men, resisted the notion that gender might be "an appropriate category of analysis for an understanding of political and social institutions."[32] Well-educated, professional women "were required, in the nature of the case, to offer the fiercest and most unquestioning commitment [to their field] in order to compensate for any lingering doubts evoked by their gender."[33] Thus, women's growing prominence in NCSS did not necessarily indicate feminist consciousness.[34] Not until the seventies brought emergence of a new women's movement would sufficient feminist consciousness exist to put women's issues on the table as publicly acknowledged, legitimate concerns for social studies educators.

Feminist Women (and Men) Within the Social Studies

Women who built careers in the social studies during the fifties, sixties, and seventies have varied recollections about NCSS and women's place in it. Dorothy McClure Fraser Hemenway, NCSS president in 1954, stated in an interview forty years later that she remembered no instance of such discrimination in NCSS. She explained differences in the status of women and men in NCSS in these terms, "The situation in NCSS reflected that in society in general. The 'professional woman' was the exception rather than the rule."[35] Hemenway also felt that since many women did not make lifelong careers out of teaching, this factor accounted for their lower numbers in NCSS leadership positions.[36] Such a perspective suggests that many women simply accepted what they perceived to be social realities without much critique, even as they themselves transcended these norms. Other women, like Ruth Ellsworth, longtime professor at Wayne State University, bridled as she related memories of the low status of women in NCSS, in social studies generally and in elementary education in particular.[37] Jean Fair and Jean Claugus, both of whom became NCSS presidents during the sixties, echoed Ellsworth's recollections.[38] All these women's views clearly reflected the influence of the feminist movement and its critique of sex-based discrimination.

Change in many women's thinking about such matters occurred as the women's rights movement gained momentum nationally in the seventies. Claugus and Fair can be seen as transitional figures in the organization. In 1970, the president of NCSS, Shirley Engle (a man), questioned why the Task Force on Racism and Social Justice had not dealt with the "question of women's rights." He commented that the "board felt this was no time to overlook such a vital question."[39] Engle's initiative came at the prodding of a number of women and men; this would set a pattern for collective efforts yielding concerted feminist action throughout the organization. In January of 1971, the new NCSS president, John Jarolimek, sent a letter to the NCSS Board of Directors asking how such a committee might "serve the cause of social justice for women," including making suggestions concerning publications, women's role in the profession, society, and the organization.[40] Later that year, the Board approved creation of a new group, at first called the Committee on Social Justice for Women and re-named the Advisory Committee on Sexism and Social Justice (ACSSJ) in 1976, the name which will be used throughout this chapter. ACSSJ members went to work energetically pursuing a variety of goals and working collaboratively as they regularly shared the responsibility for spearheading new initiatives.[41] One of the group's first achievements occurred during Jean Fair's 1972 NCSS presidency when the Board of Directors adopted a Position Statement on Social Justice for Women.

During subsequent years, numerous participants in ACSSJ shared the view that sexism limited both men and women, believing that social justice work demanded addressing the effects of sexism on both. For the first time in NCSS history, a comprehensive effort at assessing women's place in the social studies entered its official agenda. Nevertheless, timidity in dealing with social issues can also be identified during this period when the House of Delegates failed to pass a resolution denouncing sexism, racism, and ethnocentrism in curriculum.[42] It is hard to understand what might be objectionable in such a resolution, especially at a time when the organization was regularly sponsoring clinics on racism at its conferences and promoting initiatives related to women and social justice. These initiatives include resolutions passed by the House of Delegates in support of child-care legislation (1971), peace education (1971), and the Equal Rights Amendment (ERA) (1977).[43] At the same time, it is perhaps unsurprising that NCSS made no statement concerning *Roe v. Wade* in 1973, since efforts to pass resolutions in opposition to the Vietnam War had proved so divisive.[44]

ACSSJ members sponsored many feminist activities during the seventies, explicitly calling for equity for men and women in leadership of the organization, its committees and programs, and in schools, textbooks, and curriculum. ACSSJ members encouraged women to run as candidates for president, committee chairs, or seats in the House of Delegates, sometimes running two female candidates against each other to insure that a woman was elected. Many of these women launched similar efforts within their state and regional social studies organizations as well.

Overall, among the most notable events initiated by ACSSJ during its years of operation were the following:

- Development of an NCSS "position statement" on sexism and social justice for women in 1971;
- Board adoption (November, 1972) and publication of this position statement in *The Social Studies Professional,* March 1973.

NCSS supported the following policies in response to this position statement:

- Advocating equal protection and non-discrimination against women under the law;
- Endorsing educational and professional mobility for women;
- Promoting change in female socialization so that career, educational, and personal opportunities are enhanced.

To implement these commitments, NCSS recommended these actions:

- Providing equal opportunity for women for representation at all decision-making levels in NCSS;
- Encouraging federal legislation aimed at non-discrimination based on sex in educational and personnel policies;
- Asserting influence on accreditation organizations to hold institutions to compliance standards with non-discrimination standards in their policies;
- Promoting publications, workshops, curriculum, and teaching practices dealing with social justice towards women.[45]

These actions indicate that NCSS was both acknowledging the role of women and the problem of sexism in schools, society, and its own organization. Whether the commitment of leadership to eradicating sexism in the organization was sufficiently deep or longstanding remains open to debate. Most feminists believe that sexism, like racism, is a problem that will not disappear in a generation, especially when this goal involves making changes to entrenched educational domains like curriculum. Women's achievement of leadership positions in a professional organization is more easily accomplished than overturning the normative basis of curriculum.[46] Challenging the values that support notions of "significance" in history, for example, presents difficult problems. Negative reactions often occur when the suggestion is made to introduce women's issues into the social sciences. Popular elementary and secondary social studies textbooks continue today to focus on political and economic history, giving far less emphasis to the social history that has, in recent decades, become so important to the discipline at the college level.

As feminist ferment made its presence felt throughout NCSS so, too, did multiculturalism. In 1971, Anna Ochoa, writing on behalf of the Task Force on Social Studies Curriculum, promulgated new guidelines concerning "ethnic studies":

[T]he knowledge utilized by the school has reflected the biases of the white middle class and has distorted the role of minority groups. Such distortions have prevented white people as well as members of minority groups from fully knowing themselves and their culture. Such practices are clearly inconsistent with the requirements of individuals in an increasingly complex, pluralistic society.[47]

Both multicultural and feminist scholars working in NCSS during the seventies employed the concept of knowledge construction to unveil the normative assumptions lying underneath the social studies curriculum. Their efforts moved curricular reform beyond tokenism and provided a framework for systematically assessing progress in knowledge transformation.[48] As many feminist scholars have noted, curricular transformation tended to follow an evolutionary path; small changes came at the beginning and larger ones, further down the road.[49] Early work laid a foundation for more sophisticated efforts as the knowledge base about women and the social studies grew.

In 1972 and 1973, Dell Felder of the University of Houston chaired the Advisory Committee on Social Justice for Women, followed in 1973 and 1974 by Peg Carter, social studies supervisor from Oakland, Michigan, and in 1975 by Carole Hahn, professor at Emory University.[50] The correspondence of members of the committee during the first half of the seventies demonstrates the tremendous energy, organization, and enthusiasm mustered by the group to attack sexism in the organization, schools, and society as they borrowed freely from feminist initiatives adopted by other professional organizations such as the National Council of Teachers of English and the Association for Supervision and Curriculum Development.[51]

ACSSJ members reviewed NCSS manuscripts prior to publication for evidence of sexism and produced a sizable number of publications.[52] Janice Law Trecker published a review of U.S. History textbooks in 1971, indicating the gross neglect of women's history in such works, an approach that would be repeated by Mary Kay Tetreault a decade later, with results showing less than impressive improvement.[53] In 1975, Hahn edited a special section of *Social Education,* entitled "Eliminating Sexism from the Schools: Implementing Change."[54] A number of other articles about women's issues appeared in *Social Education* during this decade.[55] Carole Hahn's 1978 article in *Theory and Research in Social Education (TRSE),* "Review of Research on Sex Roles: Implications for Social Studies Research," represents an early effort at synthesizing the growing body of literature that, Hahn argued, should inform the work of social studies educators.[56] Few articles on women and gender, however, appeared in *TRSE,* the publication of the relatively new College and University Faculty Assembly, during the seventies and eighties.[57]

A number of ACSSJ members contributed chapters to *Bulletin 48* in 1976. As such, its publication can be taken as a pivotal moment in the history of NCSS and feminism. *Bulletin 48* plainly registers a feminist consciousness in its critique of the systematic silencing of women's issues, lives, and stories within the social studies curriculum, its concern for the many ways in which gender shapes educational experiences, and its demand for a dramatic overhaul in business as usual in the social studies. Were it not for the shared feminist consciousness that gave rise to recognition of the need for these changes, the book would not have been published. Grambs' opening statement signals recognition of the socially constructed nature of gender, curriculum, and schooling, hallmarks of feminist consciousness. Still, Grambs refrains from dealing with the causes of sexism in schooling and does not name patriarchy as the causal factor explaining the problems addressed throughout the book. But she does call on teachers, many of whom were women, to play a pivotal role in "putting women back into the curriculum."[58] Clearly, only if more social studies women adopt feminist consciousness will such an achievement be realized.

As ratification of ERA stalled across the country late in the decade, NCSS decided to boycott those states that had not ratified the amendment, moving its meeting site in 1978 from Atlanta to Houston. In 1981, the House of Delegates passed a second resolution concerning ERA, calling for extension of the timetable for ratification. In 1978, Jane Bernard-Powers of San Francisco State University suggested creation of a Sex Equity Special Interest Group (SIG) as an offshoot of ACSSJ in order to expand the number of individuals who could participate in gender equity efforts.[59] This SIG, established in 1979 with Bernard-Powers and Leah Englehardt as co-chairs, held breakfasts at NCSS annual meetings well into the nineties and was responsible for publication in 1995 of a commemorative issue on the 75th anniversary of the Nineteenth Amendment.

Decline in Feminist Activity

Over the course of the 1980s, activities reflecting feminist consciousness fell off rapidly in number within the organization. As early as 1980, the ACSSJ newsletter acknowledged this decline by noting that the percentage of sessions devoted to sexism had fallen since its height in 1975–76. Of course, the numbers were quite small in both cases: 1975 — 7.5 percent compared to 1980 — 3.2 percent. The Northeast Regional Council for Social Studies did its own study of this issue, which showed a similar pattern: a highpoint of sessions dealing with sexism in 1974 (4 percent) and subsequent decline to 3 percent or less in the following years.[60] In 1982, the year in which James A. Banks was elected the first African American president of NCSS and Carole Hahn became president-elect, ACSSJ listed twenty-three members; the Sex Equity SIG organized regular events for the annual program; and members continued to make regular contributions to *The Social Studies Professional* and *Social Education*. In the early eighties, NCSS also supported resolutions in favor of enforcement of Title IX, a 1972 federal measure calling for equitable educational and athletic funding for girls and women, K-16; ratification of ERA; and celebration of Women's History Week. In Hahn's NCSS presidential year, 1982, the annual meeting featured three women general session speakers and six sessions devoted to gender equity. In 1985, Bernard-Powers traveled to Nairobi, Kenya, as NCSS representative to the United Nations conference on women. By the late eighties, however, a "sunset policy" of streamlining the organization by retiring committees perceived to have outlived their usefulness brought about the merger of ACSSJ with the Committee on Racism, combining them into the Committee on Equity and Social Justice.

How do we explain the decline in visibility of feminist activities, if not feminist consciousness, within NCSS in the eighties and nineties? Many factors, including backlash against feminism, the culture wars of the nineties, the rise of multiculturalism, or judgments about the success of the women's movement in combating sexism within the organization and in social studies more generally, may all account for the demise in visibility of women's issues in NCSS.[61]

Clearly, publication of *A Nation at Risk* in 1983 ushered in a new chapter in educational history, one that produced a call for national curriculum standards, high-stakes testing, and increased educational accountability in the nineties. Issues of gender equity were left in the wake of these "reforms." Little explicit attention to gender can be found in the NCSS curriculum standards produced during the nineties; state standards, as well, generally marked a return to more conservative curriculum and pedagogy. Similarly, an important publication, *the Handbook of Research on Social Studies Teaching and Learning,* failed to devote a chapter to gender, even though scattered references can be found to women's issues throughout the volume.[62] Likewise, the NCSS and CUFA annual meetings offered few sessions dealing with gender. Although feminist scholarship flourished in the humanities during the eighties and nineties, schools of education have, by contrast, paid little sustained attention to gender over the last decade.[63]

Again, explaining this state of affairs is not an easy task. Having once highlighted gender within social studies scholarship and NCSS operations, social studies teachers and scholars may simply believe that the most important issues have all been addressed, that most questions related to this subject have been answered, most problems solved, most curricula transformed. Many feminists within the field would claim otherwise.

Perhaps the explanation for the long rise and rapid fall of feminist activity in the social studies relates to the paradoxical connections between women and education: so many women in education, yet so little feminist consciousness, or at least, so little feminist activity by women that concerns education. Philosopher Jane Roland Martin suggests one aspect of this problem in her book, *Coming of Age in Academe:* "In coming to understand the academy's mores, I came to see that the academy charges an exorbitant admission fee to those women who wish to belong."[64] In other words, the induction process into the academy socializes women (and men) to a set of values and standards that have been inimical to consideration of the very issues that feminists take as key principles. For example, raising issues of knowledge construction, relativism, and positionality in relation to academic canons has been a suspect endeavor in traditional academic domains. Likewise, studying one's own group's history or critiquing knowledge construction is seen as social advocacy violating principles of disinterested scholarship, according to traditional norms. However, in the postmodernist cultures of many universities, these issues are often no longer as contentious as they once were. Still, in the conservative academic domain of the social studies, such enterprises may be viewed more negatively.[65] In gaining greater access to academic life and positions of power within its professional organizations, some women may compromise the critical capacities that might help sustain greater feminist activity in the field.

At the very least, in writing histories of the social studies, recognition needs to be made that the part cannot represent the whole, or, the few, the many. Lerner asserts that once this "basic fallacy of patriarchal thought—the assumption that half of humankind can adequately represent the whole—has been exposed and explained, it can no more be undone than was the insight that the earth is round, not flat."[66] Nevertheless, finding consciousness of this fact, and, thereby, a pulse for feminism in the social studies remains a challenge today.

Notes

I wish to thank Jane Bernard-Powers, Catherine Cornbleth, Carole Hahn, Christine Woyshner, Joseph Watras, and Murry Nelson for comments on earlier versions of this chapter.

1. Jean Dresden Grambs, ed., *Teaching about Women in the Social Studies: Concepts, Methods, and Materials, Bulletin 48* (Washington, DC: National Council for the Social Studies, 1976).
2. Over the last twenty years, only a few historical treatments dealing with individual women's contributions to social education have been published, e.g., Margaret Smith Crocco and O. L. Davis, Jr., eds. *"Bending the Future to Their Will": Civic Women, Social Education, and Democracy* (Lanham, MD: Rowman & Littlefield, 1999) and Margaret Smith Crocco, Petra Munro, and Kathleen Weiler, *Pedagogies of Resistance: Women Educator Activists, 1880–1960* (New York: Teachers College Press, 1999).
3. See, for example, the standard works of social studies historiography, including Hazel Whitman Hertzberg, *Social Studies Reform, 1880–1960* (Boulder, CO; 1981); Michael Lybarger, "Origins of the Social Studies Curriculum," (Ph.D. diss., University of Wisconsin, Madison, 1981); Virginia Atwood, "A Historical Perspective of Social Studies," *Journal of Thought* 17, 3 (1982); David Jenness, *Making Sense of Social Studies* (New York: Macmillan, 1990); O. L. Davis, Jr., ed. *NCSS in Retrospect Bulletin 92* (Washington, DC: 1996); and Ben A. Smith and J. Jesse Palmer, eds. "A History of NCSS: 75 Years of Service," *Social Education* 59, no. 7 (1995). The *Handbook of Research on Social Studies Teaching and Learning,* edited by James Shaver (NY: Macmillan, 1991), gives short shrift to women as well, even in a chapter, ironically, dedicated to Hazel Hertzberg. (I am grateful to Linda Levstik for pointing this omission out to me.) See, by contrast, Linda Levstik's commentary on women in social education in her chapter, "Woman as Force in Social Education: The Gendering of Social Studies in the Twentieth Century," in *New Research in Curriculum History,* ed. Sherry L. Field and Lynn Burlbaw (Greenwich, CT: Information Age Publishing, 2004).

4. To my knowledge, only one comprehensive treatment of the history of NCSS has been written in dissertation form (Louis Michael Vanaria, "The National Council for the Social Studies: A Voluntary Organization for Professional Service," Ph.D. diss., Columbia University, 1958). Although scholars have done several studies of the early years of social studies and of figures such as Harold Rugg, Paul Hanna, and George Counts, few comprehensive, thematically organized overviews have been published.

5. Margaret Smith Crocco and O. L. Davis, Jr., eds., *Building a Legacy: Women in Social Education 1784–1984, Bulletin 100* (Washington, DC: National Council for the Social Studies, 2002).

6. Gerda Lerner, *The Creation of Feminist Consciousness* (New York: Oxford University Press, 1993), 284, f.9.

7. The archives are located in Special Collections, Milbank Library, Teachers College, Columbia University, New York, NY. Those materials provide the major source of evidence for this chapter.

8. See the treatment of NEA and race found in Michael John Schultz, Jr., *The National Education Association and the Black Teacher: The Integration of a Professional Organization* (Coral Gables, FL: NEA, 1970) and the characterization of teachers given in Daniel Lortie, *Schoolteacher: A Sociological Study* (Chicago: University of Chicago Press, 1975). See also Geraldine Joncich Clifford, "Man/Woman/Teacher: Gender, Family, and Career in American Educational History," in *American Teachers: Histories of a Profession at Work,* ed. Donald Warren (New York: Macmillan, 1989): 293–343. Also, see Wayne Urban's "Courting the Woman Teacher: The National Education Association, 1917–1970," *History of Education Quarterly* 41, no. 2 (2001): 139–166.

9. Gerda Lerner, *The Creation of Patriarchy* (New York: Oxford University Press, 1985) and *The Creation of Feminist Consciousness,* 261.

10. See Nancy Cott, *The Grounding of Modern Feminism* (New Haven: Yale University Press, 1987).

11. Useful treatments of the history of twentieth century women's movements can be found in Linda K. Kerber and Jane Sherron De Hart, *Women's America: Refocusing the Past* (New York: Oxford University Press, 2000); Ruth Rosen, *The World Split Open: How the Modern Women's Movement Changed America* (New York: Viking, 2000); and Leila J. Rupp and Verta Taylor, *Survival in the Doldrums: The American Women's Rights Movement, 1945 to the 1960s* (Columbus, OH: Ohio State University Press, 1990).

12. Chara Hauessler Bohan, "Lucy Maynard Salmon: Progressive Historian, Teacher, and Democrat" (47–73), Margaret Smith Crocco, "Shaping Inclusive Education: Mary Ritter Beard and Marion Thompson Wright" (73–93), and Sherry L. Field, "Lucy Sprague Mitchell: Teacher, Geographer, and Teacher Educator" (125–149) in *"Bending the Future to Their Will,"* eds. Crocco and Davis.

13. Crocco, Munro, and Weiler, *Pedagogies of Resistance,* Chapter 1.

14. Lerner, *Creation of Feminist Consciousness,* 12.

15. Barbara Miller Solomon, *In the Company of Educated Women* (New Haven: Yale University Press, 1985); Penina Migdal Glazer and Miriam Slater, *Unequal Colleagues: The Entrance of Women into the Professions 1890–1940* (New Brunswick: Rutgers University Press, 1987); Joyce Antler, "The Educated Woman and Professionalization: The Struggle for a New Feminine Identity, 1890–1920," (Ph.D. diss., State University of New York, Stony Brook, 1977); Andrea Walton, "Women at Columbia: A Study of Power and Empowerment in the Lives of Six Scholars," (Ph.D. diss, Columbia University, 1995).

16. For recent work on such problems, see Jackie M. Blount, *Destined to Rule the Schools: Women and the Superintendency, 1873–1995* (Albany, NY: SUNY Press, 1998); Patricia A. Carter, *"Everybody's Paid But the Teacher": The Teaching Profession and the Women's Movement* (New York: Teachers College Press, 2002); Crocco, Munro, and Weiler, *Pedagogies of Resistance, Women Educator Activists, 1880–1960;* and Jana Nidiffer, *Pioneering Deans of Women: More than Wise and Pious Matrons* (New York: Teachers College Press, 2000).

17. Glazer and Slater, 7, 23.

18. Ibid., 53.

19. Ibid, 14.

20. Crocco and Davis, eds., *Building a Legacy: Women in Social Education 1784–1984.*

21. Glazer and Slater, 42.

22. Joan W. Scott, *Gender and the Politics of History* (New York: Columbia University Press, 1987), 186.

23. For more information about women presidents of NCSS, see Crocco and Davis, Jr., eds., *Building a Legacy Women in Social Education 1784–1984.*

24. Vanaria, 139.

25. See Mary L. Dudziak, *Cold War Civil Rights: Race and the Image of American Democracy* (Princeton: Princeton University Press, 2000).

26. It is difficult to make a precise judgment about the distribution of NCSS membership by gender or race during these years since the organization's records do not yield this information readily. The number of women members might be determined by counting names on membership lists during each era. African Americans formed parallel social studies organizations, in part, to deal with discrimination they faced in state and national social studies organizations; women did not. For more information on African Americans in teaching generally, see Linda M. Perkins, "The History of Blacks in Teaching: Growth and Decline within the Organization," in *American Teachers,* ed. Warren, 344–370.

27. See, for example, the comment made about publications during the Great Depression in Murry R. Nelson, "The Early Years, 1921–1937," *Social Education* 59 (November/December 1995): 399–407.

28. See the following books for excellent treatments of these decades: Dorothy M. Brown, *Setting a Course: American Women in the 1920s* (Boston: Twayne, 1987); Susan Ware, *Holding Their Own: American Women in the 1930s* (Boston: Twayne, 1982); and Susan M. Hartmann, *The Home Front and Beyond: American Women in the 1940s* (Boston: Twayne, 1982).

29. Rupp and Taylor, *Survival in the Doldrums.*

30. Linda Eisenmann, "Women, Higher Education, and Professionalization: Clarifying the View," *Harvard Educational Review* 66, no. 4 (1996): 858–873. See also Andrea Walton, "The Dynamics of Mission and Market: Debates over Co-Education at Columbia University in 1889 and 1983" *History of Education* 31, no. 6 (2002): 589–611 for discussion of the need for new histories of women in education that focus on agency and institution building rather than simply access.

31. Antler, 16.

32. Glazer and Slater, 53.

33. Ibid., 55.

34. See, for example, Bonnie G. Smith, *The Gender of History: Men, Women, and Historical Practice* (Cambridge, MA: Harvard University Press, 1998) and Helene Silverberg, ed.,

Gender and American Social Science: The Formative Years (Princeton: Princeton University Press, 1998).

35. Written responses to questions posed by the author to Dorothy Hemenway provide the foundation for this paragraph, summer 2000. See the brief biography about Hemenway by Stephanie D. VanHover, "Dorothy McClure Fraser," in *Building a Legacy*, 83–84.

36. Wayne Urban's "Courting the Woman Teacher: The National Education Association, 1917–1970" provides an extremely useful comparative perspective to the story told here. Urban notes that Charl O. Williams, female staff member at the NEA for over a quarter-century, commented in 1946 on the fact that women often did not pursue teaching as a lifelong career due to the proscription against married teachers (p. 152). Urban also recounts a story about another NEA staff member, Hazel Davis, who, like Hemenway, denied discrimination in the organization. Urban comments that Davis' oral history provides other information that "complicates this conclusion" (p. 154). Like NCSS, NEA was reluctant to discuss women's issues explicitly throughout the forties, fifties, and sixties, despite the organization's efforts to court the woman teacher, as Urban put it (p. 156).

37. Phone interview of Ruth Ellsworth by Linda Levstik, July 2000. See the brief biography of Ellsworth by Levstik in *Building a Legacy*, 99–100.

38. Barbara Slater Stern interview with Jean Claugus; Janet Alleman interview with Jean Fair, summer, 2000. See the biography of Claugus by Stern in *Building a Legacy*, 115–116, and of Fair by Alleman, 113–114.

39. Shirley H. Engle, President, "Report of the President," NCSS Archives, Series III-B, box 1, folder 8, Special Collections, Teachers College, Columbia University.

40. Excerpt from Dr. John Jarolimek's letter of January 14, 1971, John Jarolimek collection, MG 17, Administrative Files, NCSS Collection, Milbank Memorial Library, Teachers College, Columbia.

41. Interview by author with Carole Hahn, September 2001.

42. William G. Wraga, "Struggling toward Professionalization: 1968–1982," *Social Education* 59 (November/December 1995): 429–437.

43. Wraga characterizes the resolutions passed by the House of Delegates during the period 1968–1982 as "moderate-liberal" in his article, "Struggling toward Professionalization, 1968 to 1982," 433.

44. Jack L. Nelson and William R. Fernekes, "NCSS and Social Crises," in *NCSS in Retrospect*, ed. O. L. Davis, Jr. (Washington, DC: NCSS, 1996), 89–103.

45. Dell Felder, Joan Ellsberg, James Hills, Jean Lantz, and Patricia F. Spears signed "The Position Statement and Report of the Committee on Social Justice for Women." It can be found in Box 4, Carole Hahn Papers, NCSS Collection, Special Collections, Milbank Library, Teachers College, Columbia University. It is beyond the scope of this chapter to trace the effects of these recommendations on NCSS operations over time. What is significant to the argument being made here is the fact that NCSS finally engaged topics related to women in a manner signifying feminist consciousness at the instigation of a self-consciously feminist group within the organization.

46. By this I mean that curriculum rests on values concerning the knowledge that is deemed important in life and education. Feminists contend that the curriculum is systematically biased in favor of masculinist notions of importance that overlook the significance of women's work and the private realms of life in fashioning curriculum.

47. NCSS Task Force on Curriculum Guidelines, "Social Studies Curriculum Guidelines," *Social Education* 35 (December 1971): 853–874. The group included James A. Banks among its members.

48. Mary Kay Tetreault, "Integrating Women's History: The Case of United States History High School Textbooks," *The History Teacher* 19, 2 (1986): 211–252

49. See, for example, Peggy McIntosh's "Interactive Phases of Curricular Re-vision: A Feminist Perspective," Working Paper No. 124, Wellesley College Center for Research on Women, 1983.

50. Subsequent chairs of the group included Joan Ellsberg, Loretta Carney, Lucy Draper, Kathy Scott, and DeAn Hansen.

51. See Urban for description of parallel activities within the NEA, pp. 165 ff.

52. See, for example, articles about women in both the 43rd NCSS Yearbook, James A. Banks, ed., *Teaching Ethnic Studies* (Washington, DC: NCSS, 1973) and the 44th NCSS Yearbook, A. Kownslar, ed., *Teaching American History: The Quest for Relevancy* (Washington, DC: NCSS, 1974).

53. Janice Law Trecker, "Women in U.S. History Textbooks," *Social Education* 35 (March 1971): 249–61. Carole Hahn; "Social Studies with Equality and Justice for All: Toward the Elimination of Sexism," *Journal of Research and Development in Education* 13/2 (1980): 103–112; Mary Kay Tetreault, "Integrating Women's History: The Case of United States History High School Textbooks."

54. Carole Hahn, "Eliminating Sexism from the Schools: Implementing Change," *Social Education* 39 (March 1975): 133–150.

55. See, for example, Elizabeth Burr, Susan Dunn, and Norma Farquhar, "Women and the Language of Inequality," *Social Education* 36 (December 1972): 841–846; Mary W. Matthews, "A Teacher's Guide to Sexist Words," *Social Education* 41 (May 1977): 389–398; Mildred Alpern, "Images of Women in European History," *Social Education* 42 (March 1978): 220–224; Bonnie R. Crown, "Women's Lives in the Asian Tradition, "*Social Education* 43 (April 1979): 248–261.

56. Carole Hahn, "Review of Research on Sex Roles: Implications for Social Studies Research," *Theory and Research in Social Education* 6, no. 1 (1978), 73–99.

57. Besides Hahn's "Review of Research on Sex Roles," the following articles on sex/gender, women, or sexism appeared in *Theory and Research in Social Education (TRSE)* in the '70s & '80s: Judith Preissle Goetz, "Children's Sex Role Knowledge and Behavior," *TRSE* 8 (Winter 1981), 31–54; Elizabeth L. Peterson and Emily M. Nett, "Sexuality in the Classrooms of Teachers with Various Sex Role Orientations, *TRSE* 10 (Fall 1982), 29–40; Carole L. Hahn and Glen Blankenship, "Women and Economics Textbooks," *TRSE* 11 (Fall 1983), 67–76; and Murry R. Nelson, "Emma Willard: Pioneer in Social Studies Education," *TRSE* 15 (Fall 1987), 245–256.

58. Grambs, 3.

59. Jane Bernard-Powers wrote a chapter on "Gender in the Social Studies Curriculum," in *The Social Studies Curriculum: Purposes, Problems, and Possibilities,* rev. ed., ed. E. Wayne Ross (Albany: State University of New York Press, 2001): 177–197.

60. National Advisory Committee on Sexism and Social Justice, December, 1980, no. 4.

61. Of course, this state of affairs may alternatively be interpreted as a decline or may simply represent a lapse in interest in women's issues within the organization. Only time will tell whether interest in gender will re-emerge within the organization, perhaps in the same cyclical fashion that characterizes much educational history.

62. James Shaver, ed., *Handbook of Research on Social Studies Teaching and Learning* (New York: Macmillan, 1991).

63. Peggy Blackwell, Jane Applegate, Penelope Earley, and Jill Mattuck Tarule, *Education Reform and Teacher Education: The Missing Discourse of Gender* (Washington, DC: AACTE, 2000).

64. Jane Roland Martin, *Coming of Age in Academe: Rekindling Women's Hopes and Reforming the Academy* (New York: Routledge, 2000), xxiv.

65. Blackwell et al., *Education Reform and Teacher Education.*

66. Lerner, 273.

10

Avner Segall

SOCIAL STUDIES AND THE DISCOURSES OF POSTMODERNITY

Since the latter part of the twentieth century, a variety of critical[1] discourses—i.e., postmodernism, poststructuralism, feminism, postcolonialism, and cultural studies—have disrupted the predominant, modern, structural, male-dominated, colonial/colonizing discourses of knowledge and knowing and have challenged those discourses' claims to universality, transparency, objectivity, and truth. While substantial differences exist both among and within each of these critical discourses,[2] they nevertheless share the view that knowledge and knowing, and their social and disciplinary organization, are not only positioned but positioning and, thus, they share an interest in how they circulate (and circulate within) relations of power and what (and who) such circulations make im/possible. Calling into question the very foundations of knowledge and its organization, critical discourses are not about constructing coherent, linear narratives about the world, but about blasting such narratives open, rupturing their silences and highlighting their detours,[3] investigating "the degree to which what is privileged . . . may be historically and conventionally prescribed."[4] Exposing the interests underlying the questions not asked within academic disciplines, they inquire into how present absences and silences governing scholarship and its administration work to deny the link between knowledge and power and refuse to acknowledge the particular way of life they help make both possible and intelligible.[5]

While much of the academy, including all of the disciplines comprising the social studies, has, since the beginning of the 1980s, attempted to seriously engage the challenges raised by critical postmodern discourses, social studies has participated in this process only marginally and sporadically.[6] That lack of engagement is, in some ways, surprising. First, and given the progressive roots and history of social studies, one would have expected such discourses to be represented extensively in its literature.[7] Second, both areas have much in common: they are inherently inter- if not anti-disciplinary, borrowing from the disciplines yet remaining suspicious of them. Moreover, the very issues critical discourses bring to the forefront—i.e., power, representation, identity, and voice—are not only pertinent to social education and research conducted in it but are fundamental to (and are always inherent in) both. What, then, does this act of "ignoring" indicate? Where and how did it unfold? And what implications might it have for the future of social studies and of research conducted in/about it?

Answering those questions requires an engagement with the politics of absence/presence (exclusion/inclusion). To think postmodern about those politics is to ask: What is absent in that which is present in the discourse of social studies? And what presents itself as a result of the absence of that which is not present? At issue is not a desire to somehow overcome or transcend the politics of presence/absence; those will always be present. What becomes important then is to make the workings of a process that produces absence problematic, opening it up for critique and showing it in ways that it does not tend to show itself. (Certainly, my own analysis will inevitably create its own politics of presence/absence, boxing certain things and persons in and leaving others "out." I, therefore, invite readers to impose the very same analysis I provide social studies to the politics of presence/absence in my own chapter.)

To start, I should clarify how I define *social studies* as my category of analysis. That is, who do I assume speaks *for* and what speaks *as* social studies in my analysis? I chose to focus on the field's two major journals, *Theory and Research in Social Education (TRSE)* and *Social Education* as representations of the field's "official" discourse. Several aspects combine to bestow that "official" status on what are considered the two premier journals in social studies. They are not only sponsored by the National Council for Social Studies (NCSS) and the College and University Faculty Assembly (CUFA), but are also distributed to all of their members. As the "official" discourse both *in* and *of* the field, these two journals are not only where scholarship in social studies is published, but also serve as the primary source and legitimation for new scholarship and knowledge.[8] The importance of those two journals is then recursive; they produce and help re-produce knowledge and knowing in the field, providing the setting for scholarship and giving legitimation to it. As gate-keepers of new scholarship in the field, they determine what scholarship is worthy of publication, what issues should be addressed and how, demarcating the boundaries not only of the kind and quality of research in the field, but also what counts as social studies and what does not. I also examine the *Handbook of Research in Social Studies Teaching and Learning,*[9] still, the most comprehensive review of theory, research, and practice in social studies education.[10] While an examination of the field's two journals provides a portrayal of a twenty-year process, the *Handbook* provides a focused snapshot, mid-term in that process.[11]

The 1980s to the Mid-1990s

By 1985, both journals had already provided readers some exposure to critical post-modern discourses. In the winter of 1982, *TRSE* published a collection of five essays discussing different meanings, purposes, and values underlying current theory in social education as well as providing possible new theories for it. Among those essays were one by Henry Giroux, another by Cleo Cherryholmes, both drawing on Continental critical theory to consider the nature and purpose of theory in/for social education. Using Habermas (and, for the first time in *TRSE*, a bit of Foucault), Cherryholmes proposed a counter strategy to the positivist epistemological assumptions underlying social studies education, calling for an interpretive critical perspective that "assumes that the social world is in need of interpretation and interpretations are in need of criticism."[12] Invoking critical social theory of the Frankfurt School, Giroux's essay offered various modes, categories, and forms of social inquiry for developing a critical theory of social education.[13]

Three years later, *Social Education* published a special themed section (May, 1985) titled "New criticism and social education." It showcased six short essays providing critical views of society, schools, and social studies not commonly found in the literature in social education. The deskilling of teachers was the focus of two of those essays. Apple and Teitelbaum explored the deskilling of teachers resulting from various reform movements and the implications of that process for content and pedagogy in social studies, for the ability of teachers to construct a curriculum that is meaningful and relevant, and for students to engage knowledge that opens possibilities for imagining otherwise.[14] Giroux examined (and calls upon teachers to examine) the ideological and material forces contributing to the deskilling of teachers. Rather than manage externally-produced curricula, teachers, according to Giroux, should become transformative intellectuals who develop and critically appropriate curricula to fit specific pedagogical concerns, who raise questions about "what they teach, how they are to teach, and what the larger goals are for which they are striving," and who "combine scholarly reflection and practice in the service of educating students to be thoughtful, active citizens" of a democracy.[15] Critiquing *functionalism* as the dominant explanatory model with which to examine the organization of society in social studies textbooks, Gilbert not only pointed out its limitations but suggested that teachers ask in whose interests and from whose perspectives functionalism or any other theoretical framework and explanatory models underlying our understandings of the world are constructed and what and whose interests they serve.[16] Stanley examined the yet unfulfilled promises of *reconstructionism,* pointing out its current relevancy in social education. Highlighting some of the issues underlying the movement, Stanley emphasized the need for social criticism both in the content and process of social education.[17] Wexler placed social education in the context of social change and advocates the creation of a bridge between technologies of information, cultural theory and practice that would help make the politics of the process, and the public social relations underlying them, apparent.[18] Cherryholmes challenged the lack of skepticism in social studies of epistemological bases for knowledge as well as the norms and ideologies that guide and validate the search and construction of such knowledge. To make those more transparent, Cherry-holmes proposed that social education focus, in part, on discourse and criticism in order to surface and analyze existing values and commitments embedded in inter-pretations and explanations in/of our field.[19]

While some of the theoretical frameworks expressed in this special section had already been presented earlier,[20] its significance stems from its collective nature, providing readers of social studies a first comprehensive overview of a variety of ideas, issues, and perspectives underlying critical discourses at that time. The im-portance of this special issue, however, lies not only in its being a first in the field but also a last; an endeavor to present a broad collection of critical pieces of such magnitude under one umbrella in either of the two "official" journals in the field has yet to be repeated.[21]

That such scholarship was not considered inherent to the field might be illus-trated by the fact that following the endeavors of 1982 and 1985 there was very little engagement with critical postmodern discourses and the issues they raise in either of the two leading journals in the field for most of the last two decades of the twentieth century. The question, then, is "Why?" One could suggest, with some plausibility, that the particular challenges brought forth by critical postmodern dis-courses were not perceived as significant or relevant to the scholarly community in social studies at that time. One could also argue, with equal plausibility, that it is not the particular ontological, epistemological, or methodological positions ad-vanced by critical postmodern discourses that were rejected by mainstream social studies but, rather, that such a rejection was part of a broader, more general refusal to seriously explore most any ontological, epistemological, and methodological is-sues underlying social studies education and research in/about it, focusing instead, almost exclusively, on practice—at times as a genuine intellectual endeavor in and of itself, at other times as a way to retreat from theory and avoid its implications. What cannot be suggested, however, is that the absence of critical postmodern is-sues could be attributed to the lack of critical scholars engaging such discourses in the field. As the essays in the two special sections well illustrate, social studies, at the time, was not only *not* lacking scholars who could infuse the field with such dis-courses, but had some of the most prominent scholars in education to do so. Yet while the work of such scholars was able to make a significant contribution across education and beyond, social studies—the very area with which they initially affili-ated themselves (and in some cases still do today)—was probably the one to least welcome, or make use of, their contributions.[22]

The Handbook of Research on Social Studies Teaching and Learning

An illustration of the status of postmodern scholars and scholarship within social studies can be gained by looking at the *Handbook of Research on Social Studies*

Teaching and Learning, another important component of the "official" discourse in social studies education. "If there is a community of inquiry in the social studies," writes Seixas, the *Handbook of Research on Social Studies Teaching and Learning* is its "most compact documentary expression."[23] By far the most comprehensive review to date of knowledge in the field, the *Handbook* comprises 53 chapters contributed by 71 scholars representing the state of knowledge of educational theory, research, and practice of social studies education at that time.[24]

The *Handbook*'s engagement with critical postmodern discourses and issues is minimal, concentrated almost exclusively in chapters written by Cherryholmes, Popkewitz (with St. Maurice), Fullinwider and Aoki. Not surprisingly, the few references to anything or anyone postmodernly critical appear in the *Handbook*'s first section, "Issues of epistemology and methodology" where all of the above-mentioned chapters are located. That references to postmodern discourses are, by and large, absent from the *Handbook*'s seven other sections indicates that (and the degree to which) such discourses did not yet appear significant to (or in) teaching and learning social studies. An analysis of the *Handbook*'s name and subject indexes helps illustrate that point.

Of a name index containing close to 3500 authors, fewer than ten could be considered critical postmodernists. Among the estimated 10,000–15,000 author-references, only 38 (about 0.3 percent) are of scholars whose work represents critical postmodern sensibilities. Foucault, the scholar most closely identified with poststructuralism, receives only seven references, all either by Cherryholmes, Popkewitz & St. Maurice, Fullinwider, or Aoki. Other theorists significantly impacting the development of critical postmodern discourses, such as Derrida, Deleuze, Lyotard, Irigaray, and Said are also ignored in all but the chapters in the first section of the *Handbook*.

While works by many of the foundational theorists of critical postmodern discourses such as Foucault and Derrida might, as some have argued, have an overly-intellectual, inaccessible, continental flair that can drive some readers away, social studies' very own—Giroux and Cherryholmes—fared only slightly better with their colleagues. Cherryholmes' work is cited in nine of the chapters. But his most significant—and most significantly poststructural—work by that time, *Power and Criticism,*[25] was only referenced once. Giroux, by then widely recognized as one of the most thought-provoking scholars in education, is referenced 14 times. With regard to both authors, while reference to their work did extend the boundaries of the *Handbook*'s first—"epistemological"—section, most of those include only work that appeared either in social studies journals and/or before either of those authors fully and explicitly engaged critical postmodern issues.

The *Handbook*'s subject index provides a similar picture. One might, for example, expect to find among the index's close to 3500 categories and subcategories terms such as *postmodernism* or *poststructuralism*—by then, more than a decade after Foucault's *Power/knowledge,*[26] seven years following Lyotard's *The Postmodern Condition*[27]—to be at least recognized (even if not common) terms in foundational literature such as a *Handbook* in any area of education. That is not the case. Similarly, *postcolonialism* is not part of the index, more than a decade after Said's *Oriental-ism*.[28] *Feminism* appears only once in the *Handbook*'s 661 pages. *Culture* and *Identity* are absent from the index as are *difference, power, positionality,* or *discourse,* all terms which, by then, were already widely circulating in most areas of academia. *Gender,* according to the index, is addressed in only five of its 53 chapters. *Race,* as a stand-alone category, surfaces only in one chapter (though several subcategories pertaining to race appear, as might be expected, in Banks' chapter).[29]

That critical postmodern discourses coming from outside of social studies were not incorporated in any significant manner should, by now, be clear. But what about those from *within* social studies? Regardless of whether social studies scholars at the time had read any of the Continental postmodern theorists, they all had opportunities to become familiar with some of the theories, perspectives, issues, and challenges raised by critical postmodern discourses through the two essays in *TRSE* (1982) and those in the special section in *Social Education* (1985). Yet of the eight critical essays appearing in both journals, only four were cited in the *Handbook.* Three—those by Cherryholmes, Giroux, and Wexler in *Social Education*—were referenced only once each in the entire *Handbook.* Cherryholmes' *TRSE* piece was cited three times (one of them by the author himself, another by Nelson, the guest editor of the special section in which it appeared). The four other essays were not mentioned at all. What we see, then, on the part of the social studies community at the time, is not only a refusal of critical postmodern discourses from outside education, or even of those in education but outside of social education. Evident is also a refusal of those discourses appearing in the "official" discourse of the field, on the pages of the two journals from which the scholarly community in social education most draws.[30]

The Mid-1990s to the Turn of the Twenty-First Century

The "long drought" regarding critical postmodern scholarship in the "official" discourse in social studies came to an end in the mid-1990s. Since then, *TRSE* has, on a continuous basis, incorporated critical scholarship previously unseen on the pages of any journal in the field.[31] The same cannot be said with regard to *Social Education* whose silence on critical postmodern issues remains mostly unhindered.[32] Several factors combined to explain this shift. A major contributing factor could be the transition in the editorship of the journal, with E. Wayne Ross assuming responsibilities in the spring of 1996. Ross demonstrated an openness toward critical postmodern discourses by publishing a number of pieces of that kind. This trend, however, began during the latter part of Fraenkel's stint as editor. What made it happen in the mid-1990s and not earlier, however, was not as much the ideological positioning of an editor but the changing demographics and sensibilities of the community of scholars in the field. The mid-1990s signaled the "coming of age" of a new cadre of social studies scholars who, due to the breakdown of traditional disciplinary boundaries in their own doctoral preparation and the proliferation of available inter- and cross-disciplinary programs, were more inclined to incorporate a variety of critical postmodern discourses and dispositions and bring those to bear on their work in the field. Infusing their scholarship within social studies with postmodern, poststructural, postcolonial, and feminist theories—often borrowed from cultural studies, curriculum theory, women's studies, African American studies, queer studies, etc.—these new scholars were more inclined to ask new questions about social studies, use different methodologies to study the field, as well as utilize new forms of textualization to report their findings, all of which helped disturb the given and taken for granted in social studies research at the time.

A second group that helped make that "shift" a reality comprised already-established, mainstream social studies scholars who not only began to increasingly incorporate elements of critical postmodern discourses into their work but also provided encouragement—mostly through reviews—to scholarship provided by the first group.

Though the word *postmodern* was first incorporated into the title of a piece in *TRSE* only in 1998,[33] critical postmodern sensibilities had entered the journal several years earlier. Assuming varying degrees of a poststructural feminist stance, and engaging gender as a category of analysis, several pieces in a themed issue titled "Gender, feminism, and social studies education"[34] illustrated not only that poststructural feminist perspectives matter in our field but also what it means to do poststructural feminist research in social studies, what one might be able to "do" with it, and where one might arrive having embarked upon it.

In the following issue, and increasingly (though in a rather sporadic fashion) ever since, critical postmodern essays began appearing not only in "special" issues of *TRSE* but on a regular basis, among "regular" essays, and on the "regular" pages of "regular" issues. In the first of a string of such pieces, and discussing research conducted with First Nations' people of Canada to evaluate the latter's representations in social studies textbooks, Dillabough & McAlpine moved away from traditional examinations of textbooks and the methods underlying those examinations and opened new avenues for thinking about research in the field as they combined postcolonial dispositions to explore reflexively how praxical ethnographic border work can, in cooperation with marginalized cultural groups, rework "the political grounds upon which social studies research processes are negotiated and thus formulated."[35]

Returning to *TRSE* to trouble prevailing views about history, Stone, using critical scholars such as Culler, Derrida, de Certeau, Foucault, Husserl, Hutcheon, LaCapra, and White, as well as her own work, not only makes the important—postmodern—point that history is multiple and that "a unifying-diversity of history is itself a problem for inquiry"[36] but, also (and in the process of making that argument) familiarizes *TRSE* readers with some of the underlying tenets of critical postmodern theories. Contributing to ongoing efforts to challenge prevailing assumptions in our field, Bloom utilized a variety of critical postmodern feminist scholars (Benhabib, Butler, Fraser, Harding, Mohanty, Mouffe, and Stone) as she explored the politics of difference within multicultural feminism and its implications for social education.[37]

A critical postmodern disruption of another kind took place a year later with the publication of "W(R)I(t/d)ing on the border: Reading our borderspace." Using a critical postcolonial discourse and, writing in critical race theory genre that weaves family history, biography, and narrative, Chavez Chavez pushed *TRSE*'s boundaries of narrativity. As he read, and helped readers read the politics of borderspaces, Chavez Chavez also provided new—border—spaces (both in their physicality and meta-physicality) for narrativity, pushing *TRSE*'s boundaries as to how we, as researchers, tell stories—our own and those that belong to others.[38]

The last issue of *TRSE* in the 1990s to incorporate critical postmodern essays was its 1999 summer issue. There, critical essays didn't simply appear among other, "regular" pieces but, for the first time, constituted a majority—two Features, a Viewpoint, and a book review.[39] While each of those pieces utilized a different critical lens, they all shared an interest in critically exploring the production of knowledge in education and its consequences. Invoking Foucault, among others, Vinson examined how national standards operate to normalize curricula and those who engage them. My own piece explored the possibilities opened up for history/social education by critical postmodern discourses, mostly from within the discipline of history. Shannon's piece was both about reading education as a cultural practice and an example of how to conduct such readings that relate stories of everyday educational life to broader political, economic, and social discourses and practices that structure education and in/form bodies and subjectivities of those engaged in/by it. Using a Marxist postmodernist lens, Pruyn explained how a radicalized social education can "provide many of the theoretical and pedagogical tools necessary for understanding how exploitations of race, class, gender, and sexual orientation relate to both predatory capitalism and our postmodern condition."[40]

What the above examples illustrate is that although such discourses were (and are still) not the main stake of *TRSE,* the journal had nevertheless made important strides in closing rank, at least regarding the amount of space afforded such discourses, with other leading journals in education, thus opening the conversation within social studies to perspectives formerly all but excluded from it. This trend has continued into the twenty-first century; several critical pieces have been published in *TRSE* in the last two years.[41] Most notably, perhaps, are the two special issues, "Connected citizenship" and "Social studies and sexual identity," that "came out" (and I do see both as a sort of "coming out" for our field) in 2001 and 2002 respectively.

Conclusion: Into the Twenty-First Century

"Doing" critical postmodern work, as some of my examples illustrate, is primarily a reflexive process; one that critically examines its object rather than simply replaces it, and only replaces it in so far as it illuminates it in a new light, asking different questions of and about it. Less interested in *what* social studies means or even in *how* it means, those incorporating critical lenses inquire into how that *how* is an effect of the commitments and values underlying the power relations and social structures that constitute the *what*. In other words, critical postmodernists inquire how discursive practices turn the actual into the real and the intelligible and construct bodies, sensibilities, and dispositions in that process. Examining how discourses become factors of truth, one can see how social studies, as a school subject or as a site of research, constructs and conditions knowledge, making both visible and problematic the presuppositions of discourses, values, and methodologies that legitimate and enforce particular arrangements constituting social education and its relation, through power and convention, to knowledge.

To conclude, I wish to highlight some of the current critical work in social studies education that appeared beyond the substantive and temporal scope of this chapter. Since the previous section emphasized work by the new generation of scholars in our field, I will devote this part mostly to work conducted by more established, mainstream scholars, briefly highlighting some of their work and, more importantly, point to ways in which it has helped move our field in new—and I would argue, interesting—directions.

Poststructural perspectives and undertakings, as Vinson's work[42] illustrates, can be used meaningfully not only to trouble what is done in social studies but also as a methodology with which to study the field. Taking on various issues such as "standards," "high-stakes testing," or "citizenship," poststructuralism (mainly through the work of Foucault) is used to underlie an analysis of how those function to both include and exclude particular meanings and subject positions, how they exude power through their dominance, and how they render alternatives unviable. Combining Foucauldian notions of surveillance with those by Debord of spectacle, Vinson[43] suggests that education should be understood as the infusion of spectacle and surveillance, and, exploring the relationship between images of schooling and the operation of high-stakes testing, then concludes that bodies and subjectivities are disciplined as groups and individuals simultaneously monitor and are monitored by others. Using poststructuralism in that manner not only encourages the field to consider new theories, frames, and strategies for analysis, but also demonstrates the kind of questions it makes possible and where we might go once we begin using them.

Bringing cultural studies into social studies education, Werner, for one, invites teachers and students to make the practices of authorship and readership of various texts used in the social studies classroom more visible and open to critical question. Utilizing concepts borrowed from cultural studies (i.e., representation, the gaze, voice, absence, intertextuality, authority, mediation, and reflexivity) would, according to Werner, help students acquire rich conceptual tools for critically reading their world and acting within it. Such tools will also help move social education away from a prevailing emphasis on determining what is *true* and on to questions about *truth:* How is "truth" constructed, legitimated, and ruled, by whom and with what consequences?[44]

Postcolonial theory has also recently been infused more meaningfully in social education. Building upon her extensive earlier work in global education yet using postcolonial literature to depart from it, Merry Merryfield has recently called for decolonizing the mind of existing, Cold War–oriented global education. Challenging some of the assumptions underlying current manifestations of global education, Merryfield reminds us that the task does not end with inclusion. Rather, and using a postcolonial approach advocated by Willinsky,[45] she suggests an examination of how the legacy of imperialism—its assumptions and values, its classifications, divisions, and exhibitions of the Other—still shapes academic knowledge today. The challenge, she argues, is not simply to explore the impact and ramifications of colonialism on the Other but how our western ways of Othering generated by centuries of empire-building have colonized our own educational mind and limited the scope of what teachers and students are invited to explore.[46]

The infusion of postcolonialism has also raised questions about the nature of research in our field, inviting a consideration of what it might mean to do postcolonial research. Combining postcolonial literature and their own experiential dilemmas to deliberate about how one comes to know the Other, about what knowing entails, and about whose meanings count and how, Levstik and Wilson, for example, examine how the frames in which we study and compare are already saturated with categories that implicate our studies and ourselves as researchers.[47]

Possibly the most substantial current body of critical literature in social studies is that which engages gender. Attempting to further infuse existing scholarship with an exploration of gender (and more recently, sexuality) as a category of analysis, Crocco's recent work[48] invites the field to consider more seriously the agenda set forth by Tetreault.[49] Moving from a history of women to a history of gender, she adds "requires acknowledgement by those writing these histories that, when it comes to gender, there is no default option, no gender-neutral standpoint. That is, gender imbricates all of social life, and includes men as well as women."[50] Recognizing our situatedness in writing history as well as the situatedness of the pasts we inscribe and the methodologies we use to inscribe them, she proposes, "will assist in illuminating its multiple perspectives, asking different questions, searching for evidence in different places . . ."[51]

While the above examples indicate the distance scholarship in social education has already gone by incorporating critical postmodern sensibilities, they also point to where it has yet to go. I will conclude by briefly pointing to two such areas. The first centers around issues of methodology. Denzin & Lincoln define the current moment in qualitative research as a triple crisis of representation, legitimation, and power.[52] Little of that seems evident in the research currently published in social education. Clinging to a realist model with its claims to neutral technique, "transparency of representation and immediacy of experience,"[53] researchers in our field still, by and large, refrain from reflexively engaging the problematic relationship in our own studies between power and knowledge, language and the world, knower and known, and method and "results." Attending "to the politics of what we do and do not do"[54] as researchers as well as to the epistemologies underlying our practices, requires more than "keeping good field notes, making accurate maps, 'writing up' results." [55] As McLaren and Lankshear suggest,[56] it requires researchers to narrate the contingency of their research, its situatedness in power/knowledge relations, and the ways in which "their research subjects and their relationship to them become artifacts of the *epistemes* that shape the direction of their research."[57] We have yet to see a sufficient number of studies in social education that incorporate such sensibilities; studies that seriously attend to the ideologies embedded in, and the ramifications of, our research by asking and responding to questions such as the following: What do our methodologies make both possible and impossible? What and who do they render intelligible? What and who do they "invite" us to forget, ignore, marginalize, or silence? How do they encourage us to speak with/to/about/for/ others? How and what do they Other? Do (and how do) they enable us and our participants to imagine otherwise? Attending to such matters will not only provide more nuanced and situated understandings of *what* we study but also, and more importantly, make more explicit the connection between *how* we study and the knowledge we produce as a result.

Part of a critical postmodern response to the crisis of representation and legitimation has centered around issues of textualization, moving away from the monological, univocal text of the realist era toward polyphonic texts, "with fractured, overlaid, multiple soundtracks."[58] Too few such opportunities have thus far been provided by research in social education. While my own work[59] has taken some steps in that direction, Hurren's recent book, *Line Dancing,* best highlights the possible. Blurring the lines between theory and data, between academic and embodied knowing, Hurren disrupts existing notions of narrativity in social studies scholarship, illustrating not only that form and substance are inextricable but that (and how) each must be made to interrogate the other if we want to understand how our writing of the world affects and reflects how we understand and live in it.[60]

A second (and due to the limited space, last) area where there is still too little engagement with critical postmodern discourses is that which pertains to their impact on the disciplines comprising social studies and the implications they pose for social education. That is, for how we think about history, geography, anthropology, economics, sociology, etc. and their education, for how we teach them, for how we prepare teachers to teach them, for how we do research in and about them. While some engagement with the opportunities and challenges created by critical postmodern discourses has been provided with regard to history education and history teacher education,[61] the literature explored for this chapter provides no evidence that such an examination has been afforded any other of the disciplines underlying the social studies education. What might it mean, for example, to engage a geography curriculum that focuses on issues of space, place, and identity as its focal point? What kind of understandings and learning positions might it engender? How might it help make possible currently ignored inter- and cross-disciplinary connections to other social studies areas and beyond? In short, how could the enterprise of geography (or, for that matter, economics, sociology, anthropology, etc.) education be conceived otherwise if we take seriously the challenges posed by critical postmodern discourses to the disciplines we teach? Much more research is necessary not only to answer those questions but to pose other question that will help broaden our understandings of what education in those disciplines currently is (and is not) as well as of what and how it could be otherwise.

Notes

I would like to thank Steve Thornton and the editors of this book for their comments on earlier drafts of this chapter and Judy O'Brien for her editorial assistance.

1. The term "critical" is problematic on two levels. First, it glosses over important differences between the discourses it subsumes under its umbrella. Second, it is too broad and too narrow for an analysis of social studies since various discourses, some with a long tradition in the field (i.e., progressivism, revisionism, and reconstructionism) are critical in nature and share some of the goals (though not the particular theoretical frameworks, ontological dispositions, and methodological maneuvers) of their postmodern counterparts. The critical work of, for example, Goodman, Ross, and Gibson, among others, has consistently engaged many aspects resulting from, and issues pertaining to, the conditions of postmodernity. Yet it is difficult to count their work as "critical postmodern" since they normally do not identify their work with, and, in most cases don't directly invoke, the critical discourses of postmodernity mentioned at the outset of this chapter. Another kind of scholarship defying easy categorization is that in multiculturalism, particularly the work of Banks and Ladson-Billings. While their work both addresses the kind of concerns raised by postmodern discourses and often invokes some of the theories of, and those theorizing in those discourses, it is primarily based in, and builds on a rich critical discourse in American anthropology and sociology more so than in postmodern or poststructural discourses (though a strong sense of postcolonialism and feminism does permeate their work which might best be defined as critical multiculturalism).

2. For a good distinction between, for example, postmodernism and poststructuralism, see William Stanley, *Curriculum for Utopia: Social Reconstructionism and Critical Pedagogy in the Postmodern Era* (Albany: SUNY Press, 1992).

3. Henry A. Giroux, "Living Dangerously: Identity Politics and the New Cultural Racism," in *Between Borders: Pedagogy and the politics of cultural studies,* eds. Henry A. Giroux and Peter McLaren (New York and London: Routledge, 1994), 45–55, 51.

4. Stanley Aronowitz and Henry A. Giroux, *Postmodern Education: Politics, Culture and Social Criticism* (Minneapolis: University of Minnesota Press, 1991), 140.

5. Henry A. Giroux, David Shumway, Paul Smith, and James Sosnoski, "The Need for Cultural Studies: Resisting Intellectuals and Oppositional Public Spheres." (1991). http://eng.hss.cmu.edu/theory/need.html

6. Peter Seixas, "Review of Research on Social Studies," in *Handbook of Research on Teaching* (4th ed.), ed. Virginia Richardson (Washington, D.C.: AERA, 2001): 545–565.

7. Jack L. Nelson, "Contemporary Social Education Literature: An Essay Review," *Theory and Research in Social Education* 22, no. 4 (1994): 461–481.

8. James S. Leming and Murry Nelson, "A Citation Analysis of the Handbook of Research on Social Studies Teaching and Learning," *Theory and Research in Social Education* 23, no. 2 (1995): 169–182.

9. James P. Shaver, ed, *Handbook of Research on Social Studies Teaching and Learning* (New York: Macmillan, 1991).

10. Leming and Nelson, "A Citational Analysis," 169.

11. While such a focus provides an important window into the conversation in our field, it no doubt ignores the contributions of numerous other publications, many of them at the regional/state level. It also excludes the level of practice exemplified in textbooks and other curricular materials.

12. Cleo Cherryholmes, "Discourse and Criticism in the Social Studies Classroom," *Theory and Research in Social Education* 9, no. 4 (1982), 61.

13. Henry A. Giroux, "Culture and Rationality in Frankfurt School Thought: Ideological Foundations for a Theory of Social Education," *Theory and Research in Social Education* 9, no. 4 (1982): 17–55.

14. Michael Apple and Kenneth Teitelbaum, "Are Teachers Losing Control of their Jobs?" *Social Education* 49, no. 5 (1985): 372–375.

15. Henry A. Giroux, "Teachers as Transformative Intellectuals," *Social Education* 49, no. 5 (1985): 376–379.

16. Robert J. Gilbert, "Social Knowledge, Action and the Curriculum," *Social Education* 49, no 5 (1985): 380–383.

17. William B. Stanley, "Social Reconstructionism for Today's Social Education," *Social Education* 49, no. 5 (1985): 384–389.

18. Philip Wexler, "Social Change and the Practice of Social Education," *Social Education* 49, no. 5 (1985): 390–394.

19. Cleo Cherryholmes, "Language and Discourse in Social Studies Education," *Social Education* 49, no. 5 (1985): 395–399.

20. For example, Cleo Cherryholmes, "Social Knowledge and Citizenship Education: Two Views of Truth and Criticism," *Curriculum Inquiry* 10, no. 2 (1980): 115–141; Henry A. Giroux and Anthony N. Penna, "Social Education in the Classroom: The Dynamics of the Hidden Curriculum," *Theory and Research in Social Education* 7, no. 1 (1979): 21–42; William B. Stanley, "The Radical Reconstructionist Rational for Social Education," *Theory and Research in Social Education* 8, no. 4 (1981): 55–79.

21. The "special" status of these sections raises concerns regarding their *legitimacy* in, and impact on, the field. Similar to criticisms raised against boxed-in representations of women and "Other" in social studies textbooks, one might question whether the "special," segregated status afforded these (and other) sections might not invite readers to "read" their ascribed location as a legitimacy to regard them as diversions, as not inherently necessary to "real" social studies knowledge or scholarship. By not requiring readers to engage such perspectives in the pages of a "regular" issue, the designation "special" serves as scholarly guidance, warning readers it is both out of the ordinary and, at the same time, could be "dangerous," something not to be left out there, untagged, to be encountered unwarrantedly by an innocent, unsuspecting reader who, in a moment of weakness, might be caught off guard.

22. While both Giroux and Cherryholmes published widely in social studies prior to the publication of their 1982 and 1985 essays, Giroux's work has not been incorporated in either *TRSE* or *Social Education* ever since. Similarly, while contributing two short pieces to *Social Education* (in 1987 and 1990), Cherryholmes, the first editor of *TRSE*,

has only published one invited piece to commemorate the journal's 25th anniversary and one book review since 1985. Lynda Stone, a prominent poststructural feminist theorist (and a board member of *TRSE*) published only marginally in *TRSE* until the end of the century. Joe Kincheloe, one of the most prolific critical scholars in education, has, since the mid-1980s, not had any of his work published in either of the two journals in social studies—an area he still identifies with (see, e.g., Joe L. Kincheloe, *Getting beyond the Facts: Teaching Social Studies/Social Sciences in the Twenty-First Century,* 2nd ed. (New York: Peter Lang, 2001). Work by either Apple or Wexler has never again appeared in either *Social Education* or *TRSE.*

23. Seixas, "Review of Research on Social Studies," 551.

24. Leming and Nelson, "A Citation Analysis," 169.

25. Cleo Cherryholmes, *Power and Criticism: Poststructural Interventions in Education* (New York: Teachers College Press, 1988).

26. Michel Foucault, *Power/Knowledge: Selected Interviews and Other Writings* (New York: Pantheon Books, 1980).

27. Jean-Francois Lyotard, *The Postmodern Condition: A Report on Knowledge* (Minneapolis: University of Minnesota Press, 1984).

28. Edward Said, *Orientalism* (New York: Vintage Books, 1978).

29. It should be noted that there are some discrepancies between the index of the *Handbook* and that which appears in its chapters. For example, while the terms *postmodernism* or *poststructuralism* are excluded from the index, they appear in chapters by Cherryholmes and Popkewitz & St. Maurice. Similarly, *gender* actually appears more frequently in the chapters of the Handbook than in its index. Whether those omissions were deliberate (that is, consciously determined) or an oversight, their absence nevertheless sends a message about their significance (or lack thereof), at least in the eyes of the editor of this volume which not only represented the field but influenced new scholarship in it.

30. Leming and Nelson, "A Citation Analysis."

31. Critical—postmodern or otherwise—literature also appeared outside of the pages of *TRSE* in the 1990s. Among the books to be mentioned: James A. Banks, *Educating Citizens in a Multicultural Society* (New York: Teachers College Press, 1997); Jesse Goodman, *Elementary Schooling for Critical Democracy* (Albany: SUNY Press, 1992); David W. Hursh and E. Wayne Ross, eds., *Democratic Social Education: Social Studies for Social Change* (New York: Falmer, 2000); Gloria Ladson-Billings, *The Dreamkeepers* (San Francisco: Jossey-Bass, 1994); Walter Parker, ed., *Educating for the Democratic Mind* (Albany: SUNY Press, 1997); Marc Pruyn, *Discourse Wars in Gotham West: A Latino Immigrant Urban Tale of Resistance and Agency* (Bolder, CO: Westview, 1999); E. Wayne Ross, ed., *The Social Studies Curriculum: Purposes, Problems, and Possibilities* (Albany: SUNY Press, 1997); and William B. Stanley, *Curriculum for Utopia: Social Reconstructionism and Critical Pedagogy in the Postmodern Era* (Albany: SUNY Press, 1992).

32. This is particularly problematic since, as Nelson points out, it "represents a serious intellectual limit on what social studies teachers are likely to read about their field." Jack Nelson, "Contemporary Social Education Literature," 464.

33. Roland Reichenbach, "The Postmodern Self and the Problem of Developing a Democratic Mind," *Theory and Research in Social Education* 26, no. 2 (1998): 226–237.

34. Robert W. Smith, "Schooling and the Formation of Male Students' Gender Identities"; Lynda Stone, "Feminist Political Theory: Contributions to a Conception of

Citizenship"; Geert ten Dam and Rally Rijkschroeff, "Teaching Women's History in Secondary Education: Constructing Gender Identity," all appearing in *Theory and Research in Social Education* 24, no. 1 (1996).

35. Jane Dillabough and Lynne McAlpine, "Rethinking Research Processes and Praxis in the Social Studies: The Cultural Politics of Methodology in Text Evaluation Research," *Theory and Research in Social Education* 24, no. 2 (1996), 186.

36. Lynda Stone, "Response to Blum's 'Diverse' Plot of History," *Theory and Research in Social Education* 25, no. 1 (1997), 73.

37. Leslie Rebecca Bloom, "The Politics of Difference and Multicultural Feminism: Reconceptualizing Education for Democracy," *Theory and Research in Social Education* 26, no. 1 (1998): 30–49.

38. Rudolfo Chavez Chavez, "W(R)i(t/d)ing on the Border: Reading Our Borderspace," *Theory and Research in Social Education* 27, no. 2 (1999): 248–272.

39. Kevin Vinson, "National Curriculum Standards and Social Studies Education: Dewey, Freire, Foucault, and the Construction of a Radical Critique"; Avner Segall, "Critical History: Implications for History/Social Studies Education"; Patrick Shannon, "Sociological Imagination, Stories, and Learning to be Literate"; Marc Pruyn, "Social Education through a Marxist Postmodern Lens: Toward a Revolutionary Multiculturalism," all appearing in *Theory and Research in Social Education* 27, no. 3 (1999).

40. Pruyn, 421.

41. For example, Nina Asher and Margaret Crocco, "(En)gendering Multicultural Identities and Representations in Education," *Theory and Research in Social Education* 29, no. 1 (2001): 129–151; Walt Werner, "Reading Authorship into Texts," *Theory and Research in Social Education* 28, no. 2 (2000): 193–219.

42. For example, Kevin Vinson, "National Curriculum Standards and Social Studies Education"; Kevin Vinson, "Pursuing Image: Making Sense of Popular Pedagogical Representations," paper presented at the annual conference of the American Educational Research Association (Seattle, WA, April 10–14).

43. Kevin Vinson, and E. Wayne Ross, "Education and the New Disciplinarity: Surveillance, Spectacle and the Case of SBER," paper presented at the annual conference of the American Educational Research Association (Seattle, WA, April 10–14).

44. Walt Werner, "Reading Authorship into Texts"; Walt Werner, "Reading Visual Texts," *Theory and Research in Social Education* 30, no. 3 (2002): 401–28.

45. John Willinsky, *Learning to Divide the World: Education at Empire's End* (Minneapolis & London: University of Minnesota Press, 1998).

46. Merry Merryfield, "Moving the Center of Global Education," in *Critical Issues in Social Studies Research for the 21st Century*, ed. William B, Stanley (Greenwich, CT: Information Age, 2001): 179–207.

47. Linda Levstik and Angene Wilson, "Constructing History in Different National Contexts: Dialogue on Multiple Perspectives," *Trends and Issues* (A publication of the Florida Council for the Social Studies) 14, no. 3 (2002): 4–14.

48. Margaret Smith Crocco, "Introduction," in *"Bending the Future to Their Will": Civic Women, Social Education, and Democracy*, eds. Margaret Smith Crocco & O. L. Davis, Jr. (Lanham, MD: Rowman & Littlefield, 1999): 11–16; Margaret Smith Crocco, "Preface" and "Conclusion," in *Building a Legacy: Women in Social Education 1784–1984*, eds. Margaret Smith Crocco and O. L. Davis, Jr. (Silver Springs, MD: National Council of the Social Studies, 2002): 9–12, 147–149; Margaret Smith Crocco, Petra Munro

and Kathleen Weiler, eds., *Pedagogies of Resistance: Women Educator Activists, 1880–1960* (New York: Teachers College Press, 1999).

49. Mary Kay Tetreault, "Rethinking Women, Gender, and the Social Studies," *Social Education* 51, no. 3 (1987): 170–180.

50. While using gender as a category of analysis that explores the world of women and of men, femininity and masculinity (and how the two are constructed with, by, and against the other) has significant implications for our field, part of how we might measure its success might be the degree to which (and how) male scholars in our field also begin to explore (with) it. To date, too few such pieces [i.e., Keith C. Barton, "Masculinity and Schooling," *Theory and Research in Social Education* 20, no. 2 (2002): 306–312; Robert W. Smith, "Schooling and the Formation of Male Students' Gender Identities"; Stephen J. Thornton, "Does Everybody Count as Human?" *Theory and Research in Social Education* 30, no. 2 (2002): 178–189] have been published in either of the field's two "official" journals that demonstrate this understanding.

51. Crocco & Davis, *Building a Legacy,* 148.

52. Norman Denzin and Yvonna Lincoln, "Introduction: The Discipline and Practice of Qualitative Research," in *Handbook of Qualitative Research,* 2nd edition, eds. Norman Denzin and Yvonna Lincoln (Thousand Oaks, CA: Sage, 2000): 1–28.

53. James Clifford, "Introduction: Partial Truths," in *Writing Culture: The Poetics and Politics of Ethnography,* eds. James Clifford & George. E. Marcus (Berkeley: University of California Press, 1986), 2.

54. Patti Lather, *Getting Smart: Feminist Research and Pedagogy with/in the Postmodern* (New York & London: Routledge, 1991), 13.

55. James Clifford, ibid.

56. Peter McLaren and Colin Lankshear, "Critical Literacy and the Postmodern Turn," in *Critical Literacy: Politics, Praxis, and the Postmodern,* eds. Colin Lankshear and Peter McLaren (Albany: State University of New York Press, 1993): 379–419.

57. The nature of this chapter and the examples I invoke in it are evidence of my own commitments and affiliations.

58. Norman Denzin, "The Experimental Text and the Limits of Visual Understanding," *Educational Theory* 45, no. 1 (1995), 17.

59. Avner Segall, *Disturbing Practice: Reading Teacher Education as Text* (New York: Peter Lang, 2002). See also, Dawn Shinew, "Disrupt, Transgress, and Invent Possibilities," *Theory and Research in Social Education* 29, no. 3 (2001): 488–516.

60. Wanda Hurren, *Line Dancing: An Atlas of Geography Curriculum and Poetic Possibilities* (New York: Peter Lang, 2000).

61. For example, Avner Segall, "Critical History: Implications for History/Social Studies Education"; Peter Seixas, "Schweigen! Die Kinder! Or, Does Postmodern History Have a Place in the Schools?" in *Knowing Teaching & Learning History: National and International Perspectives,* eds. Peter N. Stearns, Peter Seixas and Sam Wineburg (New York: New York University Press, 2000): 19–37; Peter Seixas and Penney Clark, "Murals as Monuments: Students' Ideas about Depictions of 'Civilization' in British Columbia," Centre for the Study of Historical Consciousness, University of British Columbia, Vancouver, B.C., 2002. http://www.cshc.ubc.ca.

11

Jackie M. Blount

SAME-SEX DESIRE, GENDER, AND SOCIAL EDUCATION IN THE TWENTIETH CENTURY

Over the past century, schools have played powerful roles in assuring the normative sexuality and gender of their charges. Arguably, communities have pressed them into this service as adult caregivers have devoted ever-greater portions of their time in wage-earning activities and correspondingly less time with their own children. Schools typically have tackled these added responsibilities through a wide range of indirect and direct means. In the end, even as our culture gradually has expanded its discussion and acknowledgement of a range of sexualities and gender identities, schools have continued to emphasize to students accepted forms of heterosexuality and traditional, polarized gender behaviors and characteristics.

Schools have endeavored to control students' sexual and gender development chiefly in three ways. First, ever since persons desiring members of the same-sex came to be identified as "homosexuals," thus constituting a distinct identity group, schools have singled them out for specific treatment. Second, because cross-gender behaviors and characteristics commonly have been regarded as evidence of homosexuality, schools have defined and regulated acceptable gender identities—as indirect means of controlling sexuality. And finally, school board members and administrators have attempted to hire school workers who model acceptable sexuality and gender norms for their students. In these three ways, then, schools have provided compelling social education for normative sexuality and gender. It is social education in the sense that it concerns how students learn, live, and make sense of their sexuality and gender, especially within the deeply sexual and gendered contexts of our culture.[1]

Sexual identity is a relatively recent concept. Before the early decades of the twentieth century, school administrators and teachers—when they explicitly thought about sexuality at all—typically concerned themselves with students' sexual behaviors. It was not until the middle decades of the century that the term "homosexual" commonly came to mean a *kind of person* rather than a description of a sexual *behavior*. Simultaneously, this new identity suffered association with a variety of sexual pathologies catalogued by sexologists and psychologists. In response, schools not only sought to control students' same-sex sexual activities, but they also took seriously the work of identifying and regulating students who might be homosexuals. They also launched campaigns to promote the superiority of conventional heterosexuality and, alternatively, the dangers of homosexuality. The emergence of an identifiable class of persons prompted schools to institute programs, policies, and practices for dealing with them. In essence, with the creation of homosexual identity, schools developed new means of regulating sexuality.

Beyond sexuality, the meanings of gender also have shifted. During the late nineteenth century, conventional gender expectations fitted men and women for their unique socially constructed spheres. They also assisted women and men in identifying classes of persons with whom permissible sexual relations might be a possibility. However, during the twentieth century, one's display of appropriate gender behaviors and characteristics increasingly seemed to confirm one's heterosexuality. Conversely, cross-gender behaviors and characteristics increasingly connoted possible homosexuality. By mid-century, then, not only did schools take on the task of assuring normative sexuality, but they also sought to control students' gender identities. Students who strayed into ambiguous or unconventional gender territory risked the perception of sexual deviance. To avoid this stigma, schools reinforced polarized notions of correct gender behaviors and characteristics. Ambiguous and cross-gender qualities, then, became conflated with homosexual identity, all of which schools sought to regulate.

Finally, a significant way that schools have attempted to control students' sexual and gender identities has been through hiring school workers who supposedly model desired qualities. During the twentieth century, women increasingly needed to conform to mainstream notions of femininity. By mid-century, they also were expected to demonstrate their heterosexuality through marriage—a state that set them apart from their spinster foremothers. Men not only have needed to be married throughout the century, but after WWII they also were required to manifest strongly masculine qualities through such means as coaching, displaying executive skills, and commanding authority. This strategy of supplying appropriate models of gender and sexuality assumes that students develop their own sexual and gender identities in part by imitating admired adults, presumably including teachers and other school workers. To control students' gender and sexuality, then, schools have sought to regulate the gender and sexuality of their employees.

In the end, schools still generally do not support students or employees who adopt non-mainstream sexualities or genders. However, as Jonathan Zimmerman argues in his compelling work, *Whose America? Culture Wars in the Public Schools*

(2002), there may be some limited, grudging movement. Despite rancorous culture wars that have plagued schools and social education for at least a century, Zimmerman contends that gradually the cast of characters depicted in standard school curricula has grown larger and more diverse. Native Americans, African Americans, immigrants from many nations, persons from non-mainstream faiths, and women eventually have been included.[2] It may be that lesbian, gay, bisexual, and transgender (LGBT) persons parallel these other groups and that in time, they, too, will grace the environment and curriculum as examples of the richness of our humanity.

Zimmerman maintains, though, that these culture wars in schools have not followed a single trajectory, but rather two distinct paths of disagreement: The first, as just described, concerns identity and inclusion while the second involves whose religious beliefs and/or moral views are taught. In contrast with the first path in which school curricula have expanded gradually to include more kinds of persons, Zimmerman contends that arguments following the second trajectory have moved relatively little. Even though the beliefs, strategies, and the cast of religious characters have changed notably over the years—as have the subtleties of the debates themselves—still these battles typically concern nearly mutually exclusive worldviews about morality with little common ground. These are the debates that seem irresolvable. In some ways, this second path of vexed immobility also characterizes the status of LGBT issues in schools.

In this chapter, I will explore how social education in schools has contended with sexual and gender identities in ways that have crossed both of these paths. On one hand, some schools have begun to regard persons who identify as LGBT as members of a distinct class of persons whose existence must be acknowledged and civil rights assured. On the other, however, deep-seated cultural notions about appropriate sexual and gender behaviors—and of providing upstanding models of such sexuality and gender identity—have contributed to great resistance both to LGBT students and school workers.

Behavior Versus Identity

During the late 1800s, the notion of a distinct homosexual identity seemed alien to school workers. The term "homosexual" had only recently been coined to denote sexual activities with persons of the same sex. As the term gained broader use, public awareness of homosexual activity also increased, and that awareness quickly spread to schools. A British headmaster warned listeners in 1881 that a dangerous cancer threatened to engulf upper-class education. He charged that boys in single-sex boarding schools regularly practiced the solitary vice, and worse as he explained, they "masturbated" each other with great regularity. Outraged audience members then demanded that school authorities scrutinize boys' activities more closely. In response, elite boarding schools in England instituted a series of reforms to limit boys' opportunities for sexual experiences. Schools converted dual-occupancy dorm rooms into less private barracks; they kept lights on in sleeping quarters at night to allow better surveillance; and they packed student schedules with strenuous activities that, theoretically, would leave boys too exhausted to engage in prohibited behaviors with each other.[3] Boys' boarding schools and men's colleges in the United States dealt with the same issues because they emulated the elite British boarding school model. One writer explained in 1908 that students in U.S. schools were particularly prone to homosexual relationships. "A special observer of youthful homosexuality in America has stated that the practices of uranian boys [those who seek intimacy with other males] in school are . . . 'nowhere quite so general' as in the United States."[4] When such activity could not be eliminated, students caught transgressing were dismissed.

Over the first half of the twentieth century, popular understanding of homosexuality shifted. Earlier, anyone was thought capable of engaging in prohibited same-sex sexual activity. The behavior itself was the subject of community consternation. However, after the turn-of-the-century, sexologists, psychologists, and others who studied human sexuality shifted their focus from examining sexual *behaviors* to labeling and cataloging the *people* who engaged in these sexual behaviors. At the same time, writers, moviemakers, producers, and other artists began portraying homosexual persons in their works. Gradually, scientific, cultural, and popular understanding of homosexuality changed from an *act* to *identity*. No longer was a behavior simply deviant, but also the person who engaged in it had become deviant as well.[5]

By mid-century, the notion of homosexual identity had become so embedded in popular thought that WWII military commanders summoned psychiatrists and medical doctors who specialized in sexuality to assist in screening out homosexual recruits. Examiners looked for signs of effeminacy or open admissions of homosexual activity. Obviously, recruits who regarded themselves as homosexuals found such filtering mechanisms easy to circumvent.[6] The existence of the screening process, however, alerted all recruits to the notion that persons identified as homosexuals existed and would be singled out for rejection by the military. Homosexual identity swiftly translated into the judgment of unfitness for service. Then when Kinsey's pioneering post WWII work, *Sexual Behavior in the Human Male* (1948), revealed a much higher incidence of homosexual behavior in the general population than previously had been believed, screening for homosexuals spread beyond the military to government agencies and then to schools.[7]

Two states in particular launched high-profile campaigns to rid the schools of homosexual employees. During the 1950s and 1960s, California and Florida enacted laws enabling officials to conduct investigations into homosexuals in school employment. A Florida congressional committee searched for homosexual teachers and then stripped them of their teaching licenses. Eventually as the lengthy effort closed down, the committee reported that "That the number of deviates among the teachers of Florida is proportionately low, and that in this regard Florida is substantially better off than many of her sister states with less rigid certification procedures which are now facing up to a serious problem of moral misconduct among teaching personnel."[8] In California, state law required police to notify both the state teacher licensure board and local superintendents when homosexual sting operations netted teachers. Such teachers lost their jobs immediately even if the charges later proved to be false or there was no evidence.[9] A homosexual identity, then, had become a potent liability to persons wishing to work in schools.

Eventually, the stigma associated with a homosexual identity had become so severe that persons known as homosexuals could not teach even if they had never engaged in same-sex sexual acts. In 1972, Joseph Acanfora, an openly gay student at Penn State University, encountered stiff resistance in his pursuit of a teaching license. Acanfora had belonged to a campus "homophile" organization, which some members of the university licensing committee believed made him unfit to teach. After persistent appeals, though, Acanfora received his credential and began teaching in Maryland. However, when the *New York Times* featured a story describing the great difficulty he had faced in getting his license, school officials in his district immediately transferred him out of the classroom and into a make-work administrative position. Acanfora maintained throughout that he had never engaged in sexual acts with other men, but that he did identify as gay. He launched a protracted legal battle that eventually procured greater rights for lesbian and gay teachers, but he could never regain his own teaching position. In the end, his identity as a gay man—rather than his behavior—kept him from the profession he had chosen.[10] He was not alone. A number of other high profile cases of the time confirmed that lesbian or gay identities rather than same-sex sexual activity constituted grounds for dismissal from teaching duties.[11]

Are lesbian or gay identities possible in the absence of same-sex sexual activity? At the turn of the twentieth century, such a question would have been regarded as absurd because although homosexual acts were understood to exist, homosexual identities generally were not. The question itself hints at deep disagreements about the fundamental nature of sexuality. Is sexual identity something innate and unchanging as the color of one's eyes? Is it socially constructed and therefore open to influence and context? Or is it a set of behaviors in which one might choose to engage?

How one answers these questions carries important implications. If LGBT status is considered biological or innate, then some liken it to race or sex. LGBT persons, the argument goes, should be granted civil rights just as would any other biologically distinct group that systematically experiences discrimination. On the other hand, some activists maintain that LGBT identity is not fixed or innate. Rather, anyone can sexually desire persons of the same sex. They argue that the real strength of the LGBT rights movement will be demonstrated when members do not need to rely on the "crutch" of arguing that identity is based on intrinsic qualities, but instead can rest confident that sexuality is fluid and ever-changing, that equal rights should be assured regardless of the fundamental nature of sexuality. The danger according to other LGBT activists, however, is that arguing for the fluid nature of sexuality can be used against the LGBT rights movement. Indeed, many religious conservatives also contend that sexuality is not an innate quality, but rather a moral choice—and a sinful one at that.

The outlines of this debate are important because they determine the extent to which same-sex desire is discussed in schools, tolerated among students, or even permissible for school workers. If sexual identity is seen as a fixed quality that establishes LGBT persons as a class seeking civil rights, then some limited mention of LGBT issues may become part of the explicit school curriculum and environment. However, if sexuality is regarded as a set of choices, then some conservative community constituencies may continue lobbying against any presence of LGBT issues in schools for fear that students will be corrupted.

Contemporary scholarship in social education calls for teachers and teacher educators to examine these issues squarely in their pedagogy. Citing recent reports of widespread harassment of students on account of gender and sexuality, Margaret Crocco argues that it is a moral imperative for teachers, particularly social studies educators, to confront homophobia in schools.[12] Left unmentioned, unexamined, and unchecked, students learn powerful lessons of the hidden gender and sexuality curriculum where, for example, manhood includes "patrolling the boundaries of sex role behavior and punishing those who deviate from these prescriptions."[13] Instead, she contends that social educators must challenge students to examine the common assumption that everyone is heterosexual, that homophobic slurs are acceptable, and that no one is lesbian or gay.[14] It is upon this examination that students can begin to consider what sexuality is, who defines acceptable sexuality, and how sexual identities are created and maintained. These issues may lie within the contested terrain of morality, but given the gravity of conditions for LGBT persons in schools, Crocco and other social educators contend that avoiding them is unacceptable. Alternatively, examining them offers rich opportunity for understanding what it means to be a citizen, to live mindfully in our society.[15]

Same-Sex Desire and Gender

Through much of the past half century, conventional wisdom has dictated that ambiguous or cross-gender behaviors and characteristics are tantamount to homosexuality. Essentially, the argument goes like this: An important part of one's gender concerns one's attractiveness to the other sex. If one is attracted to one's own sex, obviously gender is reversed or confused. The logic concludes that homosexuality can be controlled if gender can be regulated. Obviously, associations between gender and sexuality are deep and intertwined.

During the early decades of the century, critics wondered about the femininity of women teachers who remained single all their lives and who agitated for suffrage. One charged that, "The female possessed of masculine ideas of independence; the viragint who would sit in the public highways and lift up her pseudo-virile voice, proclaiming her sole right to decide questions of war or religion, or the value of celibacy and the curse of women's impurity, and that disgusting anti-social being, the female sexual pervert, are simply different degrees of the same class—degenerates."[16] As single women teachers fought for and won basic political and economic rights, their antagonists claimed that they had become manly, had lost their feminine charms, and not coincidentally, sometimes indulged in questionable sexual practices.

Meanwhile, male teachers in the larger profession of women suffered questions about their masculinity. By mid-century, this air of doubt typically included concerns that some male teachers might be homosexual. A number of researchers had produced detailed accounts describing how male homosexuals could be detected by their feminine characteristics. Men with high voices, who minced when they walked, who displayed artistic abilities, and who revealed their emotions easily were suspected of homosexuality. Such men were thought to be attracted to traditionally female professions, too, including teaching.[17] During the 1950s when the nation went on alert first for communists and then for homosexuals, experts warned parents to look out for homosexuals who might prey on children or otherwise corrupt them. As such, teachers received particular scrutiny. One important way that parents were told to recognize dangerous adults was by their cross-gender behavior. Male teachers who taught young children were suspect.[18]

By the early 1960s, teams of researchers published studies contending that influential adults often contributed to children becoming homosexuals. Mothers who coddled their sons supposedly caused their homosexuality. Conversely, without intervention, girls who displayed independent and tomboyish behaviors were thought likely to become lesbians.[19] Experts cautioned parents and teachers to insure the proper gender and sexual development of their charges. The 1968 book, *Growing up Straight: What Every Thoughtful Parent Should Know about Homosexuality*, assured readers that the "cancer" of homosexuality could be reversed or prevented. One of the critical factors contributing to homosexuality, the authors argued, was impaired gender development among children. Most importantly, parents should be alert for "any weakening of a child's sense of masculinity or femininity," the most significant evidence that a child was sliding slowly toward homosexuality.[20] Similarly, teachers and school counselors learned that they needed to watch for students indulging in cross-gender behaviors or characteristics and then to find ways to interrupt these patterns.[21] To assist in the effort, schools purchased and screened a number of life adjustment films produced during the 1950s and 1960s that aimed to help adolescents develop proper gender identities. Girls were cautioned to avoid the tomboyish activities of their earlier years and to cultivate their feminine qualities. Boys were shown how to be manly, but not to stray toward recklessness, rebelliousness, or irresponsibility.[22]

By the early 1980s, a conservative Christian psychologist, George Alan Rekers, had become an influential figure in the fight to keep youth from growing into homosexuals.[23] In his books and articles he argued that male homosexuals had manifested feminine qualities in their childhoods. Conversely, he contended that, "there is a pattern of masculine identification and masculine role adoption by girls in childhood which can be distinguished from tomboyism and which places the girl at high risk for homosexual temptation in the teen-age years and adulthood."[24] Thus, if parents noticed when their children strayed into non-traditional gender development, then effective interventions could be arranged. In boys, parents were told to watch for "dressing in feminine clothing," "using feminine body gestures and gait," "talking with a high femininelike voice and/or talking predominantly about feminine topics instead of masculine ones," or "taking a female role in play constantly." The fairly predictable watch-list for girls included "repeatedly refusing to wear girls' clothing, jewelry, or cosmetics," "using masculine gestures and gait," or "projecting her voice to a masculinelike tone and/or predominantly talking about male activities."[25]

Rekers explained that, "in some cases, it is necessary to introduce treatment procedures for the child in school." Boys needed to be coached patiently in learning proper athletic behaviors. And school workers needed to model correct "sex-roles."[26] Homosexual teachers presented a grave threat to children, he warned, because they could not model correct gender behaviors and characteristics. He admonished parents to be especially wary of the gay rights movement because, as he described it, one of their main purposes was to "promote changes in sex-role stereotyping."[27]

Rekers eventually figured prominently in establishing "gender identity disorder" (GID) as a pathology recognized by the American Psychiatric Association. Individuals were diagnosed with GID if they demonstrated gender-variance or wished to have sex reassignment surgery or hormones. Gay activists later would protest that although the APA had removed homosexuality from its *Diagnostic and Statistical Manual of Mental Disorders* in 1973, its inclusion of GID amounted to a backdoor way to "pathologize transgender people and 'gender-variant' youth— i.e., those children who exhibit behavior that may be viewed as 'pre-homosexual' or 'pre-transsexual.'"[28] Rekers' research on preventing or suppressing GID led to his leadership in religious organizations that, to this day, endeavor to convert LGBT persons into gender-conforming heterosexuals. Much of Rekers' published work through the years has stressed his view that adults in children's lives must clearly demonstrate normal gender behaviors and characteristics. Otherwise, children would develop what he called "sexual problems."[29]

Transgressing the bounds of "gender-appropriateness" cost one West Virginia teacher her job in 1983. School officials told Linda Conway, a kindergarten teacher, that her demeanor was not feminine enough. Her school district dismissed her because, as officials maintained, she had developed a "reputation in the community" for being a lesbian even though she staunchly asserted her heterosexuality. Conway explains that she was fired because "I wasn't prone to wearing dresses. I'm not feminine to begin with. I'm heavy-set, and I wouldn't look good in some of the things those petite women wear." She argued that, given her working conditions, she needed to wear comfortable clothing. "I taught in cafeterias, and I had to lean over tables to teach, so I wore pants. They were colder rooms, too, so I wore a lot of blazers and sweaters. Even though I had long hair, I still looked too 'manly' to them." Apparently Conway's clothing provoked rumors. In response, the superintendent attempted to transfer Conway, but his bid failed on procedural grounds. When parents circulated a petition to pressure school officials to fire her, the superintendent hastily imposed a dress code requiring her to "wear a dress at least twice a week, no boots or manly clothes."[30]

Finally, during the 1970s, two teachers in high-profile cases were dismissed from their positions when they underwent sex-change surgery. Paula Grossman, formerly Paul Grossman, was fired from her New Jersey band teaching position after her surgery. Courts upheld the administrative decision to fire her, explaining that students would suffer psychologically from having a teacher whose sex had changed.[31] The nature of the supposed suffering was not elaborated. Similarly, Steve Dain, formerly Doris Richards, a physical education teacher, was dismissed following his surgery.[32] In both cases, school administrators claimed that by definition, the teachers were violating their gender roles by becoming the other sex—and by extension, their sexual identities were called into question. Grossman, for example, remained happily married after her surgery. However, because she then was married to a woman, she was thought to be a lesbian, a charge that Grossman denied.[33] The case of transsexual teachers, then, illustrates clearly the persistent and deep connections between gender and sexual identity in popular thinking.

By and large, schools remain gender-polarized institutions. Female and male students typically experience in vastly different ways their playtime, athletics, courses, extracurricular activities, and school rituals such as homecoming celebrations. In parallel with students, school workers also experience a deeply gender-polarized environment. Women still comprise the overwhelming majority of teachers, especially those of younger children, while men are more likely to teach high school subjects such as math and science, to coach varsity athletics, and to assume administrative positions. An important factor in the persistence of gender polarization is the largely unquestioned and continuing association in popular thinking of queer identity and cross- or ambiguous gender behaviors and characteristics. People in schools who test the bounds of gender-appropriateness risk being thought lesbian or gay, with all of the attendant consequences. As long as persons who desire those of the same sex are singled out for discrimination, harassment, and social ostracism, and as long as same-sex desire is conflated with gender-inappropriateness, then homophobia will help hold sexism in place.[34] Instead, social educators recently have called for closer attention to these intersections of gender and sexuality. By provoking students to question what gender and sexuality are—as well as how they are connected—then dangerous assumptions, sexism, and homophobia can be deconstructed and possibly rendered less virulent.[35]

Modeling Sexuality and Gender

Throughout the past century, schools have labored to hire teachers and administrators who model conventional sexuality and gender. These efforts have been provoked by periodic public perceptions that schools have failed students in their sexual and gender development. In response, hiring and other personnel practices have shifted to demonstrate strong commitment to promoting normative sexualities and genders.

At the turn of the century, single, widowed, and divorced women accounted for the overwhelming majority of all teachers in the country.[36] When critics blamed the schools for high male student dropout rates as well as for supposedly turning the few remaining boys into mollycoddles, districts campaigned for male teachers. However, by that time, few men were willing to accept the low wages, the lack of independence, and the difficult working conditions that accompanied teaching careers, especially when they enjoyed a host of other employment options. Spinster women continued to hold the majority of teaching positions for decades. Slowly, though, as public awareness of lesbianism grew during mid-century, concern mounted that many of the nation's teachers might somehow be sexually suspect, and consequently threaten the proper sexual development of their students. After WWII, this concern outweighed the tremendous benefit that inexpensive and relatively well-educated single women traditionally had performed. School districts reacted by lifting their bans on married women teachers. Then, they essentially stopped hiring single women, opting instead to hire married women to fill teaching vacancies. By 1960, the ratio of married to single women teachers greatly exceeded that of women in the general workforce, a clear sign that schools no longer wanted spinster teachers.[37]

Meanwhile, schools still wanted to hire men, but few men found the work desirable. School boards enticed male candidates to apply with the promise of rapid advancement into administrative positions offering much higher salaries, greater authority, increased independence, and substantially more community respect. For these positions, especially superintendencies, though, not just any man would do. Schools sought notably masculine men who were athletic, sizeable—and married.[38] During the Cold War hunt for homosexuals in the military, government, and schools, school boards avoided any possible taint of homosexuality among their administrators when they hired such manly men. Besides, some school administrators in turn were required to screen teaching candidates to minimize the possibility of hiring homosexuals. Who better to do this than demonstrably heterosexual school leaders? During these decades, the proportion of married male superintendents greatly exceeded that of married men in the general workforce.[39]

After WWII, men who wished to remain in the classroom rather than pursue administrative or coaching positions also needed to stay clear of any suspicion that they might be homosexuals. During the Florida and California witch-hunts for homosexual teachers in the 1950s and 1960s, investigators warned that such teachers might prey on their students. However, also of great concern was the fear that homosexual teachers would provide poor gender and sexual models for their students. Experts warned that strong female and weak male caregivers contributed to the homosexuality of their charges.[40]

Matters changed after the 1969 Stonewall Rebellion, during which LGBT persons openly resisted long-standing patterns of police harassment. Historians typically mark this event as the beginning of the modern gay rights movement in which persons claiming LGBT identities openly and collectively began resisting their social oppressions.[41] In the spirit of the movement, groups of LGBT teachers in New York City, San Francisco, Los Angeles, Denver, and Boston started organizing to increase awareness of their issues as well as to win basic rights and protections against discrimination.[42] As LGBT school workers increased their visibility, though, a vitriolic backlash movement brewed, one that tapped into decades-old panics about homosexual molestation of youth and fears that homosexual teachers might influence students to become homosexual, too.

Anita Bryant tapped this deep anxiety in 1977 when she warned Miami area residents that homosexual teachers posed a devastating threat to children. She led the charge against an ordinance protecting LGBT persons from general employment and housing discrimination and she did so by evoking the specter of schools forced to hire homosexual teachers. Bryant's "Save Our Children" campaign clearly focused on homosexual teachers. She explained her fears: "Public approval of admitted homosexual teachers could encourage more homosexuality by inducing pupils into looking upon it as an acceptable life-style."[43] A "Save Our Children" newspaper ad read: "This recruitment of our children is absolutely necessary for the survival and growth of homosexuality—for since homosexuals cannot reproduce, they must recruit, must freshen their ranks. . . . And who qualifies as a likely recruit: a 35-year-old father or mother of two . . . or a teenage boy or girl who is surging with sexual awareness?"[44]

A year later, Bryant's campaign inspired California Senator John Briggs to introduce a state initiative designed to rid the schools of LGBT school workers and their supporters. The "Briggs Initiative" stated:

> As a result of continued close and prolonged contact with schoolchildren, a teacher, teacher's aide, school administrator or counselor becomes a *role model* whose words, behavior and actions are likely to be emulated by students coming under his or her care. . . . For these reasons the state finds a compelling interest in refusing to employ and in terminating the employment of a schoolteacher, a teacher's aide, a school administrator or a counselor . . . who engages in public homosexual activity and/or public homosexual conduct directed at, or likely to come to the attention of, schoolchildren or other school employees.[45]

The wording of the initiative, then, clearly indicated a belief that school workers modeled sexuality for their students. In this case, those who were thought to be homosexual, who engaged in activism on behalf of LGBT rights organizations, or who were known to support the rights of LGBT persons were described as poor models for children. In one debate with a gay teacher, Briggs insisted, "If they're not good enough to get married, how are we to support the notion that they're to serve as role models when they can't bear children themselves?"[46] At the end of what became a bitter and protracted battle, the Briggs Initiative failed largely due to the well-organized, grass roots activism of a fledgling gay rights movement that had built broad coalitions of support.

Though over the past century, school workers have been hired partly based on the models they might provide for their students, the nature of that expected modeling has shifted. Early in the century when single women accounted for most teachers, male teachers were sought largely so they could offer masculine modeling for male students in ways that women were thought incapable. During mid-century hunts for homosexuals, single female and effeminate male teachers became suspect because they might model homosexuality and thus corrupt their students. And since the 1970s, highly visible public campaigns have called into question the employment of LGBT school workers who might model supposedly undesirable gender and sexual identities to their impressionable students. Since the 1970s, some municipalities and states have passed nondiscrimination laws that protect the rights of LGBT school workers; however, most states continue to justify their lack of such protections on grounds that school workers must serve as models of suitable gender and sexuality for their charges.

LGBT school workers, then, essentially have little protection against employment discrimination on account of their sexuality and/or gender presentation. Most conceal their LGBT identity at work to avoid dismissal, harassment, or a deteriorating work climate. Some, whose status as LGBT is known, refrain from discussing their sexuality and/or gender presentation at work. In such cases, these school workers and their school communities maintain a tacit bargain where the employee is left alone provided that nothing calls attention to her/his LGBT status. Even in states like California and Wisconsin, which have non-discrimination laws protecting LGBT persons, LGBT school workers still lose their jobs on account of their status and to win their jobs back, they must wage expensive, lengthy legal battles.[47] School workers who are allies of LGBT persons often face repercussions for their vocal support, too. With such a dangerous climate for LGBT and allied school workers, it is little wonder, then, that many teachers resist discussing issues related to sexuality and gender in their classes. Yet Margaret Crocco explains that the consequences of failing to confront these issues are too great for all members of the school community. Social educators can and must play an important role in helping students question the entrenched sexism and homophobia that haunt the halls of contemporary schools.[48]

Conclusion

Schools, then, have offered powerful forms of social education to help students form conventional sexual and gender identities. This has been true throughout the twentieth century and it remains so into the present. Most school workers continue to fear disclosing unconventional gender or sexual identities because they believe they could lose their jobs with little legal recourse. Consequently, they tend to remain quiet about issues related to sexuality and gender. This silence keeps school workers from challenging students to examine the basic nature of sexuality and gender, from debating their socially constructed aspects, from discussing the complex interconnections between them, and from coming to know something of the experiences of persons who identify as LGBT.

In contrast, however, students are claiming LGBT identities at younger ages than in the past and in their schools they are vocal about doing so. The 1990s have brought the rapid growth of gay/straight alliances at high schools around the country so that many LGBT, questioning, and allied teens are organizing to understand their identity, to socialize with supportive peers, and in many cases, to demand their civil rights.[49] Queer youth, then, have begun to alter the contours of sexual and gendered social education. Arguably, they have been able to win greater visibility, protection, and clout than have LGBT school workers. And they have done so by insisting on their basic rights as citizens. As such, organized LGBT students represent a shining example of the possibilities of social education.

Notes

1. I find instructive Margaret Crocco's broad description of social education: "We take social education to mean teaching and learning about how individuals construct and live out their understandings of social, political, and economic relations—past and present—and the implications of these understandings for how citizens are educated in a democracy." Margaret Smith Crocco, "Introduction," in *"Bending the Future to Their Will": Civic Women, Social Education, and Democracy,* eds. Margaret Smith Crocco and O. L. Davis, Jr. (Lanham, MD: Rowman & Littlefield, 1999), 1.
2. Jonathan Zimmerman, *Whose America? Culture Wars in the Public Schools* (Cambridge, MA: Harvard University Press, 2002).
3. J. R. de S. Honey, *Tom Brown's Universe: The Development of the English Public School in the Nineteenth Century* (New York: Quadrangle, 1977), 178.
4. Edward Stevenson, "1908: The Intersexes," in *Gay/Lesbian Almanac: A New Documentary,* ed. Jonathan Ned Katz (New York: Harper & Row, Publishers, 1983), 326–332, especially 329.
5. Jackie M. Blount, *Fit to Teach: Same-Sex Desire, Gender, and School Work in the Twentieth Century* (Albany, NY: SUNY Press, 2004).
6. Alfred C. Kinsey, Wardell B. Pomeroy, and Clyde E. Martin, *Sexual Behavior in the Human Male* (Philadelphia: W. B. Saunders Company, 1948), 621–622.
7. U.S. Senate, 81st Congress 2nd Session, Committee on Expenditures in the Executive Departments Document #241, "Employment of Homosexuals and Other Sex Perverts in Government," reprinted in *Government Versus Homosexual,* ed. Leslie Parr (New York: Arno Press, 1975), 4; Ralph H. Major, "New Moral Menace to Our Youth," *Coronet,* September 1950, 101–108.
8. Florida Legislative Investigation Committee, "Homosexuality and Citizenship" (1964), reprinted in *Government Versus Homosexuals,* ed. Leslie Parr (New York: Arno Press, 1975); R. O. Mitchell, *Report of the Florida Legislative Investigation Committee* (Tallahassee, FL: 1965), 8–9.
9. Karen M. Harbeck, *Gay and Lesbian Educators: Personal Freedoms, Public Constraints* (Malden, MA: Amethyst Press and Productions, 1997), 188–200.

10. "Acanfora Decision May Help Teachers," *The Advocate,* 10 April 1974, 19; "Lower Court Decision Stands: Court Refusal to Hear Acanfora Appeal May Be Hidden Victory," *The Advocate,* 20 November 1974, 20. Karen Harbeck describes this case fully in *Gay and Lesbian Educators,* 248–257.

11. "Gay Teacher Loses Appeal to High Court," *San Francisco Chronicle,* 4 October 1977, 1, 24; "Schools and School Districts: Admission of Status As a Homosexual by Teacher Held Sufficient Cause for Dismissal on the Basis of Immorality, Gaylord V. Tacoma School District No. 10, Wash. 2d, 559 P.2d 1340, Cert. Denied, 45 U.S.L.W. 3220 (1977)," *Journal of Family Law, University of Louisville School of Law* (1977–78): 129–134; "Fired Because of Rumor, Rural Teacher Fights Back," *The Advocate,* 21 June 1972, 1; Harbeck, *Gay and Lesbian Educators,* 244–248.

12. See for example, American Association of University Women, *Hostile Hallways: The AAUW Survey on Sexual Harassment in America's Schools* (Washington, DC: Author, 1993), which details a survey indicating a deep, pervasive culture of sexual harassment in schools, including homophobic slurs (especially 9–10, 19–20). More recently, Nan Stein's *Classrooms & Courtrooms: Facing Sexual Harassment in K-12 Schools* (New York: Teachers College Press, 1999) examines surveys, studies, and responses to school sexual harassment in the U.S. and abroad. Finally, Crocco cites *Hatred in the Hallways: Violence against Lesbian, Gay, Bisexual, and Transgender Students in U.S. Schools,* a report issued by the Human Rights Watch (New York: Author, 2001). This study, which is based on interviews with over 140 LGBT youth and 130 adults, indicates that LGBT youth experience profound ostracism, harassment, discrimination, and often violence on account of their sexuality and/or gender presentation.

13. Margaret Crocco, "Homophobic Hallways: Is Anyone Listening?" *Theory and Research in Social Education* 30 (Spring 2002), 220.

14. Crocco, "Homophobic Hallways," 217–232. Also, see Crocco's groundbreaking piece, "The Missing Discourse about Gender and Sexuality in the Social Studies," *Theory Into Practice* 40 (Winter 2001): 65–71.

15. Kathy Bickmore, "How Might Social Education Resist Heterosexism? Facing the Impact of Gender and Sexual Ideology on Citizenship," *Theory & Research in Social Education* 30 (Spring 2002): 198–216; Stephen Thornton, "Does Everybody Count as Human?" *Theory & Research in Social Education* 30 (Spring 2002): 178–189.

16. Quoted in George Chauncey, "From Sexual Inversion to Homosexuality: The Changing Medical Conceptualization of Female 'Deviance,'" *Salmagundi* 58–59 (Fall/Winter 1983): 141.

17. Kinsey's team warned, though, that such common accounts of the supposed connections between homosexuality and effeminacy in men were not based on rigorous scientific efforts. See Kinsey, et al., *Sexual Behavior in the Human Male,* 637–638.

18. Major, "New Moral Menace," 107.

19. Irving Bieber, *Homosexuality: A Psychoanalytic Study of Male Homosexuals* (New York: Basic Books, 1962); Ernest Havemann, "Homosexuality: Scientists Search for the Answers to a Touchy and Puzzling Question—Why?" *Life,* 26 (June 1964), 76–80; Vincent T. Lathbury, "Mothers and Sons: An Intimate Discussion," *Ladies' Home Journal* (February 1965), 43–45; and Lester David, "Our Son Was Different," *Good Housekeeping* (January 1966), 51, 113, 115, 120, 122–125.

20. Peter Wyden and Barbara Wyden, who wrote *Growing Up Straight: What Every Thoughtful Parent Should Know About Homosexuality* (New York: Stein and Day, 1968), 19, 23.

21. George Kriegman, "Homosexuality and the Educator," *Journal of School Health* 39, no. 5 (1969): 306–310.
22. Ken Smith, *Mental Hygiene: Classroom Films, 1945–1970* (New York: Blast Books, 1999).
23. See for example, *Shaping Your Child's Sexual Identity* (Grand Rapids, MI: Baker Book House, 1982); and *Growing Up Straight: What Families Should Know About Homosexuality* (Chicago: Moody Press, 1982).
24. Rekers, *Shaping*, 13.
25. Ibid., 141–142, 148.
26. Ibid., 166–167.
27. Rekers, *Growing Up Straight*, 35–36.
28. NGLTF, "NGLTF Statement on Gender Identity Disorder and Transgender People" (Washington, DC: NGLTF, December 11, 1996).
29. See for example, "The Essential Characteristics of the Father's Role for Child Adjustment and Family Strength," a paper he presented at a Congressional Hearing before the Select Committee on Children, Youth and Families, United States House of Representatives (Washington, DC, February 25, 1986), ERIC Document 275403.
30. Paula Krebs, "To Teach—Or Not to Teach: Rumor Can Get You Fired in West Virginia," *off our backs* (January 1985), 5.
31. "Transsexual Sues to Get Job," *The Advocate*, 18 December 1974, 16.
32. "Sex Change Case: State Upholds Firing of East Bay Teacher," *San Francisco Chronicle*, 10 January 1977.
33. Ibid.
34. Suzanne Pharr, *Homophobia: A Weapon of Sexism* (Little Rock, Arkansas: Chardon Press, 1988).
35. Crocco, "The Missing Discourse;" Bickmore, "How Might Social Education Resist Heterosexism?;" and Crocco, "Homophobic Hallways."
36. *Statistical History of the United States from Colonial Times to the Present* (Stamford, CT: Fairfield Publishers, 1965), 208; and John K. Folger and Charles B. Nam, *Education of the American Population: A 1960 Census Monograph* (Washington, DC: U.S. Bureau of the Census, 1967), 81.
37. Jackie Blount, *Destined to Rule the Schools: Women and the Superintendency, 1873–1995* (Albany, NY: SUNY Press, 1998), 91–110; and Folger and Nam, *Education of the American Population*, 81.
38. For example, see V. E. Leonard, "No Man's Land," *American School Board Journal* (September 1946): 21–22; and L. A. Zeliff, "Bachelor or Married Man as Small-Town Superintendent?" *American School Board Journal* (September 1947): 53, 86.
39. C. E. Feistritzer, *Profile of School Administrators in the United States* (Washington, DC: National Center for Educational Information, 1988). Also see David Tyack's compelling analysis of AASA yearbooks on the status of the superintendency in "Pilgrim's Progress: Toward a Social History of the School Superintendency, 1860–1960," *History of Education Quarterly* 16 (Fall 1976): 257–300.
40. Lathbury, "Mothers and Sons," 43–45.
41. Martin Duberman, *Stonewall* (New York: Dutton, 1993).
42. Marc Rubin, "History of the Gay Teachers Association," *Gay Teachers Association Newsletter* (January 1978), 1–4, Eric Rofes's private collection; David Lamble, "10th Anniversary: Gay Teachers Struggle for Right to Teach; Take on the City's School Board," *Coming Up* (June 1985), 5–6; "Minutes of June 17, 1976 Meeting," *Gay Teachers of Los*

Angeles, 26 June 1976, Eric Rofes' private collection; and "Political News," *Cheery Chalkboard*, Gay Teachers of Los Angeles (July 1978), 3, Eric Rofes' private collection.

43. Anita Bryant, *The Anita Bryant Story: The Survival of Our Nation's Families and the Threat of Militant Homosexuality* (Old Tappan, NJ: Fleming H. Revell Company, 1977), 114–115.

44. Quoted in Dudley Clendinen and Adam Nagourney, *Out for Good: The Struggle to Build a Gay Rights Movement in America* (New York: Simon & Schuster, 1999), 303.

45. Pat Donohue, "Initiative Measure to Be Submitted Directly to the Voters With Analysis," in "Briggs" file, June Mazer Collection; emphasis added.

46. Doyle McManus, "Briggs Debates Gay Teacher," *Los Angeles Times*, 26 October 1978, sec. 1, 3.

47. For example, see Elaine Herscher, "Even in the Bay Area, Gay Teachers are Taking a Risk," *San Francisco Chronicle*, 11 March 1998, A13.

48. Crocco, "Homophobic Hallways."

49. Dan Woog, *School's Out: The Impact of Gay and Lesbian Issues on America's Schools* (Boston: Alyson, 1995), 299–305; Kevin Jennings, "I Remember," in *One Teacher in 10: Gay and Lesbian Educators Tell Their Stories*, ed. Kevin Jennings (Los Angeles: Alyson, 1994), 19–28; Jessica Portner, "Creating a Safe Place," *Education Week*, 2 March 1994; and Gavin Daly, "Students Rally for Gay/Straight March," *Boston Globe*, 21 May 1995, 34.

12

Joseph Watras

HISTORIANS AND SOCIAL STUDIES EDUCATORS, 1893–1998

The social studies as a school subject developed through the sponsorship of the American Historical Association, and many experts contend that history should provide the center of any social studies program. Yet, historians and other scholars have complained that the social studies replaced the more academic courses in history. For example, in 1985, the historian, Diane Ravitch, argued that, after World War I, educators wanted students to learn to contribute to society rather than study subjects such as history that provided intellectual stimulation.[1] The same year, Arthur Powell and his co-authors asserted in *The Shopping Mall High School* that, by 1930, educators replaced the traditional courses of history with courses in social studies because they wanted to reduce the academic demands on students. Powell and his co-authors thought educators wanted high schools to provide custodial care for teenagers.[2] In 1988, Ravitch joined the Bradley Commission to protest that 15 percent of the high school students did not study either world history or western civilization.[3] In 1998, writing in response to the controversy four years earlier about the National History Standards, Gary B. Nash, Charlotte Crabtree, and Ross E. Dunn complained that by the mid-1930s, historians displayed little interest in the social studies as a school subject. According to Nash and his co-authors, historians concentrated on specialized research in university environments and ignored lower level education.[4] Finally, scholars have complained that state boards of education encouraged schools to ignore history. In 1998, with support from the Fordham Foundation, David Warren Saxe conducted an appraisal of history standards in 37 states. He concluded that most states lacked good history standards and that, as a result, most children never learned about their nation's heritage.[5]

To explain what they see as a shift away from history, many critics of the social studies draw on a metaphor employed by Herbert Kliebard. This image is one of a struggle among different types of scholars and educators seeking to dominate the curriculum in American schools.[6] For example, Saxe argues that from 1902 to 1916, three distinct groups battled over the teaching of history in the secondary schools. These groups included historians who wanted to maintain traditional programs, scholars who wanted to revise the traditional courses, and educators who wanted to reform all instruction in history.[7]

In order to think that groups of scholars or educators fought to control the curriculum, it is necessary to imagine such people as historians or educators as falling into distinct, uniform groups whose members held fast to specific aims and sought to have all schools affirm them. Few things in education are this clear. In this case, historians did not form a uniform group. Throughout the twentieth century, they argued among themselves as to how history should be conceived. At the same time, different social studies scholars or educators could not agree as to what constituted the social studies or how such lessons should be conducted. More significant, rather than stand apart as separate groups, many historians and educators cooperated and served together on several commissions to draft curricula aimed at reforming school practices.

If there was a pattern to the changes in the curricula, it did not come from disagreements among scholars as much as it came from the tendencies of social studies educators to imitate the ways certain historians chose to do their work. To illustrate the parallel changes among American historians and social studies educators, this chapter will compare reports during four periods. The first of these periods extends from 1890 to 1918. During this period, historians sought to make their discipline into a profession and the social studies emerged as a distinct set of courses. The second period includes the years surrounding the Great Depression when historians and social studies educators sought to use their studies to help individuals change the society. The third period is the era of what is called the Cold War in which Americans sought to overcome the threats they feared from communism. The fourth period is what might be called the civil rights movement and the subsequent conservative reaction. After the March on Washington in 1963, historians and social studies educators focused on the backgrounds of various ethnic and racial groups. But in the 1980s and 1990s, conservative historians and educators rebelled against what they saw as excessive concern with the daily lives of different peoples and urged historians and educators to return to the traditional studies of politics and international relations.

The Evolution of School Studies of History
during the 1890s and 1900s

In 1893, the National Education Association's Committee of Ten tried to determine what the appropriate subject matter should be for high school students. The committee had to coordinate the reports of nine conferences that were divided according to subject areas. One of the conferences, the Madison Conference, concerned itself with the instruction of history, civil government, and political economy. The historians in this conference decided that high school students should not study separate courses in civil government or political economy. Instead, they recommended that these subjects be integrated into various history courses. In all, they recommended that an elementary and high school program in history consist of at least six years of study that included biography, mythology, American history, Greek and Roman history, and English history. They wanted teachers to use textbooks written by experts in the subject that avoided accounts of military events or an outline of political discussions. Most texts used by schools did not meet these criteria nor did they facilitate outside reading and the preparation of topics. The historians in this conference urged teachers to use several sources and to use new methods of teaching such as one that they called the topical method. This method was so important that the committee members thought that, with the help of texts, the teachers could organize the courses so that different topics covered the necessary material.[8]

At the same time that educators tried to consolidate the instruction of school subjects, historians sought to organize their field. Although it was founded in 1884, the American Historical Association (AHA) was not a professional society at first. The bulk of the organization's constituency from 1890 to 1910 consisted of wealthy amateurs pursuing their own interests, and about 25 percent of the members held faculty positions in colleges. It was not until after World War I that the AHA required its presidents to be college professors who held doctorate degrees.[9]

In ways similar to those used by the NEA, the AHA sought to reinforce the educators' efforts to improve the instruction of history in secondary and elementary schools. Shortly after the NEA's Committee of Ten released its report, the AHA formed the Committee of Seven to survey the practices of secondary school history teachers in large cities and small towns and to make recommendations for college entrance requirements. In 1899, this committee released its report. The committee recommended that high schools offer four years of consecutive courses in ancient history, medieval and modern European history, English history and American history and civil government. Less enthusiastic about the topical method that the Madison committee had recommended, the AHA committee's members cautioned teachers against using the topical method alone because this would leave the students with unconnected information. Thus, the report of the Committee of Seven urged teachers to recognize the importance of good textbooks to maintain direction in the courses.[10]

A second committee from the AHA, the Committee of Eight, made similar recommendations about the elementary school curriculum. Released in 1909, this committee's report recommended that history teaching in the elementary schools focus around explanations of the development of American civilization. Thus, for example, studies of European history should show how people brought with them traditions and institutions when they crossed the Atlantic. Subjects that did not reflect directly on American life, such as explanations of ancient or medieval life, should demonstrate the universal heritage of humankind so the students would understand their own society.[11]

Similarities among the reports of the NEA's Madison Conference and the AHA's Committee of Seven, and the Committee of Eight derived, in part, from the fact that historians urging the same innovations served on the committees. For example, the Madison Conference included such innovative historians as Albert Bushnell Hart and James Harvey Robinson. Hart served as secretary for the Madison conference and as a member of the Committee of Seven. Most important, at about the same time that they served on these committees, Hart and Robinson championed changes in the study of history.

In 1896, Hart published the *Guide to the Study of American History* with his colleague, Edward Channing. Revised in 1912 with the help of Frederick Jackson Turner, this guide repeated the aims of historical study as determined by the Madison conference. For example, such studies aimed to cultivate the power of discrimination, strengthen logical abilities by following arguments, and improve judgment by encouraging students to compare sources. And, recognizing that historians wrote less about warfare or the development of forms of government and more about the social customs of people, Hart and his co-authors urged teachers to follow the historians by studying immigrants in factories and frontiers, and people on farms. Thus, the guide listed published books that teachers could use and subjects that students could pursue as topics. Seeking manageable subjects, Hart and his co-authors listed such topics as biographies for lower-level students and investigations of social institutions such as slavery in certain colonies for more advanced students that students could investigate using a variety of sources.[12]

James Harvey Robinson, who participated in the Madison Conference with Hart, had become famous for urging the development of what he called a new history. In a series of papers and articles, Robinson complained that historians did not help people understand changes in the past. To prove his point, he quoted six pages from a text about Italy whose author claimed to present the essential facts in due order. The material Robinson quoted was a mind-numbing list of minor kings who succeeded each other from 1309 until 1435. Despite his care in listing these relatively insignificant figures, the author barely mentioned Francesco Petrarca who Robinson credited with beginning the renaissance. Complaining that such histories did not enable people to understand their own situations, Robinson called for a new history that availed itself of the discoveries of anthropologists, economists, psychologists, and sociologists.[13]

Robinson became an important figure in the American Historical Association, and social studies educators followed him. When the NEA established the Commission on the Reorganization of Secondary Education, Robinson was a member of the Committee on the Social Studies, and his conception of the new history filled the report that the committee released in 1916.

The Committee on the Social Studies was part of the National Education Association's (NEA) Commission on the Reorganization of Secondary Education (CRSE). The CRSE grew out of a study of articulation between high schools and colleges that the NEA issued in 1911. Although the chairperson for that study, Clarence D. Kingsley, had been a mathematics teacher, his committee's report noted that many students could not successfully complete courses in mathematics and foreign languages. To allow more students to profit from high school studies the report asked that colleges accept social science and natural science in place of mathematics and foreign languages.[14]

The NEA named Kingsley as chair of the CRSE, and the report of the Committee on the Social Studies played an important part in the conception of education described in the CRSE's summary statement, Cardinal Principles of Secondary Education. This report recommended that students study the vocational areas they would like to pursue as careers. Since such programs could divide the students and separate them from each other, the CRSE urged schools to create opportunities such as athletics, social activities, and student government to bring the students together. More important, the summary statement recommended that the social studies should help students develop those qualities that would enable them to be a member of a neighborhood, a town, a state or a nation. Thus, history should treat the growth of institutions so that the students could appreciate their value, and geography could show the interdependence of human beings while showing their reliance on nature.[15]

The Committee on the Social Studies took the charges from the CRSE seriously. In its report, the members of the committee described the important aims of teaching history as helping the students develop strong and intelligent senses of patriotism and enabling the students to appreciate the contributions other nations made toward the advancement of civilization. To accomplish these aims, the committee's report quoted Robinson indicating that historians should help people understand the problems of the present. Although Robinson did not list the problems historians should explore, the committee members decided that teachers should relate instruction to those topics related to the life of the students. To illustrate how these principles could apply to the work of teachers, the report described a teacher in Philadelphia enlisting the students in an extended study of the influence Greek conceptions of art had on contemporary city planning and architecture. The lesson began with a discussion of some proposed city project. It moved to descriptions of the design of ancient Athens and the similarities among classical forms and contemporary designs.[16]

According to Edward Krug, the report of the Committee on the Social Studies preserved courses in history at a time when historians such as Carl Becker called for teachers to blend studies in history with exercises in economics, civics, and sociology.[17] Nonetheless, some contemporary historians claim that the 1916 social studies report reflects the desires of educators rather than historians. For example, Robert D. Barr, James Barth, and S. Samuel Shermis claim that the difference between the Committee of Seven and of Eight and the NEA Committee on Social Studies was that they had different types of members. These commentators argue that academic scholars dominated the AHA Committees of Eight and Seven while educators prevailed in the NEA committee. Barr, Barth, and Shermis add that academic scholars were more likely to favor a textbook orientation than were teachers who faced students daily.[18]

In making their complaint, Barr, Barth, and Shermis overlook the fact that both of the AHA's committees claimed that the majority of their members had been teachers or school administrators. More important, it is not clear that the direction of the report from the NEA differed considerably from that of the AHA. The reports were similar in at least two ways. First, the material the different reports recommended for teachers to cover seems similar. In 1894, the Madison Conference recommended students take at least six history courses while, in 1916, the Committee on the Social Studies substituted a course in civics and another in geography. But civics and political economy appeared in the courses the Madison Conference labeled history, and history appeared in courses the Committee on Social Studies called geography and civics. Second, the recommended methods of teaching seemed similar. In 1894, the historians urged teachers to consider using such innovations as the topical approach that called for students finding information and making judgments. In 1916, social studies educators urged the use of the same topical approach, but they wanted the topics to come from the present life and interests of the students.

Educators and Historians in the 1920s and 1930s

Many social studies teachers ignored the call to allow students to investigate conditions in their society. For example, in 1923, Harold Rugg complained that, although students spent considerable time on the social studies subjects, teachers did not present the material in ways that would facilitate an understanding of social conditions. He noted that the students learned the rise and fall of kings, the details of military battles, and the provisions for peace treaties in history classes. Similarly, he found that the students learned lists of facts unrelated to social developments in the countries in geography. Although courses in civics promised to open the curriculum to investigations of social problems, Rugg determined that these classes presented the details of the U.S. Constitution and the composition of federal, state, and local government. Rugg suggested that, instead of dividing the social sciences into such separate subjects as history, geography, and civics, schools should offer a unified, continuous social studies curriculum organized around social problems. He added that textbook authors should present information about problems and issues rather than present the material in such divisions of subject matter as sociology, political science, or economics.[19]

Rugg took his own advice. In 1927, he began writing and publishing textbooks, workbooks, and teachers' guides. By 1940, he had completed eight volumes in the elementary school course and six in the secondary along with workbooks and teachers' guides.[20]

While Rugg's call for a unified social studies appeared radical to many educators, it did not differ widely from the proposals that the Madison Conference made in 1894 and the Committee on the Social Studies made in 1916. Although these groups recommended that distinct subject matter courses remain, they had suggested that teachers organize the studies around topics the students could investigate. Rugg's innovation was to take the idea of topics, turn them into social problems, and make the problems the center of the curriculum.

More important to this chapter, as social studies educators sought to make instruction relevant to students' lives, the so-called new historians began to occupy prominent positions in the American Historical Association. In 1929, James Harvey Robinson served as the president of the AHA. Like-minded historians followed him in this office. From these positions, the new historians called for more attention to their perspectives and thereby caused controversy among the members.

In his presidential address, Robinson claimed that World War I had proved the historian's old ways to be inadequate. Robinson contended that historians working during the turn of the century accumulated information about the past and presented it as separate from contemporary life. According to Robinson, when historians worked in this way, they could not resist the propaganda of the day and endorsed excessive anti-German acts. Contending that the failures of earlier historians caused their successors to act differently, Robinson noted that in the 1920s, historians did not separate their work from then-contemporary events and sought to determine the ways the daily actions of people modified their societies.[21]

Two years later, in 1931, one of Robinson's supporters, Carl Becker, used his presidential address to the AHA to emphasize what he saw as the changes in the historians' mission. Entitled "Everyman His Own Historian," Becker claimed that historians had a special aim to preserve and perpetuate social traditions. This meant that historians had to write stories from which people could derive significant meanings. As a result, he criticized the effort of historians to be scientific, to present objective facts, and to expect ideas to come from this presentation. He recommended that historians help members of the wider public to understand contemporary conditions.[22]

Charles Beard, a historian who had written several texts with Robinson, continued Becker's refutation of scientific historians when he delivered his presidential address to the AHA in 1934. Entitling his speech "Written History as an Act of Faith," Beard acknowledged that historical thought should be ordered by knowledge, criticism, and the scientific method. But he asserted that all historical accounts reflected the biases of the historian who wrote them. As a result, Beard called on historians to realize the intellectual and moral perils implicit in selecting a topic, organizing evidence, or presenting conclusions and to recognize that these acts represented faith in one's perspective.[23]

Beard's address sparked controversy. At the next meeting of the AHA, Theodore Clark Smith challenged Robinson, Becker and Beard. Entitled "The Writing of American History from 1884 to 1935," Smith's paper claimed that historians writing during the fifty years under review took different approaches but shared an intellectual assumption. They believed themselves to be searching for positive evidence and thought this evidence would direct their conclusions. Smith added that Beard's call to historians to base their work on bold philosophic statements repudiated the nonpartisan search for truth and would extinguish the noble dream on which was based the American Historical Association.[24]

Smith's criticisms represented an important and fairly widespread view. During the next meeting of the AHA, Beard countered in a paper entitled "That Noble Dream" in which he contended that Smith's desire to engage in a nonpartisan search for truth was impossible and that it had never been the official credo of the AHA. Instead, Beard contended that the AHA members took different perspectives in their work. According to Beard, such pluralism should continue and he called for the AHA to encourage all historians to acknowledge the philosophic perspectives within which they worked. Beard believed that historians should take many different approaches, including the scientific approach, and dispute their findings among themselves because he thought such openness and fair competition of ideas would result in a more objective body of historical work than would come from historians agreeing to use one perspective.[25]

As the new historians began to dominate the AHA, they reconsidered the way history should be taught in schools. In 1923-1924, a survey by the AHA showed that teachers and school administrators believed the recommendations in the reports by national organizations such as the NEA and the AHA to be inadequate because they did not suggest how to deal with the changing social conditions and the increasing numbers of students. To aid the school people, the AHA gathered funds from such foundations as the Carnegie Foundation, and in 1929, set up the Commission on the Social Studies. The first thing this commission set out to do was to draft a statement of the proper objectives of the social sciences in schools.[26]

In 1932, Charles Beard wrote the statement of objectives for the commission. He claimed the purpose of the social sciences was to create rich, many-sided personalities in the students. Although this statement derived from a group of historians, Ravitch argued that it contributed to the denigration of history as a course of study because, to her, no other group would pursue such a goal.[27]

When Ravitch suggests that Beard's conception of the aim of the social studies makes no sense, she overlooks the ways that the ideal of creating many-sided personalities fit Beard's conception of history as an act of faith. First, Beard did not claim that the social sciences should remain distinct nor did he claim they should be integrated. Since historians, economists, and political scientists used each others' disciplines, these fields blended. Yet, Beard thought that the fields had distinct centers on which the scholars concentrated. Second, since the world was constantly changing, he could not determine precisely what the students should learn. He contended that students should hold sufficient information, acquire appropriate skills, develop proper habits and attitudes, build willpower, maintain courage, as well as enhance their imaginations and aesthetic appreciations. But, Beard added that these were not simple things to teach or to understand. For example, every country expected civics courses to teach students to develop the attitude of patriotism. While most political institutions implied that conformity to organizational requirements was a part of good citizenship, Beard argued that, in times of change, social inventiveness was more important. As a result, he concluded that the emphasis in the instruction in the social sciences had to be on freedom of opinion and the liberation of intelligence.[28]

Critics praised Beard's description of the *Charter for the Social Sciences,* and it sold well. Despite the opportunity to gain a considerable sum of money, Beard donated the royalties from this book to the AHA.[29] But, in 1934, praise turned to criticism when the Commission released its *Conclusions and Recommendations.* Most of the criticism focused on a section entitled the "Frame of Reference" wherein the report claimed that, "Cumulative evidence supports the conclusion that, in the United States as in other countries, the age of individualism and *laissez faire* in economy and government is closing and that a new age of collectivism is emerging."[30] Statements such as this led such educators as Franklin Bobbitt to protest that the Commission had communistic intentions.[31] Boyd Bode complained that the Commission contradicted its desire to enable students to develop their intelligence in atmospheres free of pressure to conform by calling for increased social planning. If people were intelligent and there was a need for social planning, Bode added that they should be allowed to recognize the need for the planning on their own.[32] And, in 1936, U.S. Representative Thomas L. Blanton of Texas made lengthy accusations about Frank Ballou, superintendent of Washington, D.C. schools. Blaton said that Ballou conspired to turn the schools into centers of communist indoctrination. The evidence Blanton used against Ballou was that he had been a member of the AHA Commission.[33]

Fortunately for the Commission, one of its members found a method that could deflect the conservative attacks and still hold out the possibility that the study of the social sciences could lead to social reconstruction. In 1936, Leon Marshall, author of several history texts, and his daughter, Rachel Marshall Goetz, published the thirteenth part of the report of the Commission on the Social Studies. Entitling their book *Curriculum-making in the Social Studies,* Marshall and Goetz offered a proposal for organizing the social studies. In line with Beard's earlier statement of the goal of the social studies, Marshall and Goetz felt that the social studies enabled students to develop well-integrated and full personalities because these studies helped students understand their society, showed how they could participate in it, and encouraged them to do so. Marshall and Goetz believed that the social studies could accomplish these goals if the students learned about the ways of living that were common to all societies. Acknowledging the difficulties in determining what processes all societies shared, Marshall and Goetz suggested the groups of fundamental human activities included adjusting to the external world, continuing biologically, guiding human motivation, developing social organization, directing cultural improvement, and molding personality.[34]

Rugg's idea of organizing the textbooks around social problems was less successful. He claimed that he collected a four foot long shelf of criticisms, most of which appeared from 1939 to 1940, as a direct result of his organizing theme. Since Rugg organized his texts around pressing problems in contemporary life, critics complained that his books convinced the students that life in America had failed.[35] As a result, the critics claimed he was an un-American traitor, and Rugg did not revise his textbook series in subsequent years.[36]

Although organizing the texts around social problems was simple, it may not have been as helpful as Rugg thought. For example, in writing the *Charter for the Social Sciences,* Beard warned against the problem-centered method of teaching because there were no assurances that the problems before the country at one time would remain in the future, and there were no ways to predict what would be the pressing concerns in the years to come. Worse, Beard added that there were no possible solutions for many social difficulties.[37]

According to the contemporary historian, Peter Novick, despite the extensive effort Beard and his colleagues put into the Commission on the Social Studies, the AHA never officially accepted or endorsed its report.[38] But Novick's assertion seems incorrect because the AHA continued its support of the social studies. In 1934, the AHA assumed responsibility for editing the magazine, *The Social Studies,* for teachers of history, social studies, and social sciences. This became the journal for the National Council for the Social Studies (NCSS). In 1937, the AHA relinquished its responsibility for editing *The Social Studies,* and the NCSS established the journal, *Social Education,* aimed at junior high school and high school teachers, as its official journal. Unlike the *American Historical Review,* the official journal of the AHA, *Social Education* carried articles debating the nature of the social studies, evaluating its aims, and describing appropriate methods of instruction.

More important, Novick claims that when the College Entrance Examination Board (CEEB) established a Commission on History that presented its report in 1937, the CEEB's commission paid little attention to the reports of the AHA's Commission for the Social Studies and reinforced the teaching of history as a separate subject. Novick claims that the CEEB overlooked the social studies and endorsed historical studies that included social, political, and economic subjects.[39]

Novick's account attracted followers. For example, while describing the effect of culture wars on the teaching of history, Gary Nash and his colleagues repeat Novick's claim that the members of the AHA ignored the Commission on Social Studies and separated themselves from elementary and secondary school issues.[40]

Unfortunately, Novick's description appears to be incorrect because the CEEB report to which Novick refers does not overlook the social studies. In 1934, the CEEB commission defined history in ways that made it possible for students to study history in a manner consistent with the social studies. The commission defined history as the study of human beings in society from their beginnings to the present day and added that the study should be undertaken in as broad a manner as possible. Although the commission warned against exaggerating the tendency to use history to explain current events or conditions, it asked for such courses to impart an understanding of the problems people in all societies have faced. In describing the curriculum, the CEEB report recommended four courses: the history of modern Europe, history of Europe until the sixteenth century, American history, and a course in contemporary civilization. In describing the methods of teaching these history courses, the CEEB commission recommended organizing the information in the ways that Marshall and Goetz had done in *Curriculum-making in the Social Studies*.[41]

Historians and Social Studies Educators after World War II

As the nation moved into the period known as the Cold War, historians abandoned the relativism and presentist orientation that Robinson, Becker, and Beard had urged. Instead, such historians as Richard Hofstadter, Arthur Schlesinger, Jr., and Daniel J. Boorstin repudiated their youthful sympathies for left-wing causes, decried the influences of communism, and reinterpreted American political traditions in ways that celebrated the common climate of American opinion.[42]

According to Peter Novick, the revisionist historians during the post war years displayed counter-progressive tendencies. They rejected the idea that historians should clearly expose their biases, and claimed that earlier writers such as Becker and Beard had used this notion to disguise faulty scholarship. The consensus historians sought to overcome the idea that scholarship had to illuminate present-day conditions. And in an effort to affirm the virtues of the American ideal, they portrayed such dissident groups as the agrarian populists active in the late nineteenth century as backward-looking, book-burning nativists.[43]

At the same time, a history professor at the University of Illinois, Arthur E. Bestor, Jr. started a campaign against what he called anti-intellectualism in the schools. According to Hazel Hertzberg, most of Bestor's complaints fell upon what was called life adjustment education. He directed few attacks against the social studies. Yet, she adds that in 1956, he founded the Council for Basic Education to which he drew the support of such historians as Hofstadter. And by 1966, the NCSS included Bestor's essays in yearbooks the organization published to help teachers encourage critical thinking in the social studies.[44]

Hertzberg contends that the most important influence in the Cold War was the result of the *Sputnik* crisis. In 1957, the Soviet Union sent a satellite into space. Claiming that the United States had fallen behind in the arms race, commentators blamed the schools. In response, the U.S. Congress passed the National Defense Education Act to enhance the instruction of mathematics and science. To Hertzberg, the important set of idea for these curriculum reforms came from Jerome Bruner's book, *The Process of Education*, that reported the results of a conference of scientists at Woods Hole, Massachusetts in 1959. The significant idea that Bruner proposed was that academic specialists create the textbooks and the curricula for elementary and secondary schools in ways that would encourage students to discover the structure of the subject matters or disciplines involved.[45]

In 1961, the National Science Foundation (NSF) funded two curriculum projects in the behavioral sciences, and the following year, the U.S. Office of Education announced its intention to support what it called "Project Social Studies" to encourage curriculum reform. By 1965, there were twelve project centers and other NSF programs such as Bruner's own effort to design "Man: A Course of Study" (MACOS). She claims that two scholars, Edwin Fenton and John M. Good named these efforts the "new social studies."[46]

Hertzberg argues that the new social studies programs shared similar aims. For example, the teachers sought to have children explore some topic in depth rather than cover an organized range of information in the manner of textbooks. But several problems resulted from this effort to illuminate the structure of the disciplines. The difficulties included an inability to develop materials that could move among general topics expanding from grade level to grade level. Instead, the lessons flowed within specific sets of materials. Further, oftentimes, the materials ignored the ways the subject disciplines could relate to each other, and the exercises did not help the students understand such ideals as citizenship, that had been the traditional task of the social studies.[47] According to Peter Dow, Bruner's effort to create the new social studies through MACOS fell into disfavor because conservative politicians attacked it for criticizing traditional social values.[48] But in the meantime, historians changed their approaches.

Historians and Educators during the Civil Rights Movement and the Conservative Reaction

After the 1963 march on Washington, historians and educators broke with the effort to portray American history as a movement of similar ideals. Instead, they wrote more about the problems of minorities and the need for action to reshape society. For example, in 1970, Howard Zinn sought to explain the method of what he called radical history. Zinn wanted to write history in ways that extended human sensibilities and caused them to take actions to improve the society. He thought that an important step in this effort was to intensify and sharpen people's perception of how bad things are for what he called the victims in the world. Praising the *Autobiography of Malcolm X* and the autobiography of Frederick Douglass, Zinn urged historians to add depth to problems that might seem transitory. To provide this dimension, Zinn urged historians to take the perspectives of the underdog. This meant that historians had to eschew the traditional tendency to remain privileged observers and to ignore the appeal of being objective. Zinn did not worry that such a posture would lead to biased accounts. For example, he argued that historians had used plantation diaries to write histories of slavery. As a result, most available histories of slavery came from the perspectives of the plantation owners. Telling the story from the perspectives of the slaves would fill out the story, balance the scales, and pull people from their lethargy.[49]

As Zinn urged historians to take a radical stance, social studies educators claimed that schools had to help children learn how the many different groups in U.S. society interacted. The hope was that such lessons would benefit all children whether they belonged to a minority group or not because they would learn to be more tolerant. One proposal came from James Banks, who urged that schools adopt what he called ethnic studies.[50]

According to Banks, the criterion for selecting the content of an ethnic studies course was whether the material would enable students to develop valid generalizations about their social world and to acquire the skills to influence public policy. During the study of minority cultures, Banks argued, students could learn that human beings have the same basic needs but that people in different groups learn to satisfy them in different ways. Banks thought such lessons in what he called cultural literacy were important for White children since White ethnic groups tended to think of their culture as superior to all others. He hoped that when White students understood ethnic minorities, they would appreciate the basic humanness of minority group members.[51]

Banks wanted ethnic studies to have an interdisciplinary perspective. That is, he believed students should consider ethnic problems from such disciplines as anthropology, political science, and geography. When Banks selected the important concepts that anthropology could lend to ethnic studies, he listed such ideas as cultural diversity that required many African Americans to speak Standard English on the job and Black English at home. At the same time, Banks warned about the use of history in ethnic studies cautioning teachers to help students uncover the biases of historians. He complained that history was written by the victors and not by the vanquished. As a result, he warned against students reading histories of Native Americans written by White historians who had little empathy for the culture. To correct this flaw, he urged that history be taught through the eyes of the minority.[52]

In the 1980s and 1990s, more traditional historians complained that the efforts of radical historians to focus on topics such as feminist studies or gay and lesbian concerns pushed out research on the changes of governments from university presses, historical association meetings, and refereed journals. These historians charged that this new social history threatened to transform the discipline of history from efforts to understand the rise and fall of empires, states, and republics into a series of vignettes about every day life. As a result, in 1998, several prominent historians joined together to form The Historical Society. This group dedicated itself to restore what these individuals considered free and open historical study.[53]

When The Historical Society published a collection of essays to explain its aims, Ravitch submitted an essay describing her efforts as U.S. Assistant Secretary of Education to change the national standards for the teaching of history in ways that agreed with the aims of The Historical Society. She complained that the controversy over the standards drawn up from 1991 to 1993 about the teaching of history caused the federal government and many states to avoid teaching history in favor of the more acceptable social studies.[54]

Before the conservative historians formed The Historical Society, the Lynde and Harry Bradley Foundation in 1987 had funded a commission to explore the conditions that would contribute to the effective teaching of history and to make recommendations on the role history should play in the curriculum. Named the Bradley Commission, the group included former presidents of all major professional associations in history, winners of prestigious prizes for writing and scholarship, and classroom teachers. Ravitch was among the participants.

The report of the Bradley Commission complained that 15 percent of the high school students in the United States did not take any American history courses and nearly half did not enroll in courses in either world history or western civilization. The report added that history was not the only subject to suffer dilution because, since 1982, several commissions had called for more attention to the central academic core of the curriculum. Nonetheless, the Bradley commission claimed to be the first commission to study the place of history in the contemporary curriculum. The commission members asserted that the discipline of history enabled students to understand change and to recognize the continuities between eras in the past and the present time. As a result, the commission members reasoned that history could enhance personal growth among the students by offering a sense of identity and it could encourage intelligent citizenship by providing different examples of virtue, courage, and wisdom. Thus, the commission report recommended that the social studies curriculum in elementary schools be centered on history. For grades seven through twelve, the commission recommended four years of historical studies. Although the commission did not name what history courses students should take, the members offered six themes these classes should cover: cultural diffusion; human interaction and the environment; values, beliefs, and institutions; conflict and cooperation; comparisons of developments such as feudalism or slavery; and patterns of social and political interaction.[55]

According to Gary Nash, the report of the Bradley Commission met almost no criticism. Nash contends that most Americans accepted the findings and most historians responded positively to its conclusions. He adds that the report encouraged teachers to shift from the social studies approach and focus the entire curriculum, especially in elementary schools, on historical studies.[56]

Despite Nash's assertion that the Bradley report was widely accepted, several educators complained about the report. For example, Stephen J. Thornton claimed that the Bradley Commission ignored the concerns with processes of learning that social studies educators had pursued since the 1960s. Thornton added that teachers did not accept the Bradley Commission's report. According to Thornton, there was little evidence that classroom teachers had ever accepted any curriculum reports and changed their practices as a result.[57]

Even if Nash were correct, he must explain how the history approach differed from the process approach to the social studies that Marshall and Goetz had recommended in 1936 or the current standards of the National Council of Social Studies (NCSS). That is, the six themes that the Bradley Commission recommended as the structure of all history courses seem similar to the processes of social groups that Marshall claimed should provide the framework for courses in the social studies. And they appear similar to the ten thematic strands that form the basis of the standards that the NCSS approved in 1994. For example, the theme of cultural diffusion that the Bradley Commission recommended sounds very much like the process of directing cultural improvement that Marshall and Goetz listed as one of the five processes common to all societies. And it appears identical to the thematic strand the NCSS entitled "People, Places, and Environments."[58]

Conclusion

In the twentieth century, historians and social studies educators followed similar patterns to reform their work. While historians sought different ways to illuminate social changes, social studies educators imitated the different approaches that historians took in hopes that the educational reforms would make the school lessons more relevant to the students.

In 1981, Hazel Hertzberg claimed that the reforms among social studies educators came as a result of the conditions in classrooms. According to Hertzberg, during different periods of the twentieth century, reformers tried to replace student recitation with some sort of student inquiry. Yet, she added that recitation persisted as the popular classroom style. To her, the problem was that teachers wanted the students to follow textbooks because such methods of instruction kept the students busy and quiet. The problem was that activities involving student inquiry could become chaotic.[59]

While there may be truth to Hertzberg's point about the continual reappearance of some method of student activity or inquiry in social studies reforms, those changes also take specific directions, such as the recommendation for teachers to focus on minority groups or on changes in governments. These changes in the direction of classroom materials seemed to come from educators' desires to imitate the ways that prominent historians wanted to do their work. Thus, it seems that in the twentieth century there was a type of parallel development among historians and social studies educators.

Notes

1. Diane Ravitch, *The Schools We Deserve: Reflections on the Educational Crisis of Our Times* (New York: Basic Books, 1985), 118–129.

2. Arthur G. Powell, Eleanor Farrar, and David K. Cohen, *The Shopping Mall High School: Winners and Losers in the Educational Marketplace* (Boston: Houghton Mifflin Co., 1985), 251–252.
3. Bradley Commission on History in the Schools, *Building a History Curriculum: Guidelines for Teaching History in Schools* (Np: Education Excellence Network, 1988), 1.
4. Gary B. Nash, Charlotte Crabtree, and Ross E. Dunn, *History on Trial: Culture Wars and the Teaching of the Past* (New York: Alfred A. Knopf, 1998), 39.
5. David Warren Saxe, *State History Standards: An Appraisal of History Standards in 37 States and the District of Columbia* (Washington, DC: Thomas Fordham Foundation, 1998), viii.
6. Herbert M. Kliebard, *The Struggle for the American Curriculum, 1893-1958*, 2nd ed. (New York: Routledge, 1995).
7. David Warren Saxe, *Social Studies in Schools* (Albany: State University of New York Press, 1991), 83.
8. NEA, *Report of the Committee of Ten on Secondary School Studies with the Reports of the Conferences Arranged by the Committee* (New York: American Book Company, 1894), 162–165, 188–189, 195–199.
9. Peter Novick, *That Noble Dream: The Objectivity Question and the American Historical Profession* (Cambridge, U.K.: Cambridge University Press, 1988), 47–49.
10. American Historical Association. *The Study of History in Schools*. Report of the Committee of Seven (Washington, DC: GPO, 1899), 429, 476–481.
11. American Historical Association. *The Study of History in Elementary Schools*. Report of the Committee of Eight (New York: Charles Scribner's Sons, 1909), x–xv.
12. Edward Channing, Albert Bushnell Hart, and Frederick Jackson Turner, *Guide to the Study and Reading of American History* (Boston: Ginn and Co., 1912), 6, 10–11, 228–231.
13. James Harvey Robinson, 1912. *The New History: Essays Illustrating the Modern Historical Outlook* (Springfield, Mass.: Walden Press, 1958), 3–4, 18, 24.
14. NEA, Committee on Articulation of High School and College. *College Entrance Requirements* Department of Interior Bulletin, No. 7 (Washington, DC: GPO, 1913), 103.
15. NEA, Commission on the Reorganization of Secondary Education. *Cardinal Principles of Secondary Education* Department of Interior Bulletin 35 (Washington, DC: GPO, 1918), 13–14, 22, 23.
16. NEA, Committee on the Social Studies. *The Social Studies in Secondary Education*. Department of Interior Bulletin, no. 28 (Washington, DC: GPO, 1916), 41, 44, 45.
17. Edward A. Krug, *The Shaping of the American High School, 1880-1920* (Madison: University of Wisconsin Press, 1969), 357.
18. Robert D Barr, James Barth, and S. Samuel Shermis, *Defining the Social Studies* (Arlington, Virginia: National Council for the Social Studies, 1977), 19–25.
19. Harold Rugg, "Do the Social Studies Prepare Pupils Adequately for Life Activities?" in *The Social Studies in the Elementary and Secondary School*, ed. Guy Montrose Whipple. The Twenty-Second Yearbook of the National Society for the Study of Education (Bloomington, IL: Public School Publishing Co., 1923), 1–27.
20. Harold Rugg, *That Men May Understand* (New York: Doubleday, Doran, Co., 1941), 214–220.
21. James Harvey Robinson, "The Newer Ways of Historians," *American Historical Review* 35, no. 2 (1930), 246, 247, 249, 252.
22. Carl Becker, "Everyman His Own Historian," *American Historical Review* 37, no. 2 (1932): 221–236.

23. Charles Beard, "Written History as an Act of Faith," *American Historical Review* 39, no. 2 (1934): 219–229.
24. Theodore Clark Smith, "The Writing of American History from 1884 to 1935," *American Historical Review* 40, no. 2 (1935): 439–449.
25. Charles Beard. "That Noble Dream," *American Historical Review* 41, no. 1 (1935): 74–87.
26. Charles Beard, *A Charter for the Social Sciences in the Schools* (New York: Charles Scribner's Sons, 1932), vi–ix.
27. Ravitch, *Left Back,* 92–93.
28. Beard, *Charter,* 93–117.
29. Lawrence J. Dennis, *George S. Counts and Charles A. Beard: Collaborators for Change* (Albany: SUNY Press, 1989), 55–59.
30. Commission on the Social Studies, *Conclusions and Recommendations of the Commission* (New York: Charles Scribner's Sons, 1934), 16.
31. Franklin Bobbitt, "Questionable Recommendations of the Commission on the Social Studies," *School and Society* 40 (1934): 201–208.
32. Boyd Bode, "Editorial Comment," *Phi Delta Kappan* 17, no. 1 (1934): 1, 7.
33. Dennis, *Collaborators,* 97–100.
34. Leon C. Marshall and Rachel Marshal Goetz, *Curriculum-making in the Social Studies* (New York: Charles Scribner's Sons, 1936) 2–3, 7–16.
35. Rugg, *That Men,* 71–73.
36. Kliebard, *Struggle for the American Curriculum,* 178.
37. Rugg, *Charter,* 42–45.
38. Novick, *That Noble Dream,* 190–191.
39. Ibid., 191–192.
40. Nash, et al. *History on Trial,* 37–38.
41. CEEB. "Report of the Commission on History," *The Social Studies* 27, no. 8 (1936): 546–567.
42. Novick, *That Noble Dream,* 320–333.
43. Ibid., 336–337.
44. Hazel Whitman Hertzberg, *Social Studies Reform, 1880–1980* (Boulder CO: Social Science Education Consortium, 1981), 87–94.
45. Ibid., 96–97.
46. Ibid., 101–108.
47. Ibid., 109.
48. Peter B. Dow, *Schoolhouse Politics: Lessons from the Sputnik Era* (Cambridge: Harvard University Press, 1991), 178–187.
49. Howard Zinn, *The Politics of History* (Boston: Beacon Press, 1970), 35–41.
50. James Banks, *Teaching Strategies for Ethnic Studies* (Boston: Allyn and Bacon, 1975), 5–9.
51. Banks, *Ethnic Studies,* 19–21.
52. Ibid., 53–55, 75.
53. Eugene D. Genovese, "A New Departure," in *Reconstructing History: The Emergence of a New Historical Society,* eds. Elizabeth Fox-Genovese and Elisabeth Lasch-Quinn (New York: Routledge, 1999), 6–8.
54. Diane Ravitch, "The Controversy over National History Standards," in *Reconstructing History: The Emergence of a New Historical Society,* eds. Elizabeth Fox-Genovese and Elisabeth Lasch-Quinn (New York: Routledge, 1999), 242–252.
55. Bradley Commission on History in Schools, *Building a History Curriculum,* 5, 7, 10–11.
56. Nash et al. *History on Trial,* 111–112.

57. Stephen J. Thornton, "Should We Be Teaching More History?" *Theory and Research in Social Education* 18, no. 1 (1990): 53–60.
58. National Council for the Social Studies, *Expectations for Excellence: Curriculum Standards for Social Studies* http://www.org/standards, February 2003.
59. Hertzberg, *Social Studies Reform, 1880–1980,* 167–168.

13

Stephen J. Thornton

CITIZENSHIP EDUCATION AND SOCIAL STUDIES CURRICULUM CHANGE AFTER 9/11

This chapter differs from the preceding chapters which are historical in aim. They analyze past educational activities. In a variety of ways, those chapters share a common interest in analyzing the changes in what John Dewey called "social study." That is, training in all subjects to look for "social bearings" in order "to see new possibilities and the means of actualizing them."[1]

In this chapter I consider how the social studies curriculum might effectively educate for citizenship in the changed circumstances since the terrorist attacks on the United States on 9/11/01. Citizenship is generally regarded as a central aim of the social studies curriculum (hereafter, "curriculum") in the United States. I make no attempt here to defend citizenship as a social studies aim. Rather, as the preceding chapters amply demonstrate, proponents of *all* conceptions of social studies claim their version is specially suited to citizenship education purposes.[2]

Because educating for the demands of citizenship since 9/11 depends on altering existing educational practices, I first focus on the intractable problem of curriculum change in social studies. Specifically, I present ten hypotheses about this central problem of social studies curriculum. These hypotheses arise out of a combination of the concerns raised in the chapters of this volume as well as my own long-time investigations of the problem. As may be apparent, some of these hypotheses rest on secure empirical bases while others are more speculative and are intended to provoke experimentation and further investigation. My aims with the hypotheses are to provide a forum for reflection on chapters in this volume and a context for my later discussion of social studies curriculum. Perhaps, also, the hypotheses may suggest some fruitful directions for other investigators to pursue, including researchers, practitioners, program evaluators, teacher educators, and college and university students engaged in the study of education.

Confronting Curriculum Change

Popular fashion in educational research these days tends to skirt the myriad questions of curriculum planning. In the wake of the cognitive revolution, perhaps questions of scope and sequence seem mundane.[3] But there is no getting around the fact that curriculum questions are fundamental to the educational enterprise. You can have a school without educational psychologists or administrators or counselors, without a building, a library, computers, testing, or even teachers; you cannot have a school without a curriculum. As Elliot Eisner observes, what should be taught to whom, when, and in what order are the most "important" educational questions.[4]

A compelling corpus of empirical research from the 1970s shows that curriculum decisions about content inclusion and emphasis are "a powerful . . . tool for stimulating and directing the active learning capacities which are ultimately responsible for the achievement we want from schools."[5] Why has this insight, especially in social studies — long torn by fractious curriculum debates — apparently not been influential in effecting curriculum change? To answer this question, I tersely consider ten hypotheses. Although I do not claim these hypotheses exhaust the potentially relevant dimensions of curriculum change, a number of reviewers of the curriculum literature appear to have settled on the same or similar ones.[6] It should be understood from the outset, moreover, that the meaning of "curriculum change" depends on how one defines curriculum and at what level one looks for change.[7] Since the authors in this volume evidently differ on these questions, I do not attempt to impose an arbitrary definition. Rather I consider a variety of not necessarily consistent meanings of both "curriculum" and "change" as valid.

1. The first hypothesis is sweeping, but appears borne out by the evidence, at least in broad outline: The modern social studies curriculum has been marked more by curriculum stability than change.[8] James Shaver once compared the enacted curriculum of classrooms to the floor of a deep lake, scarcely touched by the violent storms (broad curriculum change movements) roiling the water's surface.[9] This seems consistent with Chara Bohan's (authors cited without a note are from this volume) suggestion that the broad curriculum pattern laid down in the 1890s has persisted until now.

2. Tyrone Howard shows that curriculum change on divisive issues such as race and civil rights is hard to effect. Moreover, radical departures from the standard scope and sequence, such as early 1970s "mini-courses" in ethnic, women's, and environmental studies, have usually been short-lived. Incremental and additive changes, which Margaret Smith Crocco fears run the risk of

tokenism and superficiality, nonetheless may be the most effective change strategies, if effectiveness is judged by inclusion in curriculum guides, textbooks, and standardized testing.

3. As Crocco also suggests, social studies courses conceived to address the demands of contemporary social living, such as Community Civics, seem over time to gravitate toward academics. The most enduring legacy of the citizenship-oriented history committees of the 1890s Bohan analyzes, for instance, may be continuity in the curricular presence of history; there is less certainty whether it has served the citizenship role originally envisaged.[10] Similarly Problems of Democracy often ended up more like an introductory course in political science than an exercise in informed civic decision-making.[11]

4. Controversial social issues (or even issues *perceived* by some influential individuals or groups to be controversial), as Andra Makler's study of censoring the Rugg curriculum materials demonstrates, may run into political opposition from conservatives or reactionaries or both. These acts of censorship occurred in diverse regions of the United States. Other controversial material, however, appears to evoke more concern in some regions of the United States than other regions. Statewide textbook adoption, for example, is mainly practiced in the Sunbelt states and its ideological slant is generally politically conservative.

5. School culture tends to socialize teachers to norms aimed at classroom order and efficiency more than student interest in the enacted curriculum.[12] Consequently, students may be only fitfully engaged with significant subject matter. Teacher education programs often fail to persuade teachers to adopt alternative practices.[13]

6. Curriculum change implemented is not necessarily change institutionalized. Crocco notes, for example, "the rise and rapid fall of feminist activity" in the National Council for the Social Studies. Likewise, the influence of intercultural education during World War II described by Yoon Pak was soon largely terminated by a Cold War consensus about curriculum indifferent, even hostile, to the spirit of cultural pluralism.[14]

7. Studies of how curriculum development actually proceeds remain too scarce. Curriculum development is a continuum of thought and activity from the idea for an innovation, to planning and producing materials, to dissemination and implementation, to evaluation, to institutionalization, to new pressures for change.[15] Social studies research has mainly dwelled on the first few of these points on the curriculum continuum, and then frequently superficially. "Naturalistic" case studies of curriculum development would be instructive.[16] These need not be models of excellence. Far from the orderly set of procedures laid out in how-to-do-it manuals, curriculum work is untidy and seldom linear. Rather than trying to follow models that idealize how the process occurs, it may be more helpful to understand how curriculum development actually proceeds. Such cases might, for example, inform the preparation of teach-

ers. Moreover, it may help prevent the kind of costly curriculum reform attempts described by Andrew Mullen that teachers refuse to enact.

8. Both conservatives and progressives attempt to use social studies education as a vehicle for their ideology. Conservatives have tended to emphasize topics such as patriotism, free enterprise education, anti-Communism, and character education. Progressives have supported teaching topics such as gender equity, cultural pluralism, internationalism, and environmental awareness. More generally, caution should be exercised in judging the content of curriculum materials and courses from their titles or announced aims.

9. Curriculum materials have proven far easier to change than methods of instruction.[17] Methods, however, are probably a surer sign of curriculum change than materials. For example, innovative materials may be used in ways that perpetuate the practices they were designed to reform. Changes in methods, on the other hand, tend to cast curriculum materials differently even if the materials are otherwise unchanged.[18]

10. There seems little doubt that social study outside of school can be educationally potent. But as Christine Woyshner's study of the P. T. A. well illustrates, it is far easier to identify intended curriculum changes than to gauge their educational effects on individuals or groups or society as a whole.

Citizenship Education and the Social Studies Curriculum

Citizenship as a primary American educational aim is about as old as the United States. From the early days of the republic the intended curriculum in history, geography, and government aimed at cultivating civic knowledge and virtue.[19] The belief that these subjects should cultivate "good" citizenship has been widely accepted by Americans ever since, even among higher-education academicians in history, geography, and the social sciences. Although academicians sometimes regard social studies as an unwelcome curricular rival, as Joseph Watras shows, they still seem to consider citizenship education basic to the K-12 curriculum. On September 11, 2002, for instance, the well-known historians Eric Foner and Thomas Bender indicted school history teachers for failing to adequately prepare "citizens" for participating in "complex, civic conversation."[20]

Despite general agreement that social studies should educate for citizenship, precisely what this entails is controversial. What subject matter best prepares young people for citizenship? How should they encounter that subject matter? Is citizenship education a separate or integrated part of the curriculum? Should citizenship be taught primarily as an academic exercise or through participatory methods? Should civic education emphasize the problems or the exceptionalism of the American political order? These are only a few of many related questions that have been answered in sharply different ways in American education.

As the foregoing questions underscore, incorporating citizenship in the curriculum entails more than identifying a body of civic knowledge. The identification of a series of topics in American history, for instance, does not constitute a curriculum.[21] A curriculum is a plan for educational practice. It requires both content (knowledge) and activity. Activity implies that the curriculum is going to engage the student in some type of action—discussion, reading, role-playing, debating, mapping, and so on. As Elliot Eisner explains it, a curriculum is "a sequence of activities that is intentionally developed to provide educational experience for one or more students."[22] Before answering what type of curriculum—both knowledge and activity—best educates for citizenship, we must first specify what is meant by "citizenship."

In its most elementary form, the idea of citizenship originated in the communities of ancient Greece and Rome. Citizens of a city held rights, privileges, and duties not held by other people. Not all residents of a city were necessarily citizens. Citizenship was not, however, merely a matter of government control and administration of public policy. It also concerned, for example, relationships with friends and family.[23]

The relative emphasis that should be devoted to formal government versus community and interpersonal relations—and its implications for what constitute legitimate activities—has been a persistent curriculum issue in the United States. In practice, it appears that citizenship education has commonly been equated with a study of information derived from the scholarly interests of those in the field of political science and government. This has been the principal content of traditional school courses in Government or Civics and Problems of American Democracy or American Problems or Participation in Government.[24]

Attention to citizenship experiences in the community and interpersonal relationships appears to have been less common. As Julie Reuben points out, during the Progressive era this view had influential proponents such as Arthur W. Dunn. Nevertheless over the long run it seems to have been more advocated than implemented. Even when community and interpersonal relationships have been treated, they may have been used to reinforce or instill conformity to majority norms as in recent practices in "character education." Conformity undermines attention to critical thinking and appreciation of diverse perspectives in the curriculum and, therefore, runs counter to vital elements of informed and caring citizenship as well as culturally relevant pedagogy.[25]

In the painful and confusing aftermath of 9/11 critical thinking as well as an understanding and appreciation of diversity are more urgent than ever. Informed and caring citizens simply must be able to think critically about the diversity of the world. Such a goal has always entailed finding a principled balance between the demands of national citizenship and global responsibilities.[26] Growing interdependence among the world's nation-states dating from the early nineteenth century has spawned proposals to educate for internationalism—the policy or practice of cooperation among nations—in countries such as the United States and England.[27]

Inhabiting the same planet in the twenty-first century, whether voluntarily or involuntarily, places common demands on humanity. (Of course, not all nations or persons choose to respond to those demands.) Whether we like it or not, human actions today impinge on the present and future of the planet itself. Issues that may once have been considered insignificant for citizenship education now sometimes threaten sustainability of human life on earth. Some of these topics, such as acid rain, saving the whales, and protection of remaining wetlands and forests seem to have attracted significant attention in the mass media for decades. Others such as protection of bird migration corridors and destinations, which are less heard of, may be just as vital to the ecological future of the planet. Moreover, bird migration provides an excellent example of how international awareness can strengthen both local civic education efforts and global responsibility-taking.[28]

Does global interdependence imply world citizen obligations comparable to those in national citizenship? Does it imply all humanity has some responsibility for fundamental human rights or the natural environment planet-wide? Any honest response to these questions can scarcely deny that the United States is already internationalist to a significant degree. So answering these questions entails matters of "how much" and "what kind" of internationalism should appear in the curriculum rather than whether it should or shouldn't.

Thus far, I have suggested that Americans expect the social studies to educate for citizenship. This task has grown in scope and urgency with growing global interdependence. Below, I discuss how the post 9/11 curriculum can be a potent means for meeting the growing demands for, if not global citizenship, then at least global awareness. Presently Americans devote a smaller proportion of the social studies curriculum to studying other nations than comparable industrial countries.[29] The current world crisis compels, however, adopting greater global awareness as a central aim of U.S. curricula. Significantly, global awareness is both cognitive and attitudinal.

It needs to be stressed that simply providing more knowledge does not automatically produce better citizens.[30] Enhanced knowledge of world history, geography, economics, and cultures alone may not motivate young peoples' interest in internationalism. In addition, young people may need to be taught "caring about" distant peoples and places we ordinarily do not experience first hand.[31] To this end, below I present examples of how we might simultaneously address the cognitive and attitudinal dimensions of internationalism.

Possible Curriculum Changes

Meaningful curriculum change entails alterations in three dimensions: knowledge, organization, and activity (and their interrelationships, of course). Moreover, all teachers serve as curricular-instructional gatekeepers and determine the content and organization of the day-to-day curriculum to which students have access and the activities in which students have opportunities to engage. Therefore, how and for what reasons teachers tend the curricular-instructional gate matter. Otherwise the effects of curriculum change efforts will fail to reach the place they ultimately count: in the classroom.[32]

Perhaps the most obvious place to begin exploring how international-minded citizens can be produced in the social studies is to identify places in the existing curriculum where just a little tweaking may do the trick. Take the common high school global history and geography course as in New York State. Such a course already includes material on Hinduism, Judaism, Christianity, and Islam. This material could be made particularly relevant to contemporary international problems by consideration of branches of each religious tradition that became increasingly fundamentalist and aggressive as the twentieth century wore on.

Of course, fundamentalism may be highlighted already, especially in more recent textbooks. But the bigger curriculum challenge is to engage students in activity that relates this material to their experiences. Mere inclusion is a Pyrrhic victory if young people affect indifference to the topic. Activities such as eliciting students' existing knowledge (which may be stereotypical), interacting first hand with guest speakers, communicating over the Internet with people in other cultures, investigating how young people in fundamentalist groups deal with issues common to all adolescents as they come of age, may engage young people. Such activities aim at both the cognitive and affective domains. To bridge cultures and borders, global educators Merry Merryfield and Binaya Subedi write, the curriculum must extend beyond the academic.[33]

Modifying the existing curriculum constitutes a first step. As noted, more comprehensive curriculum change requires considering the meaning of educational change. Michael Fullan has suggested in this regard that changing the curriculum at the classroom level is a multidimensional exercise. At least three central components are at stake in implementing any new program or policy: (1) the possible use of new or revised *materials* (direct instructional resources such as curriculum materials or technologies) (2) the possible use of new *teaching approaches* (i.e., new teaching methods or learning activities), and (3) the possible alteration of *beliefs* (e.g., pedagogical assumptions and theories underlying particular new policies or programs).[34] Let us explore each of these three components.

New or revised materials are a standard means of curriculum change. Although we can point to failures such as the negative reaction of many teachers to the elaborate new social studies materials of the 1960s, materials are still probably the most direct lever to nudge classroom practice in new directions. Materials, both traditional and digital, give tangible form to educational aspirations. From the standpoint of internationalism, a wide variety of materials are available to lend a global perspective to standard topics such as the Industrial Revolution in existing social studies courses.[35]

New instructional methods and learning activities may or may not be required for the developers' intended uses of new curriculum materials. Since teachers tend to have their own preferences for teaching approaches with which they are comfortable, changing teaching approaches often proves among the most challenging curriculum endeavors.

One promising method for internationalism may be a project-based approach, which was common in the open education movement of the 1970s. Given a practically unbounded body of information about the world that could be studied, educating for internationalism may benefit from division of student labor. With teachers acting as organizer and planner, classes can identify a common topic and set of objectives. Individuals or groups could then take part of a large topic such as global human rights. One group might, for example, study the history of the concept of "just" wars, another group the United Nations Declaration of Human Rights, and still another group ethnic cleansing in the twentieth century. This method also allows some latitude about what a child or a group will study, thus opening up prospects for students to investigate topics that may connect to regions, periods, peoples, institutions, etc. in which they have interest.[36]

Changing teacher's beliefs such as their theories of how young people learn may be the tallest order for change.[37] Much of teachers' belief systems are unexamined or tacit and their beliefs tend to be fortified by experience.[38] For example, changing teachers' beliefs about how young people become internationally-minded is likely to be a complex process of adding and modifying some beliefs while discarding some other beliefs. Part of this process may well involve persuading teachers that information alone is frequently ineffective in changing deep-seated student attitudes. Fortunately studies documenting how such processes work can provide guidance. For example, one study of how global perspectives were brought to the teaching of Japan illustrates the complexity of changing beliefs.[39]

Conclusion

The 9/11 attacks reminded everyone of how basic social studies education is. We ignore it at our peril. The attacks on New York and Washington have been followed by American-led invasions of Afghanistan and Iraq. Domestically, the federal government has assumed new, broad powers to protect "homeland" security. The lines between domestic issues such as civil liberties and international issues such as combating terrorism have become blurred.

Educating young people to be caring and competent citizens in such a nation and world will require far more than sporadic attention to current events or beefing up the treatment of Islamic countries in a standard global history and geography course. A combination of curriculum change and retooling teacher education for the domestic and international dimensions of globalization is needed. It is too soon to say if such fundamental changes will come about. But judging by social studies changes in response to past crises as documented in this book, the most positive likely outcome may be incremental and additive changes rather than fundamental reformulation of curriculum and instruction. Nonetheless, it is worth asking what we mean by one current mantra of educational reform—"world class" standards—if we fail to adequately educate citizens for the world we live in.

Notes

1. John Dewey, "What is Social Study?" in *Teaching the Social Studies: What, Why, and How,* eds. Richard E. Gross, Walter E. McPhie, and Jack R. Fraenkel (Scranton, PA: International Textbook Company, 1969), 7.
2. Linda S. Levstik, "NCSS and the Teaching of History," in *NCSS in Retrospect,* ed. O. L. Davis, Jr. (Washington, DC: National Council for the Social Studies, 1996), 23.
3. Walter C. Parker, Akira Ninomiya, and John Cogan, "Educating World Citizens: Multinational Curriculum Development," *American Educational Research Journal* 36, no. 2 (1999): 136.
4. Elliot W. Eisner, "Who Decides What Schools Teach?" in *The Curriculum Studies Reader,* eds. David J. Flinders and Stephen J. Thornton (New York: Routledge, 1997).
5. Decker F. Walker and Jon Schaffarzick, "Comparing Curricula," *Review of Educational Research* 44, no. 1 (1974): 111.
6. See, for example, Nathalie J. Gehrke, Michael S. Knapp, and Kenneth A. Sirotnik, "In Search of the School Curriculum," *Review of Research in Education,* 18, ed. Gerald Grant (Washington, DC: American Educational Research Association, 1992); Jere Brophy, Janet Alleman, and Carolyn O'Mahony, "Elementary School Social Studies: Yesterday, Today, and Tomorrow," *American Education: Yesterday, Today, and Tomorrow* (Chicago: National Society for the Study of Education, 2000); Stephen J. Thornton, "The Social Studies Near Century's End: Reconsidering Patterns of Curriculum and Instruction," in *Review of Research in Education,* 20, ed. Linda Darling-Hammond (Washington, DC: American Educational Research Association, 1994); and "Legitimacy in the Social Studies Curriculum," in *Education Across a Century: The Centennial Volume,* ed. Lyn Corno (Chicago: National Society for the Study of Education, 2001).
7. Nel Noddings, "NIE's National Curriculum Development Conference," *Value Conflicts and Curriculum Issues,* ed. Jon Schaffarzick and Gary Sykes (Berkeley: McCutchan, 1979), 299.
8. Larry Cuban, "History of Teaching in Social Studies," in *Handbook of Research on Social Studies Teaching and Learning* (New York: Macmillan, 1991).
9. James P. Shaver, "The Usefulness of Educational Research in Curricular/Instructional Decision-Making in Social Studies," *Theory and Research in Social Education* 7, no. 3 (1979): 21–46.
10. Thornton, "Legitimacy in the Social Studies Curriculum."
11. See H. Wells Singleton, "Problems of Democracy: The Revisionist Plan for Social Studies Education," *Theory and Research in Social Education* 8, no. 3 (1980): 89–104.
12. Linda M. McNeil, *Contradictions of Control: School Structure and School Knowledge* (New York: Routledge and Kegan Paul, 1986); Stuart B. Palonsky, *900 Shows a Year* (New York: McGraw-Hill, 1986); Stephen J. Thornton, "Teacher as Curricular-Instructional Gatekeeper in Social Studies," in *Handbook of Research on Social Studies Teaching and Learning,* ed. James P. Shaver (New York: Macmillan, 1991).
13. Stephen J. Thornton, "Educating the Educators: Rethinking Subject Matter and Methods," *Theory into Practice* 40, no. 1 (2001): 72–78.
14. Frances FitzGerald, *America Revised: History Schoolbooks in the Twentieth Century* (Boston: Little, Brown, 1979).
15. This idea of a "curriculum continuum" is based on Colin J. Marsh and George Willis, *Curriculum: Alternative Approaches, Ongoing Issues* (Upper Saddle River, NJ: Merrill Prentice Hall, 2003), 161.

16. Decker Walker first described the idea of a "naturalistic" model of curriculum development in the 1970s. See "The Process of Curriculum Development: A Naturalistic Model," *School Review* 80, no. 1 (1971): 51–65.

17. Lawrence A. Cremin, *Popular Education and Its Discontents* (New York: Harper & Row, 1990), 17.

18. For an example of the differences when the same textbook was used with contrasting methods, see Stephen J. Thornton, "Curriculum Consonance in United States History Classrooms," *Journal of Curriculum and Supervision* 3, no. 4 (1988): 308–320.

19. Ruth Miller Elson, *Guardians of Tradition: American Schoolbooks of the Nineteenth Century* (Lincoln: University of Nebraska Press, 1964).

20. Quoted in David Gerwin, "Responding to a Social Studies Classic: 'Decision Making: The Heart of Social Studies Instruction'," *The Social Studies* 94, no. 1 (2003): 26.

21. For elaboration on this point, see Stephen J. Thornton, "Subject Specific Teaching Methods: History," in *Subject-Specific Instructional Methods and Activities,* ed. Jere Brophy (Oxford: Elsevier Science, 2001).

22. Elliot W. Eisner, *Educating Artistic Vision* (New York: Macmillan, 1972), 153.

23. Robert J. Pranger, "Citizenship," in *World Book Encyclopedia,* Vol. 4 (Chicago: World Book, Inc., 1991); see also Margaret Smith Crocco, "Reimagining Citizenship Education: Gender, Sexuality, and the Social Studies," in *Social Studies in the New Millennium: Re-envisioning Civic Education in a Changing World,* ed. Beth Rubin & James Giarelli (Mahwah, NJ: Erlbaum, 2004).

24. James P. Shaver and Richard S. Knight, "Civics and Government in Citizenship Education," *Social Studies and Social Sciences: A Fifty-Year Perspective,* ed. Stanley P. Wronski and Donald H. Bragaw (Washington, DC: National Council for the Social Studies, 1986).

25. See Gloria-Ladson Billings, *The Dreamkeepers: Successful Teachers of African American Children* (San Francisco: Jossey-Bass, 1994) and Nel Noddings, *Educating Moral People: A Caring Alternative to Character Education* (New York: Teachers College Press, 2002).

26. William Gaudelli, *World Class: Teaching and Learning in Global Times* (Mahwah, NJ: Erlbaum, 2003), 68–71.

27. See William E. Marsden, *The School Textbook: Geography, History and Social Studies* (London: Woburn Press, 2001), 148–166.

28. Scott Weidensaul, *Living on the Wind: Across the Hemisphere with Migratory Birds* (New York: North Point Press, 1999), 124.

29. Parker, Ninomiya, and Cogan, "Educating World Citizens," 135.

30. For analysis of this point, see John Dewey, "The Challenge of Democracy to Education," *John Dewey: The Later Works, 1925–1953,* Vol. 11, ed. Jo Ann Boydston (Carbondale, IL: Southern Illinois University Press, 1991).

31. Nel Noddings, *Starting at Home: Caring and Social Policy* (Berkeley: University of California Press, 2002), 22.

32. Thornton, "Teacher as Curricular-Instructional Gatekeeper."

33. Merry M. Merryfield and Binaya Subedi, "A Global Education Framework for Teaching about the World's Women," *Social Education* 67, no. 1 (2003), 10–16.

34. Michael Fullan, *The Meaning of Educational Change* (New York: Teachers College Press, 1982), 30.

35. See, for example, the materials developed by the "Choices" Program such as *Global Environmental Problems: Implications for U. S. Policy* (Providence, RI: Brown University, 2003).

36. For elaboration, see Theo Barker and Archie W. Flanagan, *Teaching Social Studies in Primary Schools* (Sydney: McGraw-Hill, 1971), 34–40. For an example, see John B. MacDonald, "State Curriculum Policies and Teachers' Practice: The Experiences of Three New York Social Studies Teachers," (Ed.D. diss., Columbia University, 2003), 116–118.
37. Saundra J. McKee, "Impediments to Implementing Critical Thinking," *Social Education* 52, no. 6 (1988): 444–446.
38. Stephen J. Thornton, "How Do Elementary Teachers Decide What to Teach in Social Studies?" in *Teacher Personal Theorizing: Connecting Curriculum Practice, Theory, and Research,* ed. E. Wayne Ross, Jeffrey W. Cornett, and Gail McCutcheon (Albany: State University of New York Press, 1992).
39. Toni Fuss Kirkwood, "Teaching about Japan: Global Perspectives in Teacher Decision-Making, Context, and Practice," *Theory and Research in Social Education* 30 no. 1 (2002): 88–115.

CONTRIBUTORS

JACKIE M. BLOUNT is Associate Professor of Historical, Philosophical, and Comparative Education at Iowa State University. Her work focuses on the history of sexuality and gender in schools in the U.S. She has written *Destined to Rule the Schools: Women and the Superintendency, 1873–1995* and *Fit to Teach: Same-Sex Desire, Gender, and School Work in the Twentieth Century* (SUNY Press, 2004).

CHARA HAEUSSLER BOHAN is an assistant professor in the Department of Curriculum and Instruction at Baylor University in Waco, Texas. Her research interests include social studies education, history of education, and women's studies. She has published articles in *Theory and Research in Social Education, Social Studies and the Young Learner,* and the *Journal of Curriculum and Supervision.* She is the author of *Go to the Sources: Lucy Maynard Salmon and the Teaching of History* (Peter Lang, 2004).

MARGARET SMITH CROCCO is Associate Professor of Social Studies and Education at Teachers College, Columbia University. Her books include *Pedagogies of Resistance: Women Educator Activists, 1880–1960* (Teachers College Press); *"Bending the Future to Their Will": Civic Women, Social Education, and Democracy* (Rowman and Littlefield); *Building a Legacy: Women in Social Education 1784–1984* (NCSS); and *Learning to Teach in an Age of Accountability* (Lawrence Erlbaum Associates).

STEVEN JAY GROSS is Associate Professor of Educational Administration at Temple University, Philadelphia, Pennsylvania. He is also a Senior Fellow at the Vermont Society for the Study of Education. Gross' book, *Staying Centered: Curriculum Leadership in a Turbulent Era* (1998) typifies his research and writing which focus on Turbulence Theory and initiating and sustaining deep reform in schools and other educating organizations.

TYRONE C. HOWARD is an Assistant Professor in the Graduate School of Education and Information Studies at UCLA. His research interests include access and equity in schools, social studies and multicultural education, and the schooling experiences of African American students.

BENJAMIN M. JACOBS is a doctoral candidate and instructor in the Program in Social Studies at Teachers College, Columbia University. He also serves as coordinator of the doctoral program in Education and Jewish Studies at New York University. His research focuses on social studies curriculum history and theory.

ANDRA MAKLER recently retired from the Graduate School of Education at Lewis & Clark College where she served as Associate Professor of Social Studies Education and education department chair. She has published on family history, teachers' and students' conceptions of justice, and the way justice is taught and learned. Her current research focuses on the work and life of journalist Agnes DeLima.

ANDREW MULLEN is Chair of the Department of Education at Westmont College. His current scholarly interests include the history of the social studies curriculum, teacher education, and the cultivation of nationalism and/or patriotism in American schools.

YOON K. PAK is Assistant Professor of Educational Policy Studies and Asian American Studies at the University of Illinois at Urbana-Champaign. She has published in journals such as *Theory and Research in Social Education*, *Educational Theory*, and *Urban Education*. Her most recent book publication is entitled, *"Wherever I go I will always be a loyal American:" Schooling Seattle's Japanese Americans during World War II* (New York: Routledge Falmer Press, 2002). She was also a recipient of the 2002–2003 National Academy of Education/Spencer Postdoctoral Fellowship.

AVNER SEGALL is an assistant professor in the department of Teacher Education at Michigan State University. His research and teaching combine critical theory and pedagogy, teacher education, and social/cultural studies. His book, *Disturbing Practice: Reading Teacher Education as Text,* a critical study of learning to teach social studies, was published by Peter Lang in 2002.

STEPHEN J. THORNTON is Associate Professor of Social Studies and Education at Teachers College, Columbia University. He recently completed a second edition of *The Curriculum Studies Reader* (Routledge, 1997) with David J. Flinders. Thornton's new book on teachers' roles in social studies curriculum development, *Social Studies Curriculum That Matters,* will be published by Teachers College Press in late 2004.

JOSEPH WATRAS is Professor of Social Foundations of Education at the University of Dayton. Recently, Allyn and Bacon published two texts he wrote concerning the history of curriculum. The first is *The Foundations of Educational Curriculum and Diversity, 1565 to the Present.* The second is *Philosophic Conflicts in American Education, 1893 to 2000.*

CHRISTINE WOYSHNER is Assistant Professor of Education at Temple University. She has published articles in *Teachers College Record, Theory and Research in Social Education,* and *International Journal of Social Education.* She is co-editor, with Holly Gelfond, of *Minding Women: Reshaping the Educational Realm* (Harvard Education Publishing Group) and author of the ASCD Curriculum Handbook on social studies (2003).

INDEX